Preface

Bana Bhatta was a great writer of Sanskrit. His prose writing and depiction is unique. Bana Bhatta has written two books Harsh Charita and Kadambari. Harsha Charita is based on incidents took place in life of king Harshavardhana. In first three chapters of Harsh Charita he has described his own life. Harsha Charita is a historical book. Kadambari is a literary work of Bana Bhatta. Though Kadambari is a fable but there are large number of facts representing society and culture of seventh century. A true researcher of history can create history of seventh century with the help of Harsha Charita and Kadambari. Both the books have literary impact. The researcher has to separate historical facts from literary impact.

Bana Bhatta has given much political information in Harsh Charita. Describing personality of king Harsha, he has written; a lion to the Huna deer, a burning fever to the king of the Indus land, a trouble to the sheep of Gujrat, a bilious plague to the elephants sent by the lord of Gandhara, a looter to the lawlessness of the Lats, an axe to the creeper of Malwa's glory. This description gives detail of neighbouring states of king Harsha, which were under influence of him.

The description of family chart and ancestors of king Harsha given by Bana Bhatta is supported by Madhuvan inscription (Samvat 25-231) of king Harshvardhana. It is also supported by copper-seal of Harshvardhana found from Sonepat.

Bana Bhatta is the only writer who has given information of killing of last Maurya king Brihadratha by his army chief Pushyamitra at the time of inspecting army. He has also given information of killing of last Sung king Vasudev by his army chief Devabhuti. Chandragupta killed the king of Sakas in his city by a sword concealed in his mistress and saved his elder brother wife. He has given a very long list of such information but yet we have not recognized them.

Bana Bhatta has described many administrative officers. The posts of these officers are supported by many inscriptions and the Arthashastra written by 'Kautilya'. For instance, Amatya, Rajamatya and Kumaramatya named officers are mentioned in Devbarnak inscription of Jivitgupta Second.

Bana Bhatta also depicted emotions and feelings of government officers in Harsha Charita. Administrative pressure and bad working environment disgusted them. A survey carried on recently by Centre for Good Governance, Hyderabad revealed the same result.

Bana has described many weapons used by soldiers. Those are tallied by the description of Hiuen-Tsang and Kautilya.

Bana has described 'Skandhavar'. He has described market infront of Skandhavar. It can be compared with the Urdu Market of Chhavani (camp) in front of Red Fort in Delhi.

Royal palace described by Bana can be compared with the Mughal period Red Fort Delhi and Hampton Court Palace in London (16-17th century). His description is supported by later Royal palaces of different kings.

Bana Bhatta has described many social aspects of seventh century of India. He was first revolutionary writer, who criticized and opposed Sati custom. He has imagined 'The Women era', women dominated society. He was a great supporter of women.

He has described garment worn by people during seventh century. He has illustrated Chandatak, Svasthan, Pinga and Satula. These were different types of trousers. These garments are found in Mathura Art. A female dancer has worn svasthan type trouser of narrow cuff and flower painted in the temple of Devagarha. Varbana and chincholak are coats. A male idol, in cave no. 17 of Ajanta, has worn dark blue coloured Satula added with white strips resembles description of Bana. An idol of Maitreya found from Ahichhatra has worn Tarangata Uttariya illustrated by Bana. Kanchuk was an upper garment described by Bana. In cave 1 of Ajanta Chamargrahini, who has stood left of Padmapani Avalokiteshwar has worn blue Kanchuka long up to foot. Thus garments described by Bana are found in idols, painting and statues found from different places.

Bana Bhatta has described different type of ornaments worn by people of that time. He has described an ornament named Balpasha, which was a head ornament. This ornament is shown in the painting of Ajanta in the cave-1. In this painting Balpas has were tightened on the head of Nagraj and Dravidaraj. He has described Chatula tilak, an ornament similar to recently used jewellery named Mangtika. Balpasha and Tilak are in the idol of tara found from Kurkihar (Gaya,Bihar). He has described Trikantak, ear jewellery. Such jewellery is well protected in New Delhi museum. We see many ornaments in the painting of Apsara from cave-17. She has worn Ekawali, Shesh (Necklace) in her neck, and bracelet in her wrist, Balapasha in locks of hair and chatula Tilak (Mangtika) on parting of her hair.

Thus description of Bana is proved by many idols and paintings.

Indian culture is deliberately depicted in writing of Bana Bhatta. Wedding ceremony described by Bana is similar to the wedding ceremony of Punjab and kurukshetra. He has described Vas Griha (sleeping room) where God of love was figured with his two wives Preeti and Rati. There is mention of Kamdeva with Preeti and Rati in Mandasor-Script of Bandhuvarma. Bad and auspicious omens are described by Bana. Bad and auspicious omens are also described in detail in Vrihatsamhita written by Varahmihir.

In Harsha Charita it is written about Stupa or Chaitya marked baked red terra-cotta seal, those were stored beside. Now a day in excavation of ancient Bauddh places there are found large number of this type of chaitya marked terra-cotta seals. On then one or many stupa or chaitya marks are found and generally Budda's 'ye dharma hetuprabhavah' Mantra once or many times written on it. People who went to see, they bring that type of seal with them to instigate in worship.

Bana has described 21 religious communities. Somadev has given good introduction of different religious communities and their principles in 'Yashastilak Champoo' (9th A.D.). Shri Handi has deliberated on them historically in his book. Those religious communities and their principles are also indicated in Naishadh Charit of Shri Harsha and in the act Prabodhchandralaya.

Bana has described that Harsha was follower of Hindu religion but latter he was attracted towerds Buddism. He decided to accept Buddhism after completion of his vow. It is known, from description of Si-Yu-Ki, that Harsha and his sister Rajyashri was follower of Buddhism at arrival of Hiuen-Tsang.

Bana has described three types of education centers- 1.Homes of Brahmans, 2. Abode of ascetics and 3. Educational instiutions supported by state. His description is proved by ruins of Nalanda and Vikramshila universities.

Many books are mentioned in Harsha Charita and Kadambari. He has mentioned so many writers and their books those are found today. He has illustrated- Vasavdutta written by Suvandhu, Prose-poem written by Harishchandra, Dramas written by Bhasa, Books written by Kalidas, Vrihatkatha written by Gunadhya, Sangraha wtitten by Vyadi, Nitishastra written by Kamandaka, Natyashastra written by Bharat and Kamashastra written by Vatsyayana.

Knowledge of economy of any state is based on coins found at that place. Bana has described coins of that time. In Saptam Uchchawas of Harsha Charit he has depicted a Gramakshapatalik (officer of village or Patawari) giving a bull marked new gold coin to Harsha. Fortunately, a sample of bull marked copper coin is available from sonipat. Harsha was Param Maheshwar, so this bull is sign of Nandi.

Description of Bana indicates feudatory system in administration. It is known from description of Harsha Charit that agricultural land of state was divided in three categories- 1. Land given to samantas, 2. Land directly controlled by the state and 3. Tax free land given to Brahmans. Different copper inscriptions prove his description.

Today concept of history is the depiction of different aspects of life of people. Bana is the same type of historian. Mention of dates is essential to know historical chronology. But Bana has not mentioned any date in his writing. He has given actual drawing of India of seventh century through his extraordinary writing. He has exposed every important aspect of life of people. His descriptions are also proved by contemporary historical sources. Clearly it can be said that India of seventh century could not be understood without description of Bana. Thus Bana Bhatta was not only writer but also a historian.

Dhananjay Kumar Singh

CONTENTS

Chapter - **Chapter Name**

Chapter-1 - Introduction

Chapter-2 - Bana Bhatt and Contemporary Political Study in the Seventh Century

Chapter-3 - Bana Bhatt and Indian Society during Seventh Century

Chapter-4 - Bana Bhatt and Culture in India during Seventh Century

Chapter-5 - Bana Bhatt and Religion in India during Seventh Century

Chapter-6 - Bana Bhatt and Educational Aspect in India during Seventh Century

Chapter-7 - Bana Bhatt and Indian Economy during Seventh Century

Chapter-8 - Conclusion

Bibliography

Apendix (Map , figure and diagram)

Chapter – 1

Introduction

The prose writings of Bāṇa Bhaṭṭa are valuable property of Sanskrit literature. We see his micro observation, depiction and broad description in his writing. There is real expression of Indian life in Bana's dual writings 'the Harṣacarita' and 'the Kādambarī'. Every sketch of contemporary India drawn by him in his description has a special effect.

Bāṇa Bhaṭṭa firstly wrote the Harṣacarita. He has presented his whole personality before us. He has also written about his life and time in the Harṣacarita . There is clear impact of his personality and experience in his writings. By his talent and micro-vision he has described every aspect of life of contemporary civilisation frankly and clearly. The Harṣacarita is related to the period of king Harṣavardhana .He has started his description from the rule of Prabhākaravardhana , the father of Harṣavardhana. Then he has described the rule of Rājyavardhana, the elder brother of Harṣavardhana. He has described every important incident of that time which brings historical facts up such as political system, army construction, and cabinet and its work, war policy and diplomacy. He has also described the situation in which Harṣa took charge of kingdom and marched for the subjugation of killer of his brother-in-law and set out in search of his sister.Although Harṣacarita didn't describe full life of Harṣavardhana but we can understand contemporary history in the whole and authentically through the incidents which are described in it.

Kādambarī is the best literary work of Bāṇa Bhaṭṭa. Kādambarī written by Bāṇa Bhaṭṭa was proved as a standard of prose in later days. Influenced by Bāṇa Bhaṭṭa many poets had written a number of prose among which some important writings are- ' Daskumar Caritaa' of Dandi, 'Udaysundari Katha' of Soddhala and 'Tilakmanjari' of Dhanapal. Though Kādambarī is a fable but it has large number of facts representing society and culture of seventh century. When we compare those facts with other historical facts, we find them helpful in historical explanation of the society of seventh century. We can understand historical scenario of seventh century through comparative study of facts collected from the Harṣacarita and the Kādambarī and other art and literary works of Harṣa period.

After the fall of Gupta Empire north India divided into small states. In this situation clan of Puṣyabhūti was established at Thaneshwar. Further when Harṣavardhana took power of Thaneshwar then he stopped decentralisation of power in north India and large area of north India came under the Puṣyabhūties . Harṣavardhana emerged as strong and successful emperor and earned fame like Ashoka and Samudragupta in history.

There are many sources to know about Puṣyabhūti and Harṣavardhana but the Harṣacarita and the Kādambarī written by Bāṇa Bhaṭṭa are most important. He had written Harṣacarita to tell stories of Harṣavardhana to his brothers. Harṣacarita is literature as well as first historical book written in Sanskrit. The Kādambarī is a novel written in Sanskrit. Bana Bhatt has written about his life in first two to three chapters of Harṣacarita. Bāṇa Bhaṭṭa was contemporary to Harṣavardhana . "Bana's time certainly early half of seventh century (606-648AD). Harṣa period is decided so there is no historical contrast about it".[1] "Bana's time is most important to decide historical consequence of other poets of Sanskrit because it is only a certain time that can define correct timing of former and later poets. If we do not take Bana as contemporary to Harṣa then also his time defined to seventh century by the quotation of later poets. First time Vamana (779-813AD) has quoted a long phrasal sentence from Kādambarī in his book 'Kavyalankar Sutra' that certainly proved the time of Bāṇa Bhaṭṭa in seventh century"[2]

When Bāṇa Bhaṭṭa writes about his life in Harṣacarita he describes about clan of Vātsyāyana in which he was born. By doing so, Bāṇa Bhaṭṭa satisfied the readers of Sanskrit literature who want to know about personal life of Acharyas and poets. Describing about clan of Vātsyāyana Bāṇa Bhaṭṭa attached it to 'Brahma lok' perhaps Bana has written so because he wanted to show his clan as a high profile clan. Today we also see that in India many people intend to attach their clan to 'Surya' (Sun) and 'Chandra' (Moon) and they feel good to say his clan as 'Suryavanshi' and 'Chandravanshi'. Describing about the establishment of Vātsyāyana clan he writes about curse of Durvasa from which divine Saraswati came to the earth .Saraswati reached the western bank of river Sona with her friend Sāvitrī and married to Dadhīca , son of saint Chyavana. Then Saraswati conceived and she had borne a son. After birth of the son, Saraswati manifested all knowledges to her son and went to Brahmalok. "She having departed, Dadhīca , also, pierced to the heart as by a lightning flash , went away sick with his loss to the words to live as ascetic: having appointed as his son's foster-mother a hermit's daughter named Aksamala wife to Bhratri, a Brahman of the Bhrigu race . She had born a son at the very hour when Saraswati gave birth to hers. So the two children gradually grew up together, fed without favour at the same breast. The one was named Saraswat simply the other's name was Vatsa . And between the two there existed a enviable affection like that of brother." [3]

"Now Saraswat, who through his mother's power was at the very outset of youth gifted with the full treasure of the science, conveyed it undiminished in the form of words to his dear confidant and loving twin-brother Vatsa . When Vatsa took a wife, he made for him in that same neighbourhood a mansion endearingly named The Pinnacle of Delight (Prītikūṭa): he himself ,assuming the hermit's staff, black antelope skin, bark dress, rosary, girdle and matted locks, went to join his father, the ascetic." [4]

From Vatsa a race preceded called Vātsyāyana. In Harṣacarita and Kādambarī Bāṇa Bhaṭṭa has given a list of persons those were born in this race. The list is as follows:-

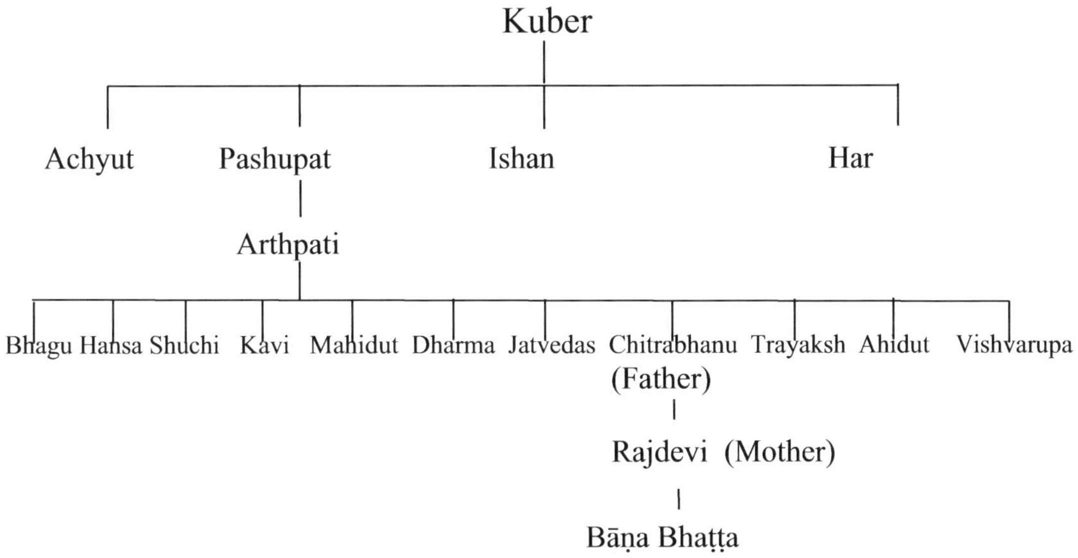

"The list of ancestors as described by Bana in Harṣacarita is different at one place from that of Kādambarī . According to Harṣacarita consequence was as - Kuber- Pashupat- Arthpati- Chitrabhanu- Bana. In Kādambarī list consequence is as -Kuber- Arthpati- Chitrabhanu- Bana. In this list Bana's grand-father's name is absent. It is assumed that the list of Harṣacarita is more authentic because poet had to work more cautiously in selection of that list." [5]

When Bana describes that Saraswati's son Saraswat traind Vatsa in all knowledge and Vātsyāyana race proceeded from Vatsa then his main aim behind it to prove every person born in this race were talented and patron of knowledge. Vātsyāyana race has expertise in all authoritative books and deep knowledge of arts. Every contemporary king had worshipped and gave honour to 'Acharyas' of this race. This honour proves that contemporary kings were obliged to this race's talent and they honour them. In Kādambarī Bana writes "I pray the feet of my teacher Bhatsunayak (Bhatsu ,Bhartsu, Bharva) that worshipped by India's ancient kingdom crown headed 'Maukharies' and that feet fingers bacame red from touching crown's top part of all landlords." [6] Here those Maukhari kings are mentioned " they should be Maukharies of Kanauj as Sharva Verma , Avanti Verma etc. Like that many Gupta kings had worshipped ancestor who born in Vātsyāyana race named

Kubera." [7] "Bana has written in Kādambarī ' Vatsa gotriya, born in Vātsyāyana race, world famous talented, forerunner in educated per sons, worshipped by many Gupta kingsand as a sparkle part of Brahma there lived a Brahman named Kubera'." [8] "Kubera was grandfather of Bana. Those who honoured him were Magadh's post Gupta kings in which family Krishnagupta ,Jivitgupta (540 AD), Damodargupta (575AD) , Mahasenagupta(600AD) and Madhavgupta (630-650AD) tradition is historically proved. Madhavgupta was friend of Harṣa ." [9]

Bana, born in Vātsyāyana race, was lived at his birthplace Prītikūṭa . His mother died at his childhood. Then his father looked after him and gave love of mother. He had said Prītikūṭa as living place of Brahmana. There is conflict among educated persons about actual place of Priticut. In an article published in 'Bhojpuri Patrika'(Ara) Shri Kamalakant Upadhyaya has given arguments in favour of Sāhābāda district (at present Bhojpur district) in which Prītikūṭa was situated. "He said that Prītikūṭa (at present Piur) and Mallkut (at present Malaur) the dual villages are present in Sāhābāda district till today. Chyavana Van today called as 'Van' and story of Chyavan-Sukanya is presently famous for that place."[10]

On other side "in his article 'birth place and race of poet Bana' (Madhuri; year 8, No-1987, whole No-96, page-722-727) Shri Parmeshwar Prasad Sharma has thought about Chyavana cottage. He has said 'searching in side of Sona nad the cottage of Chyavana rishi today known as Devkur(Devkund) is spread in middle of forest- bush near Sona Canal in Gaya district, towards east of present current of Sona, west from Gaya, situated at 14 mile north west from Raphiganj. Bana birthplace will be situated near this. After more search it is found that near this Chyavana Cottage there are many villages of Bachchhagotiya as Sonabhaddar, Parbhai, Bandhavan etc. It is assume that in these villages Sonabhaddar is old place. It is known that this village named Sonabhaddar because it is situated on bank of Sona. Those lived at that place have fame as Sona Bhaddaria who calls self as Bachchhagotia. 'Bachchhagotia' word is tempered form of Vatsa gotriya. Thinking over nearness of Chyavanashrama, Sonabhaddra on bank position, oldness of Sonabhaddara and present name of Bachchhagotia, it cannot go beyond this concept that this Sonabhaddara village was childhood playground of great poet Bana, at this place Bana wrote Kādambarī like wonderful novel and Harṣacarita like history.

In this article also written about Mayur, brother-in -law of Bana , that in Gaya district 14 mile south-west corner from Pamarganj railway station , 20 mile south-west of Chyavanashrama there is a famous place named 'Dev' where a large Sun temple reminding as worship place of Mayur. Here a festival celebrated every year sixth day of Kartik and Chaitra month on the occasion of Chhath (worship of Sun) and hundreds of people came here to get free from leprocy . The main gate of this temple is also in west direction as Chyavanashrama (Chyavana Cottage). There are many villages of local Brahman's named Marayar, those called self as from race of Mayur(Madhuri, same page-724)." [11]

Harṣacarita description proves Kamalakant Upadhyaya's view. It is written in Harṣacarita that departed from Prītikūṭa Bana reached Mallkut village after crossing Chandika vana where his friend Jagatpati welcomed and made him stay. Second day Bana crossed Ganga and halted at night in Yastigrihak village. Third day he stayed in a village named Manipur that is on bank of Rapti (Ajirawata) river where was a camp near king palace. According to this description Bana has crossed Ganga and Rapti river during journey to Kanauj from Prītikūṭa . Which proves that Bana's Prītikūṭa village, situated at west bank of Sona (Saraswati also stayed at the west bank of Sona and Saraswat made same neighbourhood a masion endearingly named Prītikūṭa) river, was definitely Peur(Piur). Translator of Kādambarī Pandey Ramtej Shastri also insisted on Sāhābāda district of Bihar as birth place of Bana. He has written in translation of Kādambarī , "ancestors of Bāṇa Bhaṭṭa lived at Prītikūṭa village on the bank of Sonabhadra river. Which was perhaps, situated in Sāhābāda district of Bihar state (Kādambarī page-5)." Here Sonabhadrariver means Sona river. On other side Shri Parmeshwar Prasad Sharma's argument proved false because accepting Bana's birth place near Devkur or Devkund (Chyavana Cottage) which is in Gaya district near Sona Canal then it would be mentioned about crossing Sona River also between journey from Prītikūṭa to Kanauj. So only on base of nearness of Chyavana Cottage, antiquity of Sonabhaddara and name of Bachchhagotia it is not justified that Prītikūṭa was situated in Gaya district.

Along with, Shri Parmeshwar Prasad Sharma has related poet Mayur with Bāṇa Bhaṭṭa which is based on a famous local story. This relation is not proved by Harṣacarita. Deep study of Harṣacarita reverses this argument and contrasts it. It is clear from description of Harṣacarita that after death of his father Bana wandered aimless, indulge in sundry youthful follies and after development of insight he came back native village Prītikūṭa . Then he got invitation from the court of Harṣa . When Harṣa called him 'petit -maitre' in fist meet then he argument in his favour and said that "from my marriage I have been a diligent householder." This description proved that Bana had married before going to Harṣa court. Poet Mayur who was a member of Harṣa court how can make relation to that Bana who was famous reproach before joining Harṣa court? And at serving time of Harṣa , Bana was married. Along with, the whole description of Harṣacarita there is not written anything about the relation between Bana and Mayur. If he was related to Bana then he would have also described about it. So story about relation of Bana and Mayur is not anything but only a local fable.

When Bana was about fourteen years old his father died. Bāṇa Bhaṭṭa has described himself becoming reproach and wandering here and there after father's death. He also described about his friend circle whose companion he got in this situation. He has written in Harṣacarita "He (Bana) through indulgence in sundry youthful follies, due either to misconduct arising from independence, to the impetuosity prevalent in youth, or to the aversion of young manhood to steadiness, came into reproach. He had friends and companions of his own years, and among them to brothers of low birth, Chandrasena and Matrisena, a dear friend the vernacular poet Icana, adherents Rudra and Narayana, preceptors Varavana and Vasavana, a descriptive poet Vnibharata, a Prakrit poet the young noble Vayuvikara, two panegyrists Anangavana and Sucivana, an ascetic widow Chakravakika, a snake-doctor Mayuraka, a betel bearer Candaka , a young physician Mandaraka , a reader Sudristi , a goldsmith Camikara, a supervisor Sindhusena, a scribe Govindaka , a painter Viravarman , a modeller Kumaradatta , a drummer Jimuta, two singers Somila and Grahaditya, a maid Kurangika , twe pipers Madhukara and Paravata , a music-teacher Darduraka, a shampooer Keralika, a dancer Tandavika , a dicer Akhandala , a gamester Bhimaka , a young actor Cikhandaka, a dancing girl Harinika , a paracara mendicant Sumati , a Jain monk Viradeva, a story teller Jayasena , a caiva devotee Vakraghona , a magician Karala, a treasure seeker Lohitaksa, an assayer Vihangama , a potter Damodara , a juggler Cakoraksa , a Brahman medicant Tamracuda. With these and others for his companions,pliant from youthfulness, smit with a passion for seeing other lands, despite the wealth sufficient for a Brahman amassed restraint and seeming bewitched by early youth through a headstrong will, he brought himself into the derision of the great."[12]

Dr. Vasudevasarana Agrawal has classified this friend circle and given a detailed list. He has written "This list of Bana's friends introduces to multi dimentional interest of a well cultured citizen and cultural sources of that time. His some friends were related topoetry and education, some were related to dance and music and some were merely helper in entertainment. Along with some were as stabilized servants. List of this friend circle is as follow:-

(A) Poet and Scholar

1. Folk poet Ishan that is intimate friend of Bana. Folk poet means song writer who writes in local or regional languages. It is known that at period of Bana, 'Apbhransa' is used for language. According to Dandi there was publicity of Apbhransa for poetry in Ahir cast etc. Great poet Pushpadanta has described about poet Ishan in preface of Apbhransa Mahapurana.

2. Varnakavi Venibharat. Word Varnakavi is not clear. According to Shankar it means who writes song in Gatha Chhand. Perhaps it means writer of folk poetry as Aalh
3. Kulputra Vayuvikar who writes in Prakrit language.

4-5. Two prisoner Anangbana and Suchibana. Prisoner's work was to read chant. There was chanted a bard in front of Dadhich mounted on horse.

6-7. Two scholar named Varbana and Vasvana. Perhaps they were Scholars related to philosophy.

8. Book reader Sudristi whose voice was sweet .After returning of Bana from Harṣa he had read the story of Vayupurana.
9. Writer Govindak.
10. Story teller Jayasena. It indicates existence of Professional story tellers of that time.

(B) Art

11. Painter Viravarman.
12. Goldsmith Chamikara.
13. Hairik Sindhusena. Shankar has called Hairik as head of goldsmiths but in my view Hairik means cutter of diamond or Begadi.
14. Pustakrit Kumardatta. That time pustakrit means making toys from clay as Bana described at another place: *pustakarmaṇāma pārthivavigrahā:*

(C) Music and Dance

15. Mardagik Jimut. Mardagik- drum or pakhavaj. Many sculptur of drummers are found from Rajghat.

16-17. Vanshik or pipers Madhukar and Paravata.

18. Dardurik Damodar, player of clay drum named Dardur.

19-20. Singers Somila and Grahaditya.

21. Music teacher Darduraka.
22. Dancer Tandavika.
23. Dancing girl Harinika.
24. Young actor (doing Bharatnatyam) Shikhandak.

(D) Sage and Hermit

25. Shiva devotee Vakraghona.

26. Jain monk Viradeva.
27. Parashari Sumati. Bana has described many places about Parashari beggars. Parashari beggars were regular practitioner of Beggar-Sutra written by Parasharya Vyas or Vedant philosophy.
28. Maskari(traveller sage) Tamrachuda.
29. Katyayanika (woman follower of Budha). Chakravakika.

(E) Doctor and Magician

30. Physician Mandaraka.
31. Jangulika (snake- doctor) Mayuraka.
32. Magician Karala.
33. Assayer (chemical drug preparer) Vihangama.
34. Asuravivaravyasani Lohitaksha. Bana has described many places about Asurvivar-Sadhan. Asurvivar's another name was Patalvivar which is described in Vikramank Prabandh the old Prabandh Sangraha. Main aim of this type of stories was to earn wealth by entering into earth wealth by entering into earth hole and having conquered (one's) desires by worshipping Yaksha or monster.

(F) Tricky

35. Akshik (dicer) Akhandala.
36. Kitav (tricky) Bhimaka.
37. Juggler Chakoraksha.

(G) Server

38. Betel- bearer Chandaka.
39. Sairandhri (shampooer) Kurangika.
40. Samvahika Keralika.

(H) Pranayi (loving adherents)

41-42. Rudra and Narayana.

(I) Two Parshav brothers

43-44. Chandrasena and Matrisena. Parshav means son of a Brahman and a Shudra woman.

Chandrasena was one of them those were most loving and credulous for Bana. Bana had given task of fooding and lodging to Chandrasena for Krishna's ambassador Mekhalak.

All these people are part of Bana's friend circle. Their names are also actual. Bana has described some of them in further references. For example, when book reader Sudristi was managing his book for telling story of Vayupurana, behind him pipers Madhukar and Paravata were present in that sitting group." [13]

Wandering here and there Bāṇa Bhaṭṭa became an experienced man and his talent sparkled like pure gold. In Harṣacarita he has written about this experience "Bana gradually thereafter by observation of great courts charming the mind with their noble routine, by paying his respects to the schools of the wise brilliant with blameless knowledge, by attendance at the assemblies of able men deep in priceless discussions, by plunging into the circle of clever men dowered with profound natural wisdom, he regained the sage attitude of mind customary among his race. After long years he returned once more to his own native soil, resort of Brahmans, shelter of the Vātsyāyana line. There, welcomed like a feast day, by kinsmen respectfully announcing their relationship and renewing after long absence their kindly affection, he found himself in the midst of the friends of his youth enjoying almost the bliss of liberation."[14]

Dr. Vasudevasarana Agrawal has written about experience of Bāṇa Bhaṭṭa in his famous book Harṣacarita : Ek Sanskritik Adhyayan. He has written that "Bana has experienced four kinds' social assemblies during his travell or wandering. First, he observed liberal behaviour of great courts and familiar to it. Second, he spent his time infamous schools or educational institutions. Bāṇa Bhaṭṭa has not named any institution but it is possible that he would certainly visited world famous Nalanda University that was situated in his state and experienced educational systems there. He mentioned educational courses of 'Divakarmitra Ashram' which he might have seen in Nalanda University. Third, he might have experienced by attendance at the assemblies of able men deep in priceless discussions. In these assemblies *educational, poetry, vina, vadya, dance* assemblies etc would present there. Fourth, he might have experienced by plunging into the circle of clever men dowered with profound natural wisdom." [15]

Describing the personality of Bāṇa Bhaṭṭa Dr. Vasudevasarana Agrawal has written that "the personality of Bāṇa Bhaṭṭa was the result of four trends. One was his mild behaviour, second was his ancestral attitude for educational love, third was his love about different art and literature and fourth was intelligence in mind. His attitude was very simple, real and full of love. In the long history of Indian writers any person whose attitude fitted with Bana, is Bhartendu Harischandra. He writes that he found himself in the midst of the friends of his youth enjoing almost the bliss of liberation." [16]

When Bana met Harṣavardhana first time we see a glimpse of his mild behaviour. After invitation of Krishna, brother of Harṣavardhana , Bāṇa Bhaṭṭa presented himself in front of Harṣavardhana then he had behaved well. Bāṇa Bhaṭṭa has given detail of this incident in Harṣacarita "But when the king heard it and saw him, he asked, filling the sky with his voice deep like roar of a lion in a mountain cave, 'Is that Bana?' The doorkeeper replied, 'As my lord commands; it is he.' 'I will not see him yet, as he has not as yet offered his tribute of respect,' so saying, he turned the long brilliance of his eye, whose pupil trembled as it inclined to the corner of the eye, as if he was shaking a curtain variegated across with white and dark silk, and said to his favourite, the son of the king of Malwa, who was sitting behind, 'He is a thorough petit-maitre.' But when the other paused for a moment in silence at this unexplained speech of the king and the courtiers were all dumb, Bana replied, 'why, my lord, do you thus addresss me, as if you did not know my character and did not believe me, as if you depended on others for guidance and did not understand the way of the world yourself? The nature and talk of people will always be wildful and various; but the great out to see things as they are. You surely will not regard me with prejudice as if I had no special claims. I am a Brahman born in the family of the Soma-drinking Vātsyāyanas.

Every ceremony was only performed, as its time came, beginning with the investiture with the sacred cord; I have throughly studied the Veda with its six angas and as far as I was able I have heard lectures on the castras, and from my marriage I have been a diligent house holder; what sign have I of being a petit-maitre ? My youth indeed was not without those follies which are not directly inconsistent with either world, so far I will not deny, and my heart on this point will confess a feeling of repentance. But now a days, when your highness, calm in mind like Buddha himself, one who carries out all the rules for the castes and orders like Manu, and bears the rod of punishment as visibly as Yama, - governs the whole earth girdled by the seven oceans and bearing all the continents as its garland, who would venture without fear even to act in his own mind the character of indecorum, that bosom-friend of open profligacy? I will not dwell on human beings, in consequence of your power even the bees drink honey in fear, even the ruddy-geese are ashamed of their too great fondness , the very monkeys are alarmed when they play their wanton tricks and even all the destructive animals eat flesh with compassion. Your highness will in time know me thoroughly by yourself, for it is the nature of the wise that their minds never act perversely.' Having said this, he was silent." [17]

Through this description it is clear that Bāṇa Bhaṭṭa defended himself humbly in front of Harṣavardhana . After so much insult Bana has not developed any bitterness in his mind for Harṣavardhana but adversely thought that it was mildness of Harṣa . He has writen in Harṣacarita- "He reflected to himself, 'king Harṣa if very gracious, since he is still fond of me, though he is vexed at the rumours which have naturally spread about my many youthful follies, if I had been really under his displeasure, he would not have honoured me with an audience. He wishes me to be virtuous, for lords teach proper behaviour to their dependents even without words by granting them an appropriate reception. Shame on me, thus blinded in my mind by my own faults, and crushed by neglect,-that I venture to indulge in various fancies concerning this most excellent monarch. Verily I will endeavour so to act that he may recognize me in time in my real character." [18] According to his thinking he overcame to his weakness of personality and after sometime received confidence of king.

After having gotten honour by the king, Bāṇa Bhaṭṭa departed from king's court and went to his village to visit his kins. It was the beginning of autumn. His brothers and other Villagers greeted warmly when he reached to Prītikūṭa . Then Bāṇa Bhaṭṭa wrote Harṣacarita on the request of his brothers. This book is an important source to make history of Harṣa period or early seventh century. This book gives us priceless knowledge to write political, social, cultural, religious and literary history of early seventh century. Along with this Bāṇa Bhaṭṭa has written a novel named Kādambarī that also makes available more knowledge to depict cultural and social aspects of that time.

In Harṣacarita we see hard work of Bāṇa Bhaṭṭa that became fruitful in Kādambarī . These two books of Bana are significantly important for literature and art and they are also important for writing history.

Bāṇa Bhaṭṭa has written Harṣacarita as *Akhyayika* and Kādambarī as *Katha*. He has written in starting of Harṣacarita that 'yet still through my loyalty to my lord, undismayed and eager in the hope of gaining my end, I venture audaciously to plunge with my tongue into ocean of narrative.' In preface of Kadanbari he has written Kādambarī as extraordinary Katha that can defeat Vasavdatta and Vrihatkatha. "In Amarkosh it is said, 'Akhyayikopalabdhartha' that means Akhyayika is a tale whose truth is known. Subject of Katha is based on imagination. Further characters of Akhyayika developed and different scholars gave their own definition of Akhyayika. After examining Harṣacarita and Kādambarī it is clear that subject of Akhyayika is related to history and subject of Katha is related to imagination or fable. According to Agnipurana Akhyayika is that which praise and describe details about clan of writer, kidnap of lady, war details, detail of calamity, love and work in very sharp words, chapter names in '*Uchchhawas*', repetition of '*Churnak*' style, '*Vakra*' and '*Apvakra*' sloka found there. (Agni-336/12-14) In katha , reverse to it , praise and details about clan of writer confined to few 'slokas' there should be other story in main story, not paragraph found and '*Lambak'* found at anywhere (Agni-336/15-17). Dandi has also tried to differentiate both in 'Kavyadarsh'. Narrator of Akhyayika is hero self but katha's hero is other; but this rule is not applicable to everywhere. Dandi was not prejudice to any of both diffferences. He thinks that there is mild difference. But Bana has accepted that both are different. He used '*Vakradi Chhanda*' in Harṣacarita and divided Chapters in Uchchhawases. In katha Bana implemented different style. Further scholars defined Akhyayika and Katha on base of Harṣacarita and Kādambarī ."[19]

It is helpful to understand contemporary Indian history on base of description of Harṣacarita and Kādambarī . Actually through his description Bana has brought polity, behaviour of people, activities of people and culture in front of us as series in form of fantasy of poetry. It is special characteristic of writing of Bana. Through his description he presented every aspect of contemporary life in front of us. When we compare and re- explain facts presented by Bana and facts that are gathered from contemporary literature and art, then whole picture of seventh century history occurs in front of us as a film. In that film we clearly saw contemporary polity, characters of kings, cabinet, army construction, judiciary, social condition, religion, education and economic condition. "He (Bana) himself said at one place in Kādambarī - svāyamutpāditānēka cintāśatākulā kavimatiriva taralatā na kiñcinnōtprēkṣatē *(Anu-198, page-202).*That means, when poet's wavy mind activates then he imagines many fantasy within him, there is nothing that does not come in it. All comes out from poet's fantasy that is present in whole behaiour of people and creation of God. It is essential to understand that indication of poet by heavy thinking and extensive knowledge." [20]

In Harṣacarita kings palace is described at the occasion of first meeting of Bāṇa Bhaṭṭa to Harṣavardhana that introduces architecture of that time. In second chapter of Harṣacarita it is described that Bana "going on the way indicated by Dauvarika crossed three rooms full of thousand kings, saw Chakrawarti king Harṣa in fourth room. He was sited at open space in house in front of Bhuktasthanmandap." [21]

Like this it is written in first part of Kādambarī that "Chandrapeeda saw his father sitting on swan like white bedstead inside a room after crossing seven rooms (dyodhiyan) those were full of thousand people."[22] From these descriptions and many descriptions that are found in both the books, it is concluded that in king palace it was to cross five rooms to reach main gate of palace to Bhuktasthanmandap and it was to cross seven rooms to reach Antahpur (inner part of palace). Through this it occures a picture of king palace in front of us which is familiar us to extraordinary structure of that palace, along with we see protection concerns behind this structure of palace. "There was horse shelter for special horses of king within main gate of palace or dyodhi. There was elephant shelter of king's own special elephant at that place. After that there were three squire crossings. In these there was external debate house of Bahya Aasthanmandap in second room. It was also called Bahya. There was living room of king or Dhavalgriha in third room of king palace. There was Bhuktasthanmandap in fourth room along with that where king met with special people after dinner. According to medieval definition Bahya Kaksha or Bahya Aasthanmandap called Divane Aam and Bhuktasthanmandap called Divane Khas."[23] There were all stablishments in king's palace for king's advantage i.e. worship house, Chatuhshal , Vithiyan, pragrivak, mirror , sleeping room, living room (Chitrashalika) , music room, chandrashala, gatekeeper room etc. The structure of palace was closely resembled to Mughal period palaces. It is clear that it was difficult to meet king and only who could meet king on whom he has special affection. Bana has written that around king there was huge security circle within which no one could enter. Kalidas has also written that, those persons can reach near king's feet for which king have special affection. Kings had taken attention about people's condition and prosperity and self met people to do away their grievances. Bāṇa Bhaṭṭa has written in first part of Kādambarī "(Tarapeed) met people in some intervals to praise people and sat on throne to do special work."[24] Kings had appointed experienced ministers and taken action on their good solutions for any situation. Kādambarī and Harṣacarita describe this type of solutions given on time to time by experienced ministers.

Till seventh century elephants were important for construction of army. According to Bāṇa Bhaṭṭa, in Harṣa 's army there were many 'Achyut' of elphants. One 'Achyut' was equall to ten thousand. "According to chinese traveller Hiuen-Tsang there weresixty thousand war elephants and a cavalry of one lakh horses in Harṣa army, that was the reason of his thirty years rulling without any disturbance. It means king had arranged a huge army before Bana had joined the royal near about the sametime. Bana's many 'Achyut Nagbal' and Hiuen-Tsang's 'sixty thousand war elephants' army, supports each other. Bana said Harṣa as 'Mahavahinipati'. This adjective is also true seeing huge army depicted by Hiuen-Tsang."[25] Elephants were important in destruction of small forts of contemporary land lords and were capable to crack front attack of cavalry. There were main reasons behind giving more importance of war elephants in army than horses.

Micro description of Indian society given by Bana in Harṣacarita and Kādambarī are praise worthy. He has described condition of every section of society, position of woman, garments and ornaments, food and beverages etc in detail. Describing about four varnas (Brahman, Kshatriya, Vaisya and shudra) of society Bana writes that Brahmans were above all in all varnas. In first chapter of Harṣacarita Saraswati says "even to Brahmans by birth merely, uninitiated in heart, respect is due."[26] There was a tradition in society to marry in its own cast. There were other casts also in society which described by Bana. There were included Tamboli , Suvarnakar, Clay toy maker , Parashar saint etc.

Women position in society is known by description of Bana. Women were educated in music, dance and painting. Bana has written with reference to Rajyashri "Meanwhile Rajyashri gradually grew up in daily increasing familiarity with friends expert in song, dance etc and with all accomplishments. In a comparatively limited period she came to maturity."[27] It is depicted as drawing picture of her beloved king Udayan by heroine Sagarika in Samrat Harṣa 's act 'Ratnawali'. Like it in 'Priyadarshika' it is given responsibility to servant Priyadarshika to train king and queen in song, dance and handle instruments. Along with these arts women were also taught religious books. Bana has written that Harṣa had requested Divakarmitra that he would comfort with his righteous discourses, and his passionless instruction which produces salutary knowledge, and his advice which calms the disposition, and his Buddhist doctrines which drive away worldly passion. "It is written in 'Life' that when Hiuen-Tsang was delivering speech on religion in front of Harṣa then Rajyashri was near his brother. This description shows that Rajyashri has interest in religious philosophy and wittiness and also presents proof that there was no tradition of Parda in women." [28] It is clear from Bana's description that girls were married early in age group of fourteen to fifteen. Two incidents of sati are described in Harṣacarita, once Harṣa mother Yashovati and second Rajyashri (who was rescued). But it is clear from Bāṇa Bhaṭṭa's description that, wish to die before her husband's death or unwidowed and to overcome from agony were reasons behind becoming Sati of women and it was not established as a tradition. In Harṣacarita Bana condemns the act of becoming Sati and he has written it as a work that leads to Hell.

Bāṇa Bhaṭṭa has given detail description about dresses and ornaments of men. In first chapter of Harṣacarita Bana has described dress of Dadhich and wrote that young youth wore Kanchuk (Labada) and tightened Uttariya of shawl (turban) on head, strip of doubled cloth was tightened knot around waist. Hiuen-Tsang also written that there was no cut and stitch in upper and lower garments of Indians. They were like Dhawal (white) garments, no coloured and diagrammed. Male wore a long cloth that hung to feet and a piece of cloth stripped to armpit tightened around waist and hand spare bare. Female mainly wore three garments Kanchuk, Lahanga and Uttariya "women of Sthanvishwar also, Bana has written, were wearing Kanchuk (Tritiya Uchchhawas-page-166). On other places Bana has written about hanging Uttariya or hanging shawl from both side of shoulder (Chaturth Uchchhawas-page-226) and in Pratham Uchchhawas (page-60) described Saraswati as concealing her heart with a portion of shawl of woven bark." [29] Hiuen-

Tsang has also written about hanged garment of women from shoulder to earth below ankle of feet.

It is clear from description of Harṣacarita and Kādambarī that men and women were amative to jevellery. Important jewellery of men were necklace of pearl, crestjewel, gems fitted ear ring, garland of Maltiflower, Shikharkhandika (head jewellery) made from lotus gems, Trikantak jewellery, ring etc. Similar to Bana's description gold ear jewellery made of emerald fitted between two pearl, is conserved in national museum New Delhi. Women ornaments described by Bana were Kardhani or Mekhala (Belt), necklace of pearl, Emerald fitted crocodile headed gold bangle, Trikantak jewellery, ear ring, Nupur a ear jewellery, Mangalsutra (locket), ring etc.

By description of Bana it is known about make-up aids that were in use in seventh century. There was tradition of make- up aids to beautify forehead, hair, lip , to colour sole and to fragrant mouth. Feet were coloured by liquid Aalta pigment.

There is also description of putting sectarial mark bearing the fragrance of civet. There is description of several applications of betel to colour lips. Liquid Aalta pigment and vermilion powder on forehead were auspicious make- up for unwidowed women. Men and women used mangoes, camphor, kakkola-fruits, cloves and coral trees to fragrant their mouth. Bana has described breathing a fragrance from Dadhīca 's mouth of these liquids and written that "His mouth, breathing a fragrance of mangoes, camphor, kakkola-fruits, cloves and coral trees." [30] Bana has described about three time bath (morning, midday and evening) in a day and use of civet, camphor and sandal liquid to fragrance body. Hiuen-Tsang also written that Indians rubbed sandal and keshar dust like fragranted materials on their body. In sequence of describing marriage of Rajyashri Bāṇa Bhaṭṭa has depicted a picture of Indian marriage system in context of seventh century which is also alive today. The description of Kautik Griha (or kohbar) ,march around the Vedi (the very flames), Vas Griha (bridegroom chamber) and provision named in the dowry etc. proves antiquity and continuity of Indian marriage system.

Describing the food of that time, Bana writes about use of vegetarian and non- vegetarian food. Important food materials used by people of that time, were - rice, bread of wheat, milk, clarified butter, sugar, khand, mustard oil, sattu, gram etc. Bana has described that people eat after bath. Hiuen-Tsang also written that Indians gave attention to their personal purity. They bathed before taking food. There is similarity between description about food material of Hiuen-Tsang and that of Bāṇa Bhaṭṭa.

Many facts related to Indian culture, tradition, astrology, charms and incantations, thinking about favourable-unfavourable condition, wealthy tradition of music, long tradition of hospitality etc found in Harṣacarita and Kādambarī . From these facts Bana has exposed special characteristics of Indian culture in front of world. Facts described by Bana, related to Indian culture, also relevant today. In Harṣacarita and Kādambarī it is written about calculation of good omen (Shubh Muhurt) to start special works on occasion of birth and wedding, departure time of kings for war and any other occasion. Bāṇa Bhaṭṭa has written about calculation by astrologers to tell future of Harṣa at time of his birth (Harṣacarita ,Chaturth Uchchhawas-page-217-18) and calculation by astrologer of good omen for wedding of Rajyashri (Harṣacarita, Chaturth Uchchhawas-page-241). It is also written in Harṣacarita and Kādambarī about antiquities of Palmistry and telling future on base of auspicious marks plotted on palm and sole. It is written in second chapter of Harṣacarita "bore signs which told of his sovereignty over the four oceans in their auspicious marks, such as the lotus, the shell, the fish and the makara." [31] Like this it is written in Kādambarī "God Vishnu like marks, the shell-wheel and auspicious lines are plotted on his both palms. His both feet were soft like new leaves of Kalpa Taru (tree of Kalpa) and decorated with auspicious mark of flag, chariot, horse, umbrella (chhatra) and lotus. These feet were able to kiss by crest-jewell of thousand kings."[32]

Bāṇa Bhaṭṭa has described rituals of Indian culture like Jatkarma, Mundan, Upnayan etc. He has described about, washing earth with cow-dung for purity, wearing holy black-magic made from nails of tiger to take liberty from ghost, keeping fast, burning lamp, rampart to concilate chandi, pacifying Mahakala, and solicit the vampire with the offering of skull by devotees of Pashupat community for recovering Prabhakara-Vardhana health, some are alive today also as heritage of Indian culture. Bāṇa Bhaṭṭa has described gesture of greetings such as, touching earth from head, to bow head towards earth, to bow on earth for some time with spread hands, touching earth by knee and palm, by touching feet, touching hand on earth, rubbing forehead on feet etc, were important. These types of greetings are also proved by description of Hiuen-Tsang.

In Harṣacarita Bāṇa Bhaṭṭa has illustrated 'Shree Parvat'. He has written that "victorious Harṣa guarded the world by a wall of fire of glorious majesty, as Shree Parvat fulfilled the desires of all the people." [33] From this description of Shree Parvat it is clear that at the time of Bana, fame of that mountain (Shree Parvat) spread every -where in seventh century which was situated in Guntoor district of Andhra Pradesh. Shreee Parvat is recently Shree Shail which is on the south bank of River Krishna 82 miles far away from Kurnul in east direction. It was famous centre for black magic, charm and incantations. It is the birth place of Mantrayan. This (Shree Parvat) is also described in Malatimadhav and Kādambarī . This place was famous in contemporary society that all desires are fulfilled at that place. It was people belief that wall of fire around Shree Parvat saves it. Bana has written about this hearsay.

In Harṣacarita Bāṇa Bhaṭṭa has written about Yampattika which he saw passing through streets of market. He has written about the content of Yampattika "whose left hand was a painted canvas stretched out on a support of upright rod and showing the lord of the death mounted on his dreadful buffalo wielding a reed-wand in his other hand, he was expounding the features of the next world." [34] This description proves tradition of different types of 'Chitrapatt' with messages which were used that time. "There are found quotations of 'Laxmipatt', 'Anangpatt' etc. Many Budhapatt contemporary to Bana are found from Millenbudh cave temple of East-Asia." [35]

It was a religious tradition in India from early civilization. Worshiping different God-Goddess has been tradition from Saindhav civilization till now. Some Gods got importance and some lost their importance in different time of history. Bāṇa Bhaṭṭa has described contemporary religious Gods, rituals, different religious communities and tradition in detail. He has described contemporary God-Goddess in which- Shiva, Vrihaspati, Katyayani, Vishnu, Kuldevtas, Narayan, Bhagwan Pravajya, Laxmi, Madhu Kaitabh, Parvati, Devmata Aditi, Bhagwati Durga, Saraswati etc were important. Performers of religious ritual put three lined auspicious mark on their forehead, wore necklace of crystal and Rudraksha. In Harṣacarita Bana has depicted current figure of contemporary 'Shaivacharyas' by describing 'Betal Sadhana' of Bhairavacharya. 'Betal Sadhana' was practice of abhorrent incantation. Again in Harṣacarita Bāṇa Bhaṭṭa has described selling of holy flesh (Mahamans) in open by princes to recover health of Prabhakara-Vardhanaa. This type of terrifying acts was in use, in Kapalik community. There is detailed description in Harṣacarita about different religious communities which were present in seventh century. This description is useful in view of religious history. In this episode "Bana has described 21 religious communities. In these only four are named and rest 17 are quoted without name. We can detect them through hidden signals of their religious principles and behavior." [36] "Somadev has given good introduction of different religious communities and their principles in 'Yashastilakachampoo'(9th AD). Shri Handi has historically deliberated in detail on them in his book. Those religious communities and their principles are also indicated in Naishadh Caritaa of Shri Harṣa and in act of Prabodhchandrodaya etc. But Bana's description belongs to first half of seventh century so it is most important. Bana's material pointed out the historical development of different philosophical theories and religious communities which were before the time of Shankaracharya. Further in Ashtam Uchchhawas Bana has enumerated names of followers of nineteen religious communities which lived at 'Divakarmitra's Ashram'. That list is helpful to understand the key of present episode. Religious experts of different sects were present in Divakarmitra's Ashram- 1.Aarhat, 2.Maskari, 3.Swetpatt, 4.Panduribhikshu, 5.Bhagawat, 6.Varni, 7.Keshlunchan, 8.Kapil, 9.Jain, 10.Lokayit, 11.Kanad, 12.Aupnishad, 13.Aishwarkarnik, 14.Karan dhami, 15.Dharmashastri, 16.Pauranik, 17.Sapt tantav, 18.Shabd, 19.Panchratrik and others. There is difference between previous list and serial number of this list but here essentially disguised the key to understand these." [37]

Describing about Ujjayini in Kādambarī it is written that 'there are Devmandir (a place of worship or temple) at the crossings of that city. There are established kalash of gold on top of those Devmandirs and above that white flags are hoisting'. This description indicates the developed form of architecture of Mandir (temple) which was started during Gupta period.

To understand education system of seventh century, the facts described in Harṣacarita and Kādambarī are most important. It is proved a long tradition of systematic education through description of Bāṇa Bhaṭṭa. Generally homes of Brahmans were centre of education. Description of taking knowledge and skill at mother-in-law's house by Dadhīca proves this fact. When gratified beyond measure by Harṣa , Bana reached at Prītikūṭa then he asked his brothers and relatives "Have you been happy all this time? Does the sacrifice proceed without hindrance, gratifying the Brahman groups by its faultless performance? Do the fires devour oblations with ritual duly and without flow performed? Do the boys pursue their studies at the proper time? Is there the same unbroken daily application to the Veda? The old earnestness in the practice of the art of sacrifice? Are there the same classes in grammar exposition, showing respect by days not idly spent in a series of emulous discussions? Is there the old logic society, regardless of all other occupations? The same excessive delight in the Mimamsa, dulling all pleasure in other authoritative books? Are there the same poetic addresses, raining down ambrosia of ever-new phrases?"[38] "These questions indicate the environment of continuous reading & studying and thinking of holy books in Brahmans families. These Brahman families do school work in ancient education system." [39]Schools were also established by states and economic aid was provided to them. Bana has written in Kādambarī that "After some time king Tarapeed established a Devmandir like school outside the city, to protect his son's mind from bad surroundings. That school was on the bank of Shipra River and had a size of half mile length and width. There was a courtyard and around that there was a white lime washed wall. That school was seen like a necklace of snow covered mountain tops. There was a vast ditch around that. There were very big and very strong doors in that school. There was only one way to enter it. There was a gym in that campus. Special efforts were made to gather teachers of all subjects to teach them. In that school king put his son as cub kept in cage. Chandrapeed has forbidden going out from school premises. In kins, there kept only teachers sons and all objects took off from there that attracts mind of children. Like this he formulate strategy that any object not to attract child's mind." [40] Bāṇa Bhaṭṭa has written in Pratham Uchchhawas of Harṣacarita about self living in the schools of the wise brilliant with blameless knowledge, from which it is assumed that, he had also lived at Nalanda University which was economically supported by state. As it there is indication three types of educational institutions- private schools, reserved school for children of king's family and government aided educational institution. There was same education system for men and women (for king's family members).

It can be prepared a long list of subjects those were taught in schools of seventh century on base of Harṣacarita and Kādambarī . Important subjects that taught that time were practice of Veda (four Vedas), education related to Yaga, Purana,, study of history, Ramayan, Mahabharat, Natyashastra, Kavya-Natak, ancient-present story, ethics of Beauty, Pithy and quotable saying of Vairagya, debate of laughing, paintings etc. Besides this there was arrangement of vocational course. Bāṇa Bhaṭṭa writes in Kādambarī "there citizen had constructed court, hostel, wells, Devmandir, bridge and machine which have instructed in Smritishastra."[41] Again Bana has written "they (people of Ujjayini) are expert in all scientific machines and architecture."[42] According to Bāṇa Bhaṭṭa, Bhojpatra and leaf of Ketaki are used as paper for writing and coal burned in liquid of leafs was used as ink to write. Bana has described about bundling book with cotton thread and reading book putting on desk of reed. Description of book reader Sudristi proves that book reading was a profession of that time.

There is given important information about contemporary economy in Harṣacarita and Kādambarī by Bāṇa Bhaṭṭa. Different aspects of seventh century economy are known on base of these informations as agriculture, animal husbandry, business, sources of income, wealth of cities etc. Describing about Shreekanth janpad (certain region) in Harṣacarita Bana has written "owing to the number of its land lotuses the ploughs, whose shares uproot the fibers as they scar the acres, excite a tumult of bees, singing, as it were, the excellencies of good soil. Unbroken lines of Pundra sugar cane enclosures seem besprinkled by the clouds that drink the Milky Sea. On every side its marches are packed with corn heaps, like extemporized mountains, distributed among the threshing floors. Throughout it is adorned with rice crops extending beyond their fields, where the ground bristles with cumin beds watered by the pots of the Persian wheel. Upon its lordly uplands are wheat crops variegated with Rajamasa patches ripe to bursting and yellow with the split bean pods. Attended by singing herdsmen mounted on buffalos, pursued by sparrows greedy for swarms of flies, gay with the tinkle of bells bound to their necks, roaming herds of cows make white its forests, reveling on Vaspachedya grass and dropping milk as if the milky sea had been drunk by the bull of Civa (Shiva) and then divided up by him into many portions through fear of indigestion."[43]Through this description it is known about doing agriculture with plough, watering land by Persian wheel and growing crops of kidney bean, wheat and rice along with it is also known that buffalos and cows husbandry was in use for milk. Like this in Saptam Uchchawas of Harṣacarita, at time of describing departure of Harṣa army it is written about illiterate Agraharik (who look after agriculture) came out of village.

In Kādambarī , describing wealthiness of Ujjayini Bana has written "that's (Ujjayini) street sides have hoard of shell, mother of pearl, pearl, coral and emerald for sell."[44] Like this in Saptam Uchchawas of Harṣacarita, it is described that some people wore Kanchuk garment of China. These descriptions are historically important and reveal the business contact from foreign countries and contemporary business.

We can imagine wealthiness of contemporary cities from description of Kādambarī in which it is written that there were big buildings and millionaire citizens in Ujjayini city. In Chaturth Uchchhawas of Harṣacarita it is written that "from the earth uprose great treasures, enclosed in cups bedecked with chains of gold (page-219)." This description is most important for knowledge of treasure that stored in underground rooms of palace.

Knowledge of wealthiness or economy of any state is based on coins found at that place. Bāṇa Bhaṭṭa has also described about coins of that time. In Saptam Uchchawas of Harṣacarita it is written about giving a bull marked new gold coin to Harṣa by Gramakshapatalik (main officer of village or Patawari). "Fortunately, a sample of bull marked copper coin is available from Sonipat. On that coin at top a bull is sitting, that's mouth, is in right direction, as Bana has described. Harṣa was *paramamāhēśvara.* So this bull is sign of Nandi. In scribed script of Rajyadhikar Mahamudra, there is a type of description about ancestors of Harṣa as found in Bansakheda-Copper plate. It is called *Purvi.*"[45]

In Harṣacarita it is written about Stupa or Chaitya marked baked red terra-cotta seal. "In excavation of ancient Bauddh places there are found large number of this type of Chaitya marked terra-cotta seals. On them one or many stupa marked and generally Buddha's 'yē dharmā hētuprabhavā:' Mantra once or many times written on it. People who went to see, they bring that type of seal with them and to instigate in worship. As Bana has written, those were stored beside." [46]

After the study of Harṣacarita and Kādambarī we are familiar with special characteristics of Bāṇa Bhaṭṭa writing. These characteristics differ him from other contemporary writers and proved him a historian along with novel writer. Special characteristics of Bāṇa Bhaṭṭa writing is his micro observation. He describes any incidents as it seems a live telecast. Description of summer, description of Harṣa 's elephant Darpashat, description of Ujjayini city etc are proof of his micro observation. In these descriptions there are many facts related to contemporary history, it is essential to find out them and examine on historical touchstone. These materials act as supplementary facts with antiquities and other materials and connect spare chains of seventh century to familiar us with total civilized history. In modern history writing there is special importance of impartial description. In Harṣacarita he is anchor of story but he called himself as 'Bana' not 'I'. This style of writing makes Bana special and expresses his commitment to impartial writing of any incident. He has not omitted fault of Bāṇa Bhaṭṭa in his description. He had described about his wandering and become reproach after the death of his father in first chapter of Harṣacarita. In second chapter of Harṣacarita he also accepted himself as reproach in open court of Harṣavardhana when Harṣa misbehaved him. This description proved that writing of a man is not partial who accepts his fault himself without any hesitation. Bāṇa Bhaṭṭa has presented history of Harṣa period impartially and doing so really he performed the task of responsible historian.

Bāṇa Bhaṭṭa has not mentioned any date at any place that is essential for history writing. In modern history writing also there is not given special emphasis on dates (as it was used in earlier history writing) but its special emphasis on every aspects of contemporary civilization as, politics, society, culture, religion and faith, economy, literature etc. In Harṣacarita and Kādambarī there are ample materials related to every aspect of contemporary civilization as polity, society, culture, religion, economy and literature etc. Total Indian panorama of seventh century can be calculated on base of these two books. The description of Bāṇa Bhaṭṭa is also important to understand Indian panorama because he was Indian and fully aware of Indian environment. It is the reason that there is not found any type of destitution in description of Bāṇa Bhaṭṭa as there is found contradiction or destitution due to misunderstanding of Indian environment and situation in description of foreign travelers. Thus, in front of us Bana emerges as a historian and study of his history writing is important to understand the history of seventh century completely.

References:-

1. Harṣa Caritaaam-Chowkhamba Vidyabhawan Varanasi-Page-6.
2. Kādambarī -Chowkhamba Vidyabhawan Varanasi-Page-8.
3. The Harsa Caritaa of Bana-Trans.by-E.B.Cowell & F.W.Thomas- Motilal Banarsidass Publishers Pvt.Ltd. Delhi-Page-29-30.
4. Do. - Page-30.
5. Kādambarī :Ek Sanskritik Adhyayan-Vasudevasarana Agrawala- The Chowkhamba Vidyabhawan Varanasi-Page-17.
6. Kādambarī -Chowkhamba Vidyabhawan Varanasi-Page-2.
7. Kādambarī : Ek Sanskritik Adhyayan-Vasudevasarana Agrawala- The Chowkhamba Vidyabhawan Varanasi-Page-16.
8. Kādambarī -Poorvabhagah-Chowkhamba Vidyabhawan Varanasi- Page-3.
9. Kādambarī : Ek Sanskritik Adhyayan-Vasudevasarana Agrawala- The Chowkhamba Vidyabhawan Varanasi-Page-16.
10. Harṣacarita: Ek Sanskritik Adhyayan-Dr.Vasudevasarana Agrawal- Bihar Rashtrabhasha Parishad Patna-Page-19.
11. Do -Page-18-19.
12. The Harsa Caritaa of Bana-Trans.by-E.B.Cowell & F.W.Thomas- Motilal Banarsidass Publishers Pvt.Ltd. Delhi-Page-32-33.
13. Harṣacarita: Ek Sanskritik Adhyayan Dr.Vasudevasarana Agrawal- Bihar Rashtrabhasha Parishad Patna-Page-28-30.

14. The Harsa Caritaa of Bana-Trans.by-E.B.Cowell & F.W.Thomas- Motilal Banarsidass Publishers Pvt.Ltd. Delhi- Page-33-34.
15. The Harsa Caritaa of Bana-Trans.by-E.B.Cowell & F.W.Thomas -Motilal Banarsidass Publishers Pvt.Ltd. Delhi-Page-27-28.
16. Do -Page-28.
17. The Harsa Caritaa of Bana-Trans.by-E.B.Cowell & F.W.Thomas-Motilal Banarsidass Publishers Pvt.Ltd. Delhi-Page- 65-67.
18. Do -Page-68-69.
19. Harṣacaritama-Chowkhamba Vidyabhawan Varanasi- Page-32.
20. Kādambarī : Ek Sanskritik Adhyayan-Vasudevasarana Agrawala- The Chowkhamba Vidyabhawan Varanasi-Page-14.
21. Harṣacaritama-Chowkhamba Vidyabhawan Varanasi- Page-118.
22. Kādambarī -Poorvabhagah-Chowkhamba Vidyabhawan Varanasi- Page-195-96.
23. Harṣacarita: Ek Sanskritik Adhyayan Dr.Vasudevasarana Agrawal- Bihar Rashtrabhasha Parishad Patna-Page-38.
24. Kādambarī -Poorvabhagah-Chowkhamba Vidyabhawan Varanasi-Page-127.
25. Harṣacarita: Ek Sanskritik Adhyayan- Dr.Vasudevasarana Agrawal- Bihar Rashtrabhasha Parishad Patna-Page-38-39.
26. The Harsa Caritaa of Bana-Trans.by-E.B.Cowell & F.W.Thomas-Motilal Banarsidass Publishers Pvt.Ltd.Delhi-Page-7.
27. Do -Page-121.
28. Rajvansh: Maukhari aur Puṣyabhūti- Pr. Bhagwati Prasad Panthari- Bihar Hindi Granth Akadamy Patna- Page-316.

29. Do -Page-324.
30. The Harsa Caritaa of Bana-Trans.by-E.B.Cowell & F.W.Thomas-Motilal Banarsidass Publishers Pvt.Ltd.Delhi-Page-17.
31. Do -Page-59.
32. Kādambarī -Poorvabhagah-Chowkhamba Vidyabhawan Varanasi-Page-154-55.
33. The Harsa Caritaa of Bana-Trans.by-E.B.Cowell & F.W.Thomas -Motilal Banarsidass Publishers Pvt.Ltd.Delhi-Page-3.
34. Do -Page-136.
35. Harṣacarita: Ek Sanskritik Adhyayan Dr.Vasudevasarana Agrawal- Bihar Rashtrabhasha Parishad Patna-Page-91.
36. Do -Page-106.
37. Do -Page-106-07
38. The Harsa Caritaa of Bana-Trans.by-E.B.Cowell & F.W.Thomas-Motilal Banarsidass Publishers Pvt.Ltd. Delhi- Page-71.
39. Harṣacarita: Ek Sanskritik Adhyayan- Dr.Vasudevasarana Agrawal- Bihar Rashtrabhasha Parishad Patna-Page-51.
40. Kādambarī -Poorvabhagah-Chowkhamba Vidyabhawan Varanasi -Page-158-59.
41. Do -Page-107.
42. Do -Page-108.
43. The Harsa Caritaa of Bana-Trans.by-E.B.Cowell & F.W.Thomas-Motilal Banarsidass Publishers Pvt.Ltd. Delhi-Page-79-80.
44. Kādambarī -Poorvabhagah-Chowkhamba Vidyabhawan Varanasi- Page-105.
45. Harṣacarita: Ek Sanskritik Adhyayan- Dr. Vasudevasaran Agrawal- Bihar Rashtrabhasha Parishad Patna-Page-141.
46. Do -Page-194.

Chapter-2

Bāṇa Bhaṭṭa and Contemporary Political Study in the Seventh Century

---

Indian political scenario in the seventh century especially Harṣa-period could not be known without help of writing of Bāṇa Bhaṭṭa, The Harṣacarita and The Kādambarī. Bāṇa Bhaṭṭa has depicted contemporary political events, position of king, qualities and duties of kings, work of ministers, bureaucracy administrative system, defense system (internal and external) and judiciary in his books. Together with he had given authentic and important information about revenue system, expansion of state, relation with neighboring countries and foreign policy. Other contemporary books and inscriptions also support description given by Bāṇa Bhaṭṭa. There are some unexplained facts, which can be understood only by the writings of Bāṇa Bhaṭṭa.

The complete political scenario of seventh century can be described by the description of Bana under following subtitles:-

Puṣyabhūti dynasty: Political Events and expansion of Empire:-

The information about the position of kings, their merits and demerits and duties to the subject is received from the Harṣacarita and The Kādambarī. In The Harṣacarita there is illustration about the Puṣyabhūti dynasty, personality and works of king Harṣa, by dint of which the political system of Harṣa-period can be understood easily. On the other hand the story described in the Kādambarī gives detail information about contemporary political behavior, policy of the state, duties of a king etc.

In the Harṣacarita Bāṇa Bhaṭṭa has written that Puṣyabhūti Dynasty was emerged in Shrikanth Janpad. The capital of this janapad was Sthaneshwar. According to The Harṣacharit Puṣyabhūti was the first king in Sthaneshwar. Bāṇa Bhaṭṭa has written about the dynasty started with king Puṣyabhūti that "as the Harivansha started from yaduking Shoor undefeatable i.e. a dynasty containing Vishnu and Balram (dynasty with undefeatable army) so a dynasty started with Puṣyabhūti."[1] In context of king Puṣyabhūti , there is description in Harṣacarita about obtaining a sword named Atthas from Bhairavacharya, event of Betal and defeat of Shrikanth Nag (on which that Janpad was named), from these it is concluded that after defeating the ruler of Shrikanth Janpad king Pushybhuti has laid the foundation of Pusyabhuti dynasty. About this conclusion of Prof. Bhagwati Prasad Panthari seems absolutely correct. He writes that "probably Shrikanth Janpad was basically under control of Nags and Pusyabhuti snatched it from Nags and took it in his control. After describing the incident of defeating Shrikanth Nag Bana describes about giving a boon to Pusyabhuti by Laxmi that he (Pusyabhuti) will be founder of great dynasty through his elevation of strength and superlative devotion to the holy lord Shiva and like a third added to the Sun and Moon - *'anēna satvōtkarṣēṇa bhagavacchiva bhaṭṭārakabhaktvā cāsādhāraṇayā bhavāmbhuvi sūryacandramasōstṛtīya -mahatō rājavaṁśasya kartā bhaviṣyati'* (Harṣacarita, tritiya uchchhawas, page-196)

It is clear that founder of Sthanvishwar & Kanauj's great Puṣyabhūti dynasty was a heroic man named Puṣyabhūti and he was worshipper and great devotee of lord Siva."[2] It is described in Fourth Uchchhawas of The Harṣacarita that "the whole world depending on the visible creatures is produced from Vishnu, in the same way many kings born in this dynasty."[3]

"In the consequence of these kings a king emperor named Prabhakara-Vardhana became the ruler whose other name was Pratapshil."[4]

Here Prabhakara-Vardhana is called king emperor where as former rulers are called kings. Obviously the former rulers were not so dignified (they were dukes) or they were not independent rulers. Prabhakara-Vardhana became famous by expanding his kingdom by dint of political wisdom and rivalry (obvious by second name Pratapshil). He developed unused land to establish Samanti system and worked for welfare of the people. His personality and works were described in the Harṣacarita as follows –"a lion to the Huna deer, a burning fever to the king of the Indus land, a troubler of the sleep of

Gujarat, a bilious plague to that scent-elephant the lord of Gandhara, a looter to the lawlessness of the Lats, an axe to the creeper of Malwa's glory. From his members of royalty the coronation water purged no foulness but filthy lucre. Even an enemy's life, that coward's darling, when kept like a straw in the mouth of battle, filled him with shame. It was torture to him to be accompanied in battle even by his image in the sword-blade which his hand bore, torture that even his bow bent to the foe in conflict. A proud man, he was vexed by his proud ambitions. Steadfast he kept his royal majesty, as if pinned by the implanted arrow-points of countless foes. Leveling on every side hills and hollows, clumps and forests, trees and grass, thickets and anthills, mountains and caves, the broad paths of his armies seemed to portion out the earth for the support of his dependants. By deterring all enemies his own prowess annoyed him as much as that of others, leaving his passion for battle ungratified. In the seraglios of slain rivals his valour was, as it were, materialized in the form of the five elements, fire in the women's hearts, water in the hollows of their eyes, wind in their sighs, earth upon their forms, ether in the vacant solitude. As in a mirror, his glory was matched in those gems among ministers who attended him. Once more: - his greatness was made to glow by the fire of his valour, his success was digested by the heat of his courage, the growth of his race was fostered like a bamboo by the water of the sword's edge, his valorous deeds were proclaimed by the mouths of the wounds which his steel dealt, his grasping of tribute by the callosity of the bow string. A furious onslaught he counted a present, war a favour, the approach of battle a festival, a foe the discovery of a treasure, a host of enemies the acme of prosperity, a challenge to conflict a boon, a sudden onset an ovation, the fall of sword strokes a shower of wealth. Beneath his rule the golden age seemed to bud forth in close packed lines of sacrificial posts, the evil time to flee in the smoke of sacrifices meandering over the sky, heaven to descend in stuccoed shrines, Dharma to blossom in white pennons waving over temple minarets, the villages to bring forth progeny of beautiful arbours erected on their outskirts for meetings, alms' houses, inns, and women's marquees, Mount Meru to crumble in a wealth of utensils all of gold, a very cornucopia to bear fruit in bowls of riches lavished upon Brahmans."[5]

Describing political events in Harṣacarita Bāṇa Bhaṭṭa has written that from father Prabhakara-Vardhana & Patrani Yashomati a child had born named Rajya-Vardhana. After that at length in the month Jyaistha on the twelfth day of the dark fortnight, the Pleiades being in the ascendant, just after the twilight time, when the young night had begun to climb that time Harṣa-Vardhana born. On this occasion astrologer Taraka said to king about Prabhakara-Vardhana that "O king! It was on a day like this, free from the taint of all evil conjunctions such as malignant aspects of the sun and moon, at a moment like the present, when all the planets were similarly at their apexes, that Mandhatri came to birth. Since then in all the intervening time no second has in the whole world been born at a conjuncture so fit for a universal emperor's birth. The son now born to your majesty shall be coryphaeus of the Seven Emperors, bearer of the Seven Imperial Signs and the Great Jewels, lord of the Seven Oceans, performer of all sacrifices of Seven Forms, the peer of him of the Seven Steeds."[6]

From above quotation it is clear that in Harṣa period there was also tradition of an ancient thinking about Chakravarti king. Probably, conception of Chakravarti king in Indian politics was urged to give a distinguished position to king and to contain divine powers in king. This thinking is also behind the tradition of different types of Yagyas (Ashwamegh, Rajsuya, and Vajpey etc.) and the tradition of ostentationally coronation. By doing those rituals kings were enable to create fear and respect to self in their subjects.

Describing further incidents it is written in Harṣacarita that "When he (Harṣa) could just manage five or six paces with the support of his nurse's finger and when Rajya-Vardhana was about six year old then queen Yasomati became pregnant with Rajyashri such as Narayana's statue with the earth."[7] From this description it is clear that Rajya-Vardhana was about five years older than Harṣa-Vardhana and there was two years difference between age of Harṣa-Vardhana and Rajyashri.

We obtained family chart of Puṣyabhūti dynasty according to description of Bāṇa Bhaṭṭa as follow:-

Puṣyabhūti

Prabhakara-Vardhana→Yashomati (Patrani)

↓

Rajya-Vardhana

Harṣa-Vardhana Rajyashri

Family chart presented by Bāṇa Bhaṭṭa is incomplete because he has not given any name between Puṣyabhūti and Prabhakara-Vardhana.

To complete this deficiency in the information we have get information from other important historical sources as description of Manjushreemulkalp and Madhuvan inscription of king Harṣa-Vardhana. "According to description of Manjushreemulkalp the family chart of Puṣyabhūti dynasty is as follow:-

Aditya-Vardhana

↓

Prabhakara-Vardhana

↓

Rajya-Vardhana HarṣaVardhana

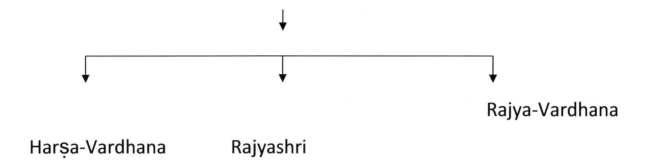

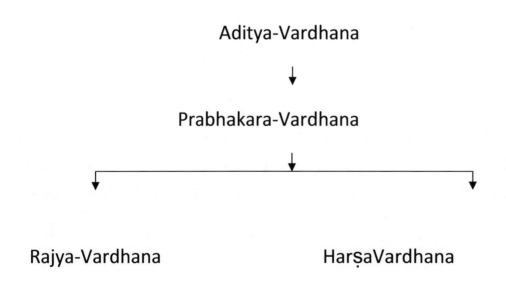

In Madhuvan inscription (sambat 25-231) of king Harṣa-Vardhana, names of his ancesters are given as follow:-

Nara-Vardhana ——— Vajrini Devi

↓

Rajya-Vardhana (Pratham) ——— Apsaro Devi

↓

Aditya-Vardhana ——— Mahasengupta Devi
(sister of Latter
Gupta king Mahasenagupta)

↓

Prabhakara-Vardhana ——— Yashomati Devi

His family chart is also written on Sonepat copper-seal of Harṣa-Vardhana but first line of inscription is omitted so there is no name of Narvardhan. Great Sun devotee king shree Prabhakara-Vardhana name is written in second line and Param Sugat Param Bhattarak great king emperor shree Rajya-Vardhana name is written at last."[8]

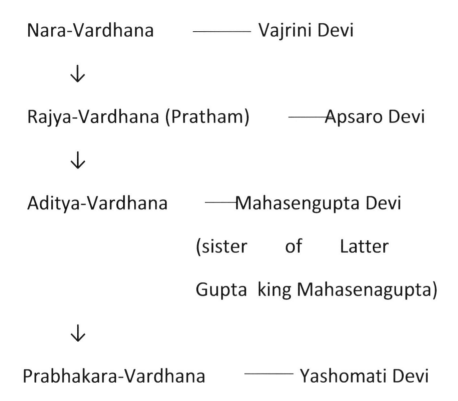

There are differences among opinions of scholars about the cast of the kings of Puṣyabhūti dynasty. The main reason of this difference is the description of contemporary Chinese traveler Hiuen-Tsang, in which he has written that "The reigning king is of the vaisya caste. His name is Harṣavardhana. A commission of officers holds the land. During two generations there have been three kings. (The king's) father was called Prabhakara-Vardhana; his elder brother's name was Rajya-Vardhana (Ho-lo-she-fa-tan-na)."[9]

But description of Harṣacarita does not support it. Contrary to it, description of Harṣacarita proves that cast of the kings of Pusyabhuti dynasty was Kshatriya. Describing about Sthanvishwar's king (establisher of Puṣyabhūti dynasty) Bana has written that "He (king Puṣyabhūti) hold bow to support all varnas including Brahmans as Indra holds a bow that have different type of varnas (=colours) - '*tatra ca sākṣātasahastrākṣa iva sarvavarṇadharama dhanurdadhāna :*'"[10] Here 'holding a bow to support different varnas including Brahmans' means holding a weapon by kshatriya varna in varna system.

In this consequence, describing the event of giving a sword named Attahasa to king Puṣyabhūti by disciple of Bhairavacharya, Bana has written that "One day however he entered with something wrapt in white rage, and, having sat down as before, spoke after a pause: - 'Most fortunate king, his reverence informs your majesty that he has a Brahman disciple named Patalasvamin, who from the hand of a Brahmaraksasa took a great sword called Attahasa. Pray accept of this, a weapon befitting your majesty's arm'"[11]

From this description it is clear that Bhairavacharya wanted to give sword to king Puṣyabhūti taking it from a Brahman as he thought that king was suitable possessing authority of sword of king was related to Kshatriya caste. In Indian literature Kshatriya Varna is depicted as a ruler who protects kingdom.

Again, describing actual affection of king Puṣyabhūti to weapon Bāṇa Bhaṭṭa writes "The king took it in his hand, and gazing at it for a while, seemed as it reflected his image, to be given the weapon a loving embrace."[12] Certainly, people of Kshatriya caste had affection to weapons because they were responsible for protection of kingdom.

"Describing childhood of Harṣa Bana has written that his neck was ornamented with a row of great tiger's claws linked with gold, which might expressed his natural kshatriya strength –' *samabhivyajyamānasahajakṣātratējasīva hāṭakabaddha-vikaṭavyāghranakhapaḍiktamaṇḍitagrīvakē*'(Harṣacarita, Chaturth Uchchhawas, page- 228).

Like this, on other place Bāṇa Bhaṭṭa has said Rajya-Vardhana as '*vīrakṣētra sambhavatvācca janmana :*' (Shashtham Uchchhawas, page-322) – born in brave family and calling out to Harṣa as virtuous Rajarshi (*āvisaṁvādina: rājarṣima*) & title of virtuous

Rajarshi(Dwitiya Uchchhawas, page-119 and Tritiya Uchchhawas, page-155)

In Six Uchchawas of Harṣacarita Bana has said Harṣa as worthy of the nobility fostered in Puṣyabhūti's line of his own inborn valour- *'puṣyabhūtivaṁśasambhūtasyābhijanasyābhijātyasya sahajasya tējasō'* (do- page-350). These quotations present indisputable evidence for Puṣyabhūties as kshatriya.

In Chaturth Uchchhawas Bana has said Puṣyabhūti and Maukhari dynasty like that of the Sun and Moon houses, is sung by all the world to the gratification of wise men's ears-' *tējōmayau sakalajagadagīyamāna- budhakarṇānandakāriguṇagaṇau sōmasūryavaṁśāviva puṣyabhūtimukharavanśau'* (page-250).

In this context a wise Brahman attached to the king Prabhakara-Vardhana named Gambhir likely said to the husband of Rajyashri Grahvarma that you are one to be supported, like the moon by Shiva, on king (Prabhakara-Vardhana) – *'idānī tu śaśīva śirasā paramēśvarēnāsi vōḍhvyō jāta :'*-do). Description of holding Grahvarman like a moon on head by Prabhakara-Vardhana indicates Maukharies as Somvarshi Kshatriya. So it is clear that Maukharies were Chandravanshiya Kshatriya and Sun devotee Prabhakara-Vardhana and his ancestors were Suryavanshiya Kshatriya of Puṣyabhūti family."[13]

Important political events related to Puṣyabhūti dynasty is obtained from description of Harṣacarita. These events are also proved by description of Hiuen-Tsang and inscriptions. Systematic study of these events is important part of seventh century's history. Impact of these events was on the changing geographical scenario of that time, along with these events paved the way to Harṣa-Vardhana to become great king of north India. So study of these events is important for historical point of view.

After establishment of Puṣyabhūti dynasty by king Pushyabuti there is no mention in Harṣacharit about middle rulers. Again there is mention of Prabhakara-Vardhana who is called Rajadhiraj (king of kings or emperor) in Harṣacarita and his second name was called Pratapshil. Along with mentioning victory of Prabhakara-Vardhana there is description about his effect on Hunas, Sindhudesh, Gurjar, Gandharraj, Lat desh, Malav desh etc. About this description Prof. Bhagawati Prasad Panthari's view is that " from this short description it is difficult to inference that Prabhakara-Vardhana has established permanent supremacy on Sindh, Gandhar, Gurjarpradesh(Gujrat), Lat and Malva or to oppress them from his terror. In Harṣacarita (Tritiya Uchchhawas; page – 154) Bana has called 'Sindhu Rajajwaro' for Prabhakara-Vardhana, but announced Harṣa as absorber of his treasurury and to make one's own after churning pride of Sindhuraj ('Sindhurajam pramashya laxmi-ratmikrita'- Tritiya Uchchhawas , page-154). From this sentence, it can be said about Harṣa in context of Sindhuraj, it is clear that Prabhakara-Vardhana has terror-stricken Sindhuraj (other) but not conquered him. So it seems that probably establishing supremacy on greater part of Panjab Prabhakara-Vardhana has subdued and terror-stricken neighbour states by his growing power, but he was not able to make them his subject."[14] In Harṣacarita it is mentioned that Prabhakara-Vardhana leveled land and distributed it in his dependants. In description of Bāṇa Bhaṭṭa it is also written about works of Prabhakara-Vardhana those were useful to the people. By these descriptions it is clear that Prabhakara-Vardhana was first king who established Puṣyabhūti dynasy.In Harṣacarita it is written that Prabakarvardhan had appointed Kumargupta and Madhavgupta, sons of the Malwa king as servants of his sons. There is written about beloved son of the Malwa king who was seated back to Harṣa at time of first meet of Bāṇa Bhaṭṭa to king Harṣa-Vardhana whom Harṣa said about Bana that he is a thorough 'petit-maitre'. According to events, one day, introducing these two Kumaras to his sons Rajya-Vardhana and Harṣavardhan, Prabhakara-Vardhana has told "I have appointed to wait upon your highnesses the brothers Kumaragupta and Madhavagupta, sons of the Malwa king, inseparable as my arms from my side; they are men found by frequent trials untouched by any taint of vice, blameless, discreet, strong, and comely. To them your highnesses will also show a consideration not enjoyed by the rest of your dependants."[15]

About the king of Malwa, who is mentioned in above event, Prof. Bhagwati Prasad Panthari writes-"Here it seems that the king of Malwa means king Mahasengupta, the latter king of Gupta dynasty of Magadh and Malwa. According to Dr. D.C. Ganguli, study of Kalchurie's inscription it appears that up to year 590 and year 595 Malwa gone into the hand of Kalchuri from Guptas. Probably round about year 595 Sankargana, son of the Kalchuri king Krishnaraja was defeated away latter Gupta king Mahasenagupta and snatched Malwa from him. In this clash probably king Mahasengupta was killed which led his both sons to become without support and so they would have to take shelter at home of their paternal aunt. Here it remembers that Mahasenagupta, mother of Prabhakara-Vardhana, was sister of latter Gupta king Mahasenagupta. Perhaps Prabhakara-Vardhana would attack on Kalchuri Sankargana by side of his maternal uncle Mahasengupta and make effort to drive away him from Malwa. But immediately after death of Prabhakara-Vardhana the king of Malwa attacked on Maukharies and Puṣyabhūties, from which it is clear that Prabhakara-Vardhana had not succeeded against the king of Malwa, so that Kalchuries have managed to rule on Malwa for some time(till year 608-609). So, from 'Malavlaxmilataparashu' it seemed Prabhakara-Vardhana's enemity to that royal family of Malwa possibly that was particularly Kalchuri family."[16]

Based on these facts Prof. Bhagawati Prasad Panthari has concluded the sons of the Malwa king were certainly near relative so that Prabhakara-Vardhana has compared them with his two arms of his body and directed to not behave like other simple servants. The view of Prof. Panthari is not correct in light of facts described in Harṣacarita and Kādambarī. Clearly it is written in Harṣacarita that introducing sons of the Malwa king Prabhakara-Vardhana has said at beginning that my dear sons, it is difficult to secure good servants, the first essential of sovereignty (*vatsau ! prathamama rājyāngama, durlabhā: sadabhṛtyā:- Harṣacarita, Chaturth Uchchhawas, page- 234*). He told them as men found by frequent trials (*Bahudhopdhabhih pareekshitauh-do-page-235*).After that Prabhakara-Vardhana directed his sons and said that I have appointed to wait upon your highnesses the brothers Kumargupta and Madhavagupta, sons of the Malwa king, inseparable as my arms from my side. To them your highnesses also will show a consideration not enjoyed by the rest of your dependants (*anayōrupiri bhāvadbhayāmapī nānya- parijana samavṛtibhyā̃ bhavitavyama -do-page-236*). After this, describing Kumargupta, Bāṇa Bhaṭṭa has written that he derived a dignity from senses conquered even in boyhood and, like conquered foes, kept well under his control (*'śaiśava ēva nirjitairindriyairaribhiriva saṁyatai: śōbhamānama'*-do-page-237). From these descriptions it can be said clearly that two sons of the Malwa king were captured in war, appointed as faithful servant founded by frequent trails. They were faithful and king has great affection to them so he directed his sons not to behave like other servants. Here Prabhakara-Vardhana said them as inseparable arms of his body that means he had very much trust on sons of the Malwa king because of their virtue. If Prabhakara-Vardhana has nearest relationship to these sons of the king then Bāṇa Bhaṭṭa certainly mentioned about it as he written about Bhandi. Introducing Bhandi Bana writes "About this time Yashomati's brother presented his son Bhandi, a boy about eight years of age, to serve the young princes."

This type of event is also described in Kādambarī that is helpful to understand this context easily. There is an event described to appoint a female servant named Patralekha as betel bearer for prince Chandrapid. It is written that she was daughter of the Kulut king whom (In childhood) king Tarapid has taken as a prisoner along with female servants after defeating capital of Kuluteshwar. Considering as an orphan daughter of the king the queen (mother of Chandrapid) looked after her with great affection like her daughter. To handing over Patralekha as betel bearer and giving message of queen to Chandrapid, Kanchuki said "Now she is ready to become your betel bearer, so I am sending her to you. You have not to treat with her as other female servants and take care of her as a child (*na cāsyā māyu ṣmatā parijanasāmānya dṛṣṭinā bhavitavyama. bālēva lālanīyā.*)"[17]

On base of conjecture it can be drawn some conclusions about recognition of sons of the Malwa king. Kalchuries have established control over Malwa after defeating Malwa's king Mahasenagupta then Prakarvardhan would have attacked on Malwa because he was near relative of Mahasenagupta. During invasion probably Kalchuri king (that time who was Malwa king) would have run away and his two sons Kumargupta and Madhavagupta would have kept in his palace and take care with great affection like sons of king. Latter after frequent trials they were appointed as dependents of Harṣa-Vardhana and Rajya-Vardhana. From description of Harṣacharit it is also seems that Prabhakara-Vardhana was not defeated Malwa entirely but rather particularly some money or land of Malwa has come to his hand (*mālavalakṣmīlatāparaśu:* –Harṣacarita, Chaturth Uchchhawas, page-203). Later on the Malwa king was successful in acquiring power and after attacking on Malwa killed Grahavarman (husband of Rajyashri). Then attacking on the Malwa king Rajya-Vardhana eradicated him.

Wedding of Rajyashri and Grahvarma was important event for political point of view. Discussing about marriage of Rajyashri Prabhakara-Vardhana said to his wife "In general too, though a bridegroom may have other merits, the wise especially incline towards good family. Now at the head of all royal houses stand the Maukharies, worshipped, like Siva's foot-print, by all the world of that race's pride, Avantivarman, the eldest son, Grahavarman by name, who lacks not his father's virtues, a prince like the lord of planets descended upon earth, seeks our daughter. Upon him, if your majesty's thoughts are like wise favorable, I propose to bestow her."[18] After discussing about this relationship Prabhakara-Vardhana weds Rajyashri to Grahavarman. This matrimonial relationship was essential and important to diplomatic point of view for both royal families (Maukharies of Kanauj and Puṣyabhūties of Thaneshwar). Now they were in position to attack jointly on their enemies and defeat them. On this relationship Prof. Bhagawati Prasad Panthari has written "this matrimonial relationship was important to political point of view, because great dynasty of Thaneshwar and Kanauj now jointly can oppose with hardness of their same enemies Hunas and Malwas (Kalchuries). Matrimonial relationship to The Maukhary dynasty that was a great ancient royal family also displays extended political power of Prabhakara-Vardhana."[19]

It is written in Harṣacarita that Rajya-Vardhana has departed towards Uttarapath to attack the Hunas. Ahout this Bāṇa

Bhaṭṭa has written "Subsequently the king one day summoned Rajya-Vardhana, whose age now fitted him for wearing armour, and, as a lion dispatches his whelp against the deer, placed him at the head of an immense force and sent him attended by ancient advisers and devoted feudatories towards the north to attack the Hunas."[20] From this event it is concluded that Hunas had become powerful again, whom Prabhakara-Vardhana had defeated or subdued (*'hūṇahariṇakēsarī'* - Harṣacarita, Chaturth Uchchhawas, page-203) once. Rajya-Vardhana had been sent to defeat Hunas along with an immense force and a team of devoted and experienced ministers (feudatories). Here it is right to think that Prabhakara-Vardhana had not departed self for war because of his old age and unhealthiness as possibility expressed by Prof. Bhagawati Prasad Panthari. He writes " Probably 'Huna-Harinkesari' was not able to enter in top hills himself because of his old age and unhealthiness , so that he had to send crown king Rajya-Vardhana along with force and his old experienced minister and feudatories towards Uttarapath."[21]

Bāṇa Bhaṭṭa has clearly written that Prabhakara-Vardhana had sent Rajya-Vardhana to attack the Hunas as a lion dispatches his whelp against the deer (*'hariṇāniva harirhariṇēśakiśōraparimitabalānuyātaṁ'* –Harṣacarita, Pancham Uchchhawas, page-257). From this statement it can be concluded that Prabhakara-Vardhana had sent Rajya-Vardhana on war under a strategy to gain experience about this type of circumstances and to hand over responsibility on his shoulders.

According to description of Harṣacarita Prabhakara-Vardhana felt unwell after Rajya-Vardhana had gone to attack Hunas. Harṣavardhan backed home after receiving this news. After reaching there held a conversation between Harṣa and Prabhakara-Vardhana this displays a father's love expression, which is on bed of death, to his son. On this occasion Prabhakara-Vardhana said to his son Harṣa-"I know my boy, your filial love and exceeding tender heart. At times like this overmastering, all-afflicting family affection distracts even a sober man's mind. For this reason you must not give yourself over to sorrow. Consumed as I am by the fever's fierce heat, I am still more so by your distress. Your leanness cuts me like a sharp knife. Upon you my happiness, my sovereignty, my succession, and my life are set, and as mine, so those of all my people. The sorrows of such as you are a sorrow to all people on earth; for no families of small worth are adorned by your like. You are the fruit of stainless deeds stored up in much another life. You bear marks declaring the sovereignty of the four oceans, one and all, to be almost in your grasp. By your mere birth my end is attained, I am free from the wish to live. Only deference to the physicians makes me drink their medicines. Furthermore, to such as you, who through the merits of a whole people are born for the protection of all the earth, fathers are a mere expedient to bring you into being. In their people, not in their kin, are kings rich in relatives. Rise therefore, and once more attend to all the needs of life. Not till you have eaten will I myself take my diet.'"[22]

On base of Prabhakara-Vardhana's expression to Harṣa, V. Smith has imagined that in Thaneshwar there was a conspiracy to enthrone Harṣa on royal seat but this plan did not become successful because Rajya-Vardhana returned on time. He writes that "There are indications that a party at court was inclined to favor the succession of the younger prince, but all intrigues were frustrated by the return of Rajya-Vardhana who ascended the throne in due course."(The Early History of India, 3rd ed. P. 336).

The conclusion of V. Smith is not correct because this is not matched to the description of Harṣacarita, but contradicted it. In this context Prof. Bhagawati Prasad Panthari's argument is absolutely correct. He thinks this imagination throughout wrong. He writes "From love-melted heart's expression of a father, who was on bed of death in praise of Harṣa, it not suitable in perspective of Harṣacarita's whole description to reach on this fact that Prabhakara-Vardhana wanted to enthrone Harṣa on royal seat by deprived Rajya-Vardhana from right of succession. So based on these expressions to reach on this conclusion like V. Smith that there was a conspiracy to enthrone Harṣa in place of Rajya-Vardhana and that was frustrated by immediate return of Rajya-Vardhana- is completely wrong and nonsense."[23]

To make this fact clearer Prof. Bhagawati Prasad Panthari writes "First thing it should be remembered that Harṣa himself had sent messenger to call back Rajya-Vardhana. All officers and courtiers were distressed by lack of desire for kingdom by Rajya-Vardhana, remorseful of father's death, and himself Harṣa (who,

V. Smith thinks, was active to obtaining kingdom by conspiracy) was anxious about lack of desire for kingdom by Rajya-Vardhana and distressed by fact of giving right of succession to him. He thought that his elder brother was not thinking him as born in Puṣyabhūti line, son of Prabhakara-Vardhana and his younger brother, so this type of proposal had been submitted in front of him.

The lack of desire and proposal of brother was compelled Harṣa to think that perhaps some one has told something about him to his brother, so he seems impure in it. From these expressions of Harṣa it is clear that he was not indulge in any conspiracy against his brother Rajya-Vardhana, but rather from brother's expression he certainly thought as some one has conspired against him to make his brother reluctant to kingdom.(see Harṣacarita, Pancham Uchchhawas, page-277, Shasth Uchchhawas, page-314-320).

From description of Harṣacarita it is clear that Rajya-Vardhana had not any anxiety towards Harṣa, but rather Harṣa was anxious about it that perhaps remorseful of father's death, Rajya-Vardhana might not take shelter in forest for ascetic practice developing due to lack of desire for kingdom.(' *bhrātṛgatahṛdayaścācintayata api nāma tātasya maraṇama mahāpralayasadṛśāmidamupaśrutya āryō vāṣpajalasnātō na gṛhaṇīyādvalkalē . nāśrayēdvā rājarṣirāśramapadama'*(Pancham Uchchhawas, page-304). Harṣa's anxiety became true and only after compelled by the circumstances, those were created by the king of Malwa, Rajya-Vardhana could be ready to take arms or the royal throne-‘ *śastragrahaṇamuditarājalakṣmī ....”............gatō ahamadyaiva malāvarājakulapralayāya . idamēva tāvadvalkalagrahaṇamidamēva tapa: śōkāpagamōmpāyaścayamēva yadatyantāvinītārinigraha:*’ (Shashth Uchchhawas, page-322-324).

Panikkar has expressed his view correctly that Rajya-Vardhana had not any anxiety towards Harṣa for his right of succession; so “Rajya-Vardhana did not abandon the field of war in order to hasten to the capital where he knew the administration will be conducted in his name by Harṣa.”(Shri Harṣa of Kanauj, K. M. Panikkar, p. 52).

Bana has written that Rajya-Vardhana’s red cheeks blazed with anger, as if Sovereignty, delighted by his taking up arm, were celebrating an ovation by scattered vermilion powder-‘ *śastragrahaṇamuditarājalakṣmī kriyamāna piṣṭavṛddhividyutasindūradhūliriva kapila: kapōlayōradṛśyata śēṣarāga:*’(Shashth Uchchhawas, page-323).” [24]

In changing events Yashomati burnt herself to die for desire to die before husband death when she saw that her husband was about to die and after that Prabhakara-Vardhana died. From these events Harṣa became anxious. On the other hand he sent messenger to call back brother Rajya-Vardhana and had fear that he would not develop absence of desire for throne. Rajya-Vardhana came back after defeating Hunas then according to Harṣa's anxiety actually announced to abandon weapon and directed Harṣa to take over power.

In this context, abandoning throne by Rajya-Vardhana and Harṣa's decision to follow his brother silently are expressions of brother love that is a long tradition and identity of Indian culture.

After death of Prabhakara-Vardhana, Rajya-Vardhana and Harṣa got the news of murder of Grahvarma by the Malwa king and emprisonment of Rajyashri. Two brothers became angry with this event. Then Rajya-Vardhana departed with Bhandi and ten thousand cavalry to punish the killer of brother in law.

From description of Harṣacarita it is clear that after many days of Rajya-Vardhana's departure Harṣa-Vardhana got imformation from a horseman named Kuntal that "though Rajya-Vardhana had uprooted the Malwa army with ridiculous ease, had been allured to confidence by false civilities on the part of the king of Gauda, and then weaponless, confiding, and alone, dispatched in his own quarters."[25]

In context of above event there are different opinions of scholars about identification of the Malwa king and the king of Gauda and conspiracy behind killing of Rajya-Vardhana. There would be no scope of this type of different opinion if there would be mention of their names in Harṣacarita. Even so after thinking on different opinions about this event there should be effort to find a certain conclusion.

About the Malwa king "Dr. Radhakumud Mukharjee has guessed that probably this Malwa king was Shiladitya son of western Malwa king Yashodharman Vikramaditya and he had attacked on Kanauj with Devagupta the king of eastern Malwa which mentioned in Madhuvan inscription of Harṣa."[26] According to another argument, many scholars think Malwa king the killer of Grahvarma was probably Devgupta of Harṣa's Madhuvan inscription. Prof. Bhagawati Prasad Panthari has identified the Malwa king as Kalchuri Buddharaj based on some evidences. He writes "About year 595 Kalchuri king Shankargana had control on Malwa. After Shankargana his son Buddharaj had accession to the Kalchuri throne. From Mahakut pillar inscription of the Chalukya king Mangalesh, which considered year 502, it seems that he had defeated a king in war named Buddha. This Buddha is considered the Kalchuri king Buddharaj. So it is clear that Buddharaj had assigned to the throne of his father about year 602. From Vidisha inscription of this Buddharaj, which is dated in Kalchuri samvat 360 or year 607-08, it is known that as his father he had also control on Malwa Pradesh. It is also known from other inscriptions of Buddharaj that in addition to Malwa he had control on Lat and Gujrat for some period and at last approximately in year 628-29 the Maitrik kings of Saurastra or Ballabhi took away Kalchuries from there. (Journal of Bihar & Orissa Royal Society)."[27]

Based on these facts Prof. Panthari has identified the Malwa king as Kalchuri King Buddharaj which seems absolutely correct.

In description of Harṣacarita name of the Gauda king is not directly mentioned. By referring a sentence of Sastha Uchchhawas- *'prakaṭakalanka mudayamānama viśankataviṣānōtkīrṇapanka- sankaraśankarabarkuraśankarakakuda kūṭaśankāśamakāśatākāśē śaśānkamaṇḍalama'*, English translators of Harṣacarita E.B.Cowell &F.W.Thomas have written "The rising clear-flecked moon (cacanka) shone like the pointed hump of civa's tame bull, when blotted by mud scattered by his broad horns", the commentator himself supplies us with the allusion, as he tells us in his note on the opening verses of chap. VI, that cacanka was the name of the dishonored Gauda king against whom Harṣa was marching."[28]

Contemporary Chinese traveler has also written "At this time the king of Karnasuvarna (kie-lo-na-su-fa-la-na); a kingdom of Eastern India-whose name was Sasangka (she-shang-kia), frequently addressed his ministers in these word; "If a frontier country has a virtuous ruler, this is the unhappiness of the (mother) kingdom." On this they asked the king to a conference and murdered him."[29]

Certainly Bāṇa Bhaṭṭa has written name of the Gauda king in his ornamental language. In Harṣacarita describing control of the king named Gupta on Kushsthal (Kanyakubja) Bāṇa

Bhaṭṭa has written that "After his majesty Rajya-Vardhana was taken to paradise and Kanyakubja was seized by the man named Gupta, queen Rajyashri burst from her confinement and with her train entered the Vindhya forest."[30] In Madhuvan and Banskheda inscription of Harṣa it is also indicated king Devgupta as head of kings and like wicked horse. From these descriptions it is clear that "The Gauda king's full name was Shashankgupta or Devgupta Shashank."[31] 'Shashank' name also confirmed from description of Hiuen-Tsang.

There is not detail description about the conspiracy behind Rajyvardhan's killing but it is clear from statement of horseman named Kuntal that Rajya-Vardhana took false hospitality by the Gauda king and killed in his own room in armless condition.

From this description it is clear that the Gauda king tempted something for Rajya-Vardhana to take in his net and killed him alone in armless condition. In Banskheda and Madhuvan inscription of Harṣa, there is also mention of killing Rajya by misleads. Shankar, commentator of Harṣacarita, has also mentioned fraud killing of Rajya-Vardhana (covet to his daughter) by the Gauda king. Despite these proofs, Shri Raybahadur R.P. Chanda's and Shri R.C.Majumdar's conclusion, that Rajya-Vardhana was defeated in lawful war, is not justifiable.

Describing event of Rajya-Vardhana's killing by the king of Gauda, Bāṇa Bhaṭṭa has written in Harṣacarita "From the man (Chief officer of cavalry named Kuntal) he learnt that his brother (Rajya-Vardhana), though had routed the Malwa army with ridiculous ease, had been allured to confidence by false civilities on the part of the king of Gauda, and then weaponless, confiding, and alone, dispatched in his own quarters."[32] Considering on contemporary political events, Prof. Bhagawati Prasad Panthari has written about those circumstances which led Shashank to take help of fraud. He writes "It can be estimated from description of Harṣacarita that after defeating the king of Malwa at any place between Thaneshwar and Kanauj, Rajya-Vardhana was gone towards Kanauj to take control on Kanauj and to free his sister Rajyashri, but before reaching his destination he was killed in the way by the king of Gauda."[33]

"Perhaps, inspired from situation of decentralized Aryavarta, the Gauda king Shashank (Devgupta) came towards Kanauj to expand kingdom. Probably Shashank was also fearful from crush of the Malwa king (Buddharaj) and other feudatory princes of Malwa by 'Rajya' and so he had no courage to fight alone to the heroic king of Thaneshwar. So it seems that he had taken shelter of diplomacy and killed Rajyavarthan by trickery. Throwing light on this incident Hiuen-Tsang also written that at the time; when Rajya-Vardhana was on the throne, the king of Karnasuvarna, in Eastern India, whose name was Sasankaraja, hating the superior military talents of this king, made a plot and murdered him."[34] Throwing light on cause of making use of trickery instead of open fight, Shri Basak has written "......It maybe presumed that after the Malwa king's defeat by the enormous army of Rajya, Sasanka did not consider it expedient to enter into an open fight."(History of North Eastern India, Page-14). Throwing light on cause of foully murder of Rajya-Vardhana by Shashank Shri Panikkar has written"A better motive could perhaps be found in the fact that Rjyavardhana, after defeating the Malwa king, attempted to extend his territory eastward and conquer the king of Karnasuvarna, who finding himself unable to meet the Raja of Thaneswar in open field foully murdered him after making a show of submission" (Harṣa-Pnikkar, p.13).

Next day Harṣa's anger reached on ultimate limit from news of Rajya-Vardhana's killing by the Gauda king. Bāṇa Bhaṭṭa has written that first time Harhsa's great anger appeared in his vigour (*pūrvāgamaḫ iva pōruṣasya*) .Meanwhile friend of Harṣa's father and army chief Sihnad also motivated by encouraging him to go on expedition against enemies. After that Harṣa took vow to clear this earth of Gaudas.

It is clear from these descriptions that political events full of sorrow and sadness compelled Harṣa to take that great vow and go on expedition for war (*kĩ punarīdṛśē durjātē jātē jātāmarṣanibharē* - Harṣacarita, Shashth Uchchhawas, Page-342). Harṣa was in deep sadness and angry from events of father's death, murder of brother and brother-in-law and imprisonment of sister. These events reminded him again and again and make cry of his heart.

In perspective of these events when we evaluate personality and mental status of Harṣa then it is clear that Harṣa-Vardhana was a person with steadfastness who had potential to finish challenges. In this difficult situation he also obtained strength from these grieves. This difficult situation purified personalities of Harṣa as gold purified in heat. He resumed his expedition by understanding responsibility of a king.

In succession of his expedition for conquest of territory in all directions, Harṣa first halted on bank of Saraswati. At this place messenger of king Bhaskardyuti (his other name was Bhaskarvarma), the king of Pragyajyotishpur (Assam), Hans Vega met Harṣa-Vardhana. He presented an umbrella named Abhog to Harṣa which was sent by his king. Abhog named umbrella has some special features as :- Fire does not burn it, nor wind bear it away, nor water wet it, not dust defile it, nor age corrode it. Along with umbrella other gifts were also presented to Harṣa in which some important were- ornament, cloth made from kshom silk, drinking vessels, bucklers, pillows, cane stools ,books, green betel nut fruits etc. Along with these gifts messenger read message of king in which the king of Pragyajyotisheshwar expressed desire of an imperishable alliance. Accepting friendship of the king of Pragyajyotishpur Harṣa-Vardhana said " How could the mind of one like me possibly even in a dream show aversion, Hansavega, when such a great and noble spirit such a treasure of virtue and captain of the worthy, bestows his love as an absent friend upon me?"[35] Along with, Harṣa desired to see the prince soon.

It is clear from description of Harṣacarita that Harṣa acknowledges his supremacy on Bhaskarvarma. Bhaskarvarma was a ruler of small state which has status as an independent king. Telling the message of the king of Pragyajyotishpur, Hansvega said "Now from childhood upwards it was this prince's firm resolution never to do homage to any being except the lotus feet of Shiva, such an ambition, so difficult of attainment in the three worlds, may be reached by one of three means, by a conquest of the whole earth, by death or by a friend like your majesty, peerless hero of the world, burning the heavens with a blaze of impetuous valour. The friendship of monarchs again commonly has regard to utility. And what possible contribution of utility could incline your majesty to friendship?"[36] From this description it is clear that there was no equal relationship between Bhaskarvarma and Harṣa-Vardhana. Bhaskarvarma himself understood Harṣa-Vardhana bigger and more powerful than himself. In sequence of giving description of Kamrupa, Hiuen-Tsang has also written about calling of Bhaskarvarma by king Shiladitya (Harṣa) and Bhaskarvarma presented himself to serve the king Shiladitya. Quoting Bhaskarvarma he has written "But now Siladitya raja is in the county of Kajughira (kie-ehu-hoh-khi-lo) about to distribute large alms and to plant deeply the root of merit and wisdom. The Sramans and Brahmans of the fire Indies, renowned for their learning, must needs come together. He has now sent for me. I pray you go with me!"[37] The event, in which Bhaskarvarma presented himself in court of Harṣa, is also mentioned in the life of Hiuen-Tsang. This description also proves supremacy of Harṣa on Bhaskarvarma.

From historical point of view it is important to think here on this fact that in which circumstances Bhaskarvarma had sent umbrella and other gifts to Harṣa and urge to form friendly relationship. Different scholars have presented their views on friendly relationship of Harṣa and Bhaskarvarma. C.B. Vaidya has presented his view that "Kumar-raja of kamrupa was perhaps previously the enemy of Sasanka, for which reason he allied himself with the emperor of Sthaneswara."(H.M.H.J; Vol. I, p.10) In this context Dr. Ramashankar Tripathi has written "He (Bhaskarvarma) was in great fear of his powerful neighbor, Sasanka, and this was probably the reason why he so readily extended the hand of friendship to Harṣa at the initial stage of his campaigns."(History of Kanauj, P. 104). About this friendship R.D. Banarjee has written that "Bhaskarvarman of Assam might have felt the weight of Sasanka's arms before he sent an ambassador to Harṣa to seek his alliance."(History of Orissa, Vol.I, P.129)

On this relationship, conclusion of Prof. Bhagawati Prasad Panthari is absolutely correct. He has written that "According to Harṣacarita, before expedition Harṣa had sent message to let all kings prepare their hands to give tribute or grasp swords, to seize the realms of space or chowries, let them bend their heads or their bows, grace their ears with either my commands or their bowstrings, crown their heads with the dust of my feet or with helmets ....I am gone abroad."-' *sarvēṣāma rājñāma sajjīkriyantāma karā: karadānāya śastragrahaṇāya vā ....namantu śirāsi*

.........śēkharībhavantu pādarajānsi śirastrāṇi vā .... Parāgatōhama'
(Shashth Uchchhawas, P.344)

Based on this message it can be directly assumed that repressed by increasing power of Harṣa Bhaskarvardhan sent his ambassador Hansvega with offerings and request for friendship. Bhaskarvarman was also aware of enemity of Harṣa to Shashanka. He also could doubt that Harṣa could attack on Kamrupa after acquiring the Gauda. Again it was natural that the king of Kamrupa was anxious due to increasing power of anti Budha Shashanka, the king of Gauda. So Harhsa's friendship was an essential option for him. So it is clear that Bhaskarvarman had friendship with Harṣa like powerful king for self benefit and self protection. It is clear from the gift of umbrella named 'Abhoga' by Bhaskarvarma, that he was considered Harṣa as a soverign Chakravrti and this was the reason, he had not to use hereditary umbrella named 'Abhoga' to himself instead giving it to Harṣa."[38]

After sending Hansavega ambassador of Bhaskarvarma, Harṣa resumed his army's march. One day he heard from a letter- carrier that Bhandi had arrived with the victorious army of Rajyavardhana, which conquered Malwa and encamped quite near. Harṣa welcomed Bhandi and inquired the facts of his brother's death. After hearing detailed he wanted to know about Rajyashri then Bhandi replied "after his majesty Rajya-Vardhana was taken to paradise and Kanyakubja was seized by the man named Gupta, queen Rajyashri burst from her confinement and with her train entered the vindhya forest."[39]After information that Rjyashree is in Vindhya forest, Harṣa-Vardhana decided to go there. Along with, he ordered Bhandi to attack on Gauda.

There is some confusion about identity of Bhandi. Actually this confusion is due to misinterpretation of facts. In his travel account Hiuen-Tsang has described an event of Kanauj in which there is discussion to hand over throne to Harṣa after death of Rajya-Vardhana. About this event he writes- "The people having lost their ruler, the country became desolate. Then the great minister Po-ni, whose power and reputation were high and of much weight, addressing the assembled ministers, said, "The destiny of the nation is to be fixed today. The old king's son is dead: the brother of the prince, however, is humane and affectionate, and his disposition, heaven-conferred, is dutiful and obedient. Because he is strongly attached to his family, the people will trust in him. I propose that he assume the royal authority: let each one give his opinion on this matter, whatever he thinks." They were all agreed on this point, and acknowledged his conspicuous qualities."[40]

Po-ni of above mentioned event is called Bani by Julien. Connecting this Po-ni or Bani to Harṣacarita's Bhandi, some scholars have presented their conclusion. This type of conclusion is opposite to facts those are given in Harṣacarita. It is described in Harṣacarita that brother of Prabhakara-Vardhana's wife Yashomati has sent his eight year old son to serve as attendant of Rjyavardhan and

Harṣa. (Harṣacarita, Chaturth Uchchhawas, Page-230). This Bhandi grew along with Rajya-Vardhana and Harṣa-Vardhana and latter he was appointed as army chief. When Rajya-Vardhana departed to take revenge of the death of his brother-in-law Grahvarma then Bhandi was also with him with ten thousand cavalry. (Shashth Uchchhawas, Page-324-325) Again when Harṣa-Vardhana was on war-expedition against the king of Gauda then Bhandi met him in way with conquered army of the Malwa king. Harṣa again sent Bhandi for war with the Gauda and he himself departed to Vindhya forest in search of Rajyashri. (Harṣacarita, Saptam Uchchhawas, Page-404). From these events of Harṣacarita it is clear that Bhandi was the army chief of Thaneshwar, not the great minister of Kanauj. From Harṣacarita's description it is also clear that Puṣyabhūti clan ruled on thaneshwar and after death of Grahvarma Kanauj was also included in Thaneshwar in absence of successor. From begining, by mistake, Hiuen-Tsang has described Puṣyabhūti clan as ruler of Kanauj. During the visit of Hiuen-Tsang in India, Kanauj was the capital of Harṣa-Vardhana's state. Probably this was the reason that he mentioned Puṣyabhūti as ruler of Kanauj.

Thomas watters also said Po-ni of Hiuen-Tsang as Bani or vani. He has written- "When the latter (Prabhakara-Vardhana) died he was succeeded on the throne by his elder son named Raja (or Rajya) vardhan. The latter soon after his accession was treacherously murdered by Sasanngka, a persecutor of Buddhism. Here upon the statesmen of kanauj, on the advice of their leading man Bani (or Vani), invited Harṣa-Vardhana, the younger brother of the murdered king, to become their sovereign. The prince modestly made excuses, and seemed unwilling to comply with their request."[41]

In view of above mentioned facts it can be certainly said that Bhandi and Bani were not the same person. Bhandi was the army chief of Thaneshwar and maternal brother of Harṣa. Bani was, probably, powerful minister of kanauj and in absence of successor played his important role to give throne of Kanauj to Harṣa.

To searchout Rajyashri, Harṣa-Vardhana reached in Vindhya forest where he got information that a women was ready to became Sati. When Harṣa-Vardhana reached there he saw Rajyashri is ready to enter in fire. After escaping Rajyashri Harṣa first partook her food and then afterward ate himself. Then attendant told full story- "how she was sent away from Kanyakubja, from her confinement there during the Gauda trouble, through the action of a noble named Gupta, - how she heard the news of Rajya-Vardhana's death, and refused to take food, and then how, faint for want of food, she wandered miserably in the Vindhya forests and at last in her despair resolved to mount the funeral pile."[42]

"Who was man of noble family named Gupta? It can not be said surely. It certainly seems that he would be a senior officer of army under the Gupta, the Gauda king or Devgupta (Shashank), so that he was present there during seizure of kanauj by the Gauda king and after receiving an opportunity he set free Rajyashri silently to went away from Kanyakubja. Probably man of noble family named Gupta, as it is clear from his good behavior; he was feeling affection, respect and friendship to Puṣyabhūties and Maukharies. Perhaps he was a youth of the latter Gupta clan, which was added in affectionate-bond with dual Puṣyabhūties and Maukharies through matrimonial relationship. Shri Harnol also think that noble man of Gupta family, Kumar and Madhav were related to that clan of latter Gupta which has feeling of friendship to Puṣyabhūties and Maukharies and Devgupta was related to that clan of latter Gupta which has enemity to Puṣyabhūties and Maukharies. (Journal of Royal Asiatic Society, 1903, P.562)."[43]

Harṣa-Vardhana introduced Rajyashri to Acharya Divakarmitra and told her that Baudh Acharya was your husband's childhood friend impressed with Acharya Divakarmitra, Rajyashri requested Harṣa to give permission to assume the red robe. Harṣa remain quiet but Divakarmitra suggest Rajyashri that she must obey the decree of Harṣa in any case. Then Harṣa-Vardhana said to Acharya Divakarmitra "From this day forth, while I discharge my vow, and console my subjects in their sorrow for my father's death, I desire that she should remain at my side and be comforted with your righteous discourses, and your passionless instruction which produces salutary knowledge, and our advice which calms the disposition, and your Buddhist doctrines which drive away worldly passions. At the end, when I shall accomplish my design, she and I will assume the red garments together."[44]

After that Harṣa-Vardhana took Rajyashri with Acharya and went back, in a few marches, to his camp. Along with this the story of Harṣacarita is ended. We have not got information about latter events from Harṣacarita. After writing the Ashtham Uchchhawas of Harṣacarita and Purvabhag of Kādambarī, probably Bāṇa Bhaṭṭa was suddenly dead. His son Pulinbhatt completed unfinished story of Kādambarī after adding Uttarbhag but Harṣacarita remained incomplete. In this situation, it is felt inconvenience, in lack of Harṣacarita like wide range source, to know remaining events of Harṣa's life.

There is mention of the solemn conferring performed by Harṣa-Vardhana on interval of five years. Describing the characteristics of Harṣa-Vardhana Bāṇa Bhaṭṭa writes " his breast was wrapped in a fold of rays from the pearls in his necklace as if it were a strip of cloth put on to signify the solemn conferring as a special gift of all the property gained during every five years (*jīvitāvadhigṛhītasarvasvamahādānadīkṣā cīrēṇēva hāramuktāphalānāma kiraṇanikarēṇa prāvṛtavakṣa: sthalama*)"[45] Discussing that the solemn conferring, Hiuen-Tsang writes that "At the present time siladitya-raja, after the example of his ancestors, distributes here(Prayaga) in one day the accumulated wealth of five years."[46] From these descriptions it is concluded that till Harṣa-

Vardhana period there was a tradition of the solemn conferring on every five years which was also performed by the ancestors of Harṣa. In this context Dr. Vasudevasharan Agrawal has written "This type of tradition of the solemn conferring on every five years was in use in Gupta period or after some latter. In Divyavadan the word 'Panchvarshik' is used for these events. Kalidas also mentioned the solemn conferring yagya of Raghu."[47]

In Harṣacarita there is also important information about expansion of state by the king of Puṣyabhūti clan and relation with neighbor states. It is easy to determine geographical boarder of Vardhan dynasty based on the historical facts given by Bāṇa Bhaṭṭa in Harṣacarita.

It is known from Harṣacarita that Prabhakara-Vardhana was first real founder of Vardhan dynasty. In his period Vardhan dynasty had witnessed special growth in fame. Praising Prabhakara-Vardhana Bāṇa Bhaṭṭa writes- " who (Prabhakara-Vardhana) was a lion to the Huna deer, a burning fever to the king of the Indus land, a troubler of the sleep of Gurjar, a bilious plague to that scent-elephant the lord of Gandhara, a looter to the lawlessness of the Lats, an axe to the creeper of Malwa's glory(*tēṣu caivamutpādyamānēṣu kramēnōdapādi hūṇahariṇakēsarī sindhurāja – jvarō gurjaraprajāgarō gāndhārādhipagandhadvipakūṭapākalō lāṭapāṭavapāṭaccarō mālavalakṣmīlatāparaśu: pratāpaśīlaiti prathitāparanāmā prabhākaravardhanō nāma rājādhirāja:).*"[48]

In this description ornamental language is used and not written anything clearly. But it can be assumed something on base of used ornamental words. A lion to the Huna deer means there was a war conducted between Prabhakara-Vardhana and Huna in which Hunas were defeated and frightened by him they paid taxes. But based on this description it can not be said certainly that Hunas were included in dynasty. From description, that Sindhuraj, Gurjars and Gandharraj were having any type of fever to Prabhakar, it can be concluded that three kings have encountered with Prabhakara-Vardhana, so they were frightened from him. In this situation, despite Free states, they paid him taxes regularly. To end the wisdom of Lat state means Prabhakara-Vardhana has control on Lat state. From comparison of Prabhakara-Vardhana with an axe for the creeper of Malwa's glory, it infers that Prabhakara-Vardhana had attacked on Malwa state and successfully captured that wealth and land but not defeated totally. Here we should remember that two sons Kumargupta and Madhavgupta of the Malwa king had been also captured during this war. In this matter conclusion of Prof. Bhagawati Prasad Panthari is correct that "probably, Prabhakara-Vardhana had depressed neighbouring states by his growing power of terror after acquiring maximum area of Panjab but he was not succeeded to capture him."[49]

After Prabhakara-Vardhana, Rajya-Vardhana also played important role in expansion of the state. Particularly, once Prabhakara-Vardhana had sent him towards Uttarapath to attack on Hunas. When he came back after defeating

Hunas (*Hun nirjay samara*- Harṣacarita, Shashth Uchchhawas, Page-309) at least Prabhakara-Vardhana was dead. After death of father and mother committed sattee, Rajya-Vardhana felt alienation and abandoned weapon. Then hearing news of brother-in-law's murder by the Malwa king and imprisonment of sister Rajyashri. Angered again Rajya-Vardhana taken up arm and alone gone to punish the Malwa king with ten thousand cavalry along with Bhandi. Rajya-Vardhana was completely successful in expedition of the Malwa victory but the Gauda king murdered him by trick.

It is clear from this description of Harṣacarita that after the victory on Huna and Malwa, Vardhan dynasty was expanded. Victory of Malwa was not permanent because Rajya-Vardhana was murdered.

Harṣa-Vardhana became ruler after death of Rajyavardha. After becoming ruler Harṣa, distressed from death of father and mother and angered from murder of brother in law and brother, vowed for conquest of the world. In this vow he proclaimed to clear this earth from Gaudas, and make it resound with fetters on the feet of all kings who were excited to insolence by the elasticity of their bows. Along with he sent letters to the four directions to all kings to prepare their hands to give tribute or grasp swords to fight with him.

In Dwitiya Uchchhawas of Harṣacarita, Bāṇa Bhaṭṭa has mentioned that every five year Harṣa organized festival of charity. This fact is also proved by Chinese traveler Hiuen-

Tsang. “Hiuen-Tsang has written that every five years Harṣa organized the great festival of charity. In year 634, along with Harṣa, Hiuen-Tsang also participated in festival of charity organized in Prayaga. This festival was sixth festival performed that time. It is clear from calculation, based on this fact, that first festival of charity performed in Prayaga was first performed in year 612 or 613. To start festival of charity in Prayag by Harṣa, it is self accomplished that Prayag janpad was included in Harṣa’s state and probably he has control on Prayag till year 612 or before it. Triumph of Prayaga echoed this fact that under that period (year 613) starting from neighbouring states of kanauj to Saket (Ayodhya) in east and up to Prayag janpad were included in Vardhana dynasty, were integral part of it. In Harṣacarita, as simile for Harṣa, Bana has written that streams of the united Ganga and Yamuna had come of their own accord to anoint him-“ *prayāgapravāhavēṇi kāvāriṇēvāgatya svayamabhiṣicyamānama*” (Dwitiya Uchchhawas, page-127)

This sentence or simile indicates rule of Harṣa on Ganga-Yamuna doab or Aryavarta.”[50]

In his vow for conquest of the world Harṣa-Vardhana vowed to clear earth from the Gaudas. That time there were five Gaudas – (1) Saraswat Mandal or Saurashtra (Punjab and Kashmir), (2) Kanyakubja (area from Uttarapath to Narmada in south were included in it), (3) Gauda (Bengal), (4) Mithila and (5) Uttkal (Odisa,

Ganjam). In Harṣacarita there is no information about victory of the Gaudas. About this Hiuen-Tsang has written that after six years Harṣa subdued the Five Indies.

From Harṣacarita it is known that Harṣa conquered the king of Sindh. About victory of the Sindh Bāṇa Bhaṭṭa has written "by churning pride of the king of Sindh, best of men, Harṣa, made his wealth own (*atra purūṣōttmēna sindhurājama pramathya lakṣmīrātmīkṛtā* - Harṣacarita, Tritiya Uchchhawas, Page-153-154). From this description it seems that Sindh state was attached in Harṣa's dynasty. But it is not proved by description of Hiuen-Tsang. About the king of Sindh, Hiuen-Tsang has written that "The king is of the Sudra (Shu-to-lo) caste. He is by nature honest and sincere, and he reverences the law of Buddha."[51] It is clear from this description that Sindh was also a separate state at that time. Probably the king of Sindh had status of a feudal king under Harṣa.

"In Harṣacarita Bana has mentioned another king that is defeated by Harṣa beside the king of Sindh, who was squeezed in trunk by his famous Mahanag (great elephant) Darpshat, after be defeated in war and whom Harṣa freed from Gajraj as king of the demons freed Mahanag Basuki-" *ata balinā mōcitabhūbhṛdvēṣṭanō muktō mahānāga:"* (Harṣacarita, Tritiya Uchchhawas, Page-154).

Who was this king and where he ruled, this is not mentioned in Harṣacarita.But which similarity showed by simile of freeing him from Gajaraj and freeing Mahanag Basuki from Bali, it seems that probably Harṣa had defeated any Nag king of Aryavarta.

This is also revealed by Bana that Harṣa has accepted kar from 'Durgam TusHarṣail' or he has accepted kar (collected tax) from unattainable janpads of the Himalaya as the supreme lord Siva has accepted kar of Durga, daughter of Himalaya-" *atra paramēśvarēṇa tuṣāraśailabhuvō durgāyā gṛhīta: kara:*" (Harṣacarita, Tritiya Uchchhawas, Page-154)."[52]

There is not unity of opinion in scholars about this 'TusHarṣailbhu'. It was Nepal in opinion of R.K. Mukharjee, K.M.Pnikkar, Bular and V.A.Smith. Other side Dr. R.S.Tripathi thinks 'TusHarṣailbhu' as Tukhar or Tushar state and derives meaning from simile, that is given here, that Harṣa married to daughter of any powerful mountaineer king.

A different opinion, referring the event which is written in the life of Hiuen-Tsang, Prof. Bhagawati Prasad Panthari has presented an argument which seems appropriate in every way. He writes "based on description of Hiuen-Tsang's biography it seems that probably Harṣacarita's 'TusHarṣailabhu' meaning is related to Kashmir. It is described in 'Life' (The life of Hiuen-Tsang) that there was the remains of Buddha's tooth with Kashmir sangharama. Harṣa reached on boarder to see and worship that holy tooth and wanted permission to the king of Kashmir to do so. Sangharam hide the tooth but frightened from Siladitya's power the king of Kashmir himself searched the tooth and handed over it to Harṣa. Harṣa was overwhelmed by seeing the remains of tooth and by forcibly took it with him. The mention of snatching remains of tooth forcefully by Harṣa clearly indicates defeat of the king of Kashmir in front of Harṣa."[53]

It is known from Harṣacarita that in way of the expedition of Harṣa against the Gauda, Bhaskarvarma, the king of Pragjyotish (the king of Assam), had desire to establish relation of friendship by sending umbrella named 'Abhoga' with other gifts to king. Harṣa accepted his friendship. From this description it is clear that Bhaskarvarma accepted submissiveness of Harṣa.

Describing conversation of princes those were along with the king, during Harṣa's expedition for conquest of the world, Bāṇa Bhaṭṭa writes "It was the famous Mandhatri who opened the way to world-conquest. With the irresistible onset of his chariot Raghu in a brief time setted the world at peace. Seconded by his bow, Pandu imposed tributed on the array of kings haughty in the pride of inherited prowess, nobility, and wealth. Having crossed the realm of China, the Pandava Arjuna, in order to complete the Rajasuya sacrifice, subdued Mount Hemakuta, whose caves resounded with the twang of the bow-ends of the angry gandharvas. No obstacle saved resolution do the conquests of heroes know. Though shielded by Himalaya with all its snows, the impotent Druma, fearing a trial of strength, bore like a servant the exactions of the Kuru king. Not too ambitious, surely, of conquest were the ancients, seeing that in a small part of the earth there were numerous monarchs such as Bhagadatta Dantavakra, Kratha, Karna, Kaurava, Sisupala, Salva, Jarasandha, and Sindhuraja. King Yudhisthira was easily content since he endured quite near at hand the kingdom of the Kimpurushas, when the conquests of Dhananjaya had made the earth to shake. A fainéant was Candakoca, who, having subdued the earth penetrated not into the Amazonian realm. How insignificant the distance between the Snowy Range and Gandhamadana! The land of the Turuskas is to the brave but a cubit. Persia is only a span. The Saka realm but a rabbit's track. In the Pariyatra country, incapable of returning a blow, a gentle march alone is needed. The Deckhan is easily won at the price of valour. Mount Malaya is hard by the Dardura rock, whose cave temples are pleasant with the fragrance of sandal branches tossed by the wind from the southern ocean's waves; and Mahendra joins Malaya."[54]

"In this description many facts are important from geographical point of view. According to Sabhaparva, during conquest of North direction, Arjuna conquered countries of Wahlik, darad and Kamboja(Valkh, Gilgit and Pamir) then entered into Param kamboj country (north-east of kamboj) and from there into country of Rishak or Yuchies where became a terrible fight with rishaks like Shiv and Tarkasur. There is not name of the China in the main Mahabharata but Bana has written that Arjuna went to the China, and that is also correct; because in fifth century B.C., that time this context is, Yuchi or Rishik were in the north China. The scholars of the Mahabharata, contemporary to Bana, were well informed this fact that Arjuna went to China to defeat Rishaks. Coming back after defeating Rishaks Arjauna came in Kimpurushdesh and from there went to Hatakadesh, where lake was named Manasha. Hatakadesh was a part of Tibet and there was also Hemkut Mountain. Though, there is no name of Hemkuta in the Mahabharata but clearing the geography of the Mahabharta time, Bana has mentioned that.

In this context mention of Alasshachandakosh is very important. Shrisilvan Levi has identified it as Alsand or Sikandar. The full story-sea of Sikandar related tale has spread from Yunan to Abyssinia (Africa) and to Iran. According to that, after conquering the whole earth, at last Sikandar had defeated by sending a letter to the state of women named Amejan, but not enter self into that. This state of women was in Asia Miner on the bank of Black sea and Agien Sea. According to kartias, history writer of Yunan, by conquering when Sikandar came in Asia then Thlestris, the queen of Amejan country, came to meet him. This story of Sikandarnama became famous that by bringing the state of women in his control from far away, Sikandar has abandoned it without touch. Bana has mentioned that story.

In his own style, Bana has given short geographical background of that relationship of India to foreign countries, which was in early half of seventh century. Chinese Turkistan was the country of Turushks, where Uigur Turk, who were Buddhist, they were lover of Indian culture and patron of art and literature. Many proofs of their culture and remain of literature were found in excavation of desert cities of Chinese Turkishtan. In west there was country of Iran of Sasani age, which was called country of Parsik which is also mentioned in the Raghuvans (4/60) of Kalidasa. Shak place was at eastern border of Iran. In second century B.C. when Shak were removed towards south from Bahlik in pressure of Hunas, then they settled on border of eastern Iran and Afghanistan. Singh titled Kharoshthi lipi inscription of first century A.D. found from Mathura mentions their native country Shaksthan by telling the history of Shak kshatraps of Mathura and Takshashila. Ardent Guptas rooted out the state of Shahanushahi Shakas and their branch Murunda and at time of Bana there was not any state of Shakas. Even so, there remained that name of Shaksthan as Varahmihir has also (Vrihatsamhita, 14/21) described about janpad of west direction.

Harṣa's state was established in Malwa Pradesh of Pariyatra Mountain. But he did not achieve his purpose in Dakshinapath due to Challukya king Pulkeshin."[55]

The map of Vardhan dynasty can be sketched by dint of Bana's description of expedition of conquest of world. In Vardhan dynasty whole Aryavarta (Doab of Ganga-Yamuna), grater part of Punjab(in which south Punjab and east Rajputana were included), Lat and Gandhar state, Pariyatra (Malwa state) etc were included which were directly controlled. Beside those the king had indirect control on states of Sindhu, Kashmir and Kamrupa. These states supported Puṣyabhūti dynasty through taxes and with army on time of war. This dynasty touched Dakshinapath in south India so Bana has written-' *śauryaśulka: sulabhō dakṣiṇāpatha:. dakṣiṇārṇavakallōlānila calitacandanalatāsaurabha sundarī kṛtadarīmandirāddardurādadrērnēdīyasi malayō malayalagna ēva ca mahēndra:'* (Harṣacarita Saptam Uchchhawas, page-381).

Bana has mentioned neighboring states of this dynasty. According to description Chinese Turkistan was the country of Turushkas, in west, the Iran country of Sasani age (=country of Parasiks) and Shaksthan named country was situated on east border of Iran.

King: Position, merit-demerit, and duties :

There is adequate light thrown on position of kings in description of Harṣacarita and Kādambarī. King was the supreme officer of administration. In contemporary polity whole events were conducted around the king. Kings were associated to Kshatriya family and there was tradition to make king from the same clan. Vardhan royal family of Harṣa-Vardhana was also associated to Kshatriya family. There was tradition of appointing crown prince. After death of king that crown prince had to become king. In absence of heir, courtiers of king, Samant, ministers and army chief etc had jointly elected the king. Sardars of Kanyakubja have invited Harṣa-Vardhana to take charge of royal duties in absence of heir after death of Grahvarma.

The coronation (as crown king) of elder son of the king was conducted. Probably, tradition of coronation was continued to establish respect for king in subjects. Describing pomp, at time of coronation, Bāṇa Bhaṭṭa has written in Kādambarī about coronation of Chandrapid-"After that, some day's latter one auspicious day royal-priest has presented all auspicious materials of coronation. Then along with minister Shuknas and many thousand kings, king Tarapid has coroneted crown king by taking auspicious pitcher in his hand filled with purified holly water of all religious places, all rivers and all oceans and all medicines, all fruits, all type of soil, all gems, blessed tears and all mantras."[56]

Contemporary kings were taken on different titles. Giving information of messenger, sent by Harṣa-Vardhana's brother Krishana, Bana's Parshav brother Chandrasena has said "A renowned courier is waiting at the door, sent to you by Krishana, the brother of ShriHarṣa, Maharajadhiraj Parameshwar, the Adhipati of the four oceans, whose toenails are burnished by the crest gems of all other monarchs, the leader of Chakravarti kings."[57] From this description it is clear that generally contemporary kings have taken on titles of Chakravarti. Harṣa was the leader of those Chakravarti kings. He was called Maharajadhiraj Parmeshwar. From this it infers meaning that generally king or feudal were called 'Maharaj' whenever the king taken on title of Maharajadhiraj Parameshwar who had supremacy on them. Kings were also adorned noun of Purushottam, Rajarshi, Pushyarajarshi, Prajapati, Loknath etc.

Clearing the characteristics of Chakravrti kings, giving context of king Shudrak in Kādambarī, Bana has written "There was a king, similar impressive like second Indra, named

'Shudrak'. Contemporary all kings, were followed his orders by bowing their heads. He was the lord of four oceans like sacred thread wearer earth. All feudal kings were under his control due to love for his valour. King Shudrak had all characteristics of Chakravarti (world-wide) as declared by the sastras of palmistry."[58]

Thinking on suitability of this type of titles A. L. Basham has written "Chakravarti kings emerged to conquer whole Jambu dwip and to rule with justice and prosperity. Jainies have also idea of chakravarti king and there are many ancient kings in Mahakavyas as Yudhishthir and Ram have called Digvijayi or conqueror of four directions. Chakravarti king was a divine man placed on a special level in world-system. So he was worshiped on half divine level. This tradition was stimulus for ambitious kings in medieval age, some kings had himself announced chakravarti king."[59]

Early half of seventh century kings were considered respectful and fearful. Countless money from royal treasury was spent on these kings's daily life and they lived luxurious life. In descriptions of Harṣacarita and Kādambarī there is mentioned several contexts which describe privileges of kings. Story of Kādambarī is based on fable but it can be estimated about life of king's grandeur and luxurious daily life which described in it. There is a similarity in daily life of Harṣa which is described in Harṣacarita and daily life of kings which is described in story of Kādambarī.

Servants were appointed on every step in royal building for personal pleasure of kings and they had to take care of his every comfort.

There is also mention in Harṣacarita and Kādambarī about desire of contemporary kings. Different main desires of kings were doing daily exercise, riding on horse, riding on elephant (kings had taken good horse and good elephants for their own use i.e. Harṣa's favorite elephant was Darpshat), regular exercise of weapons(day after day their hands, begrimed with the marks of sword play, seemed defiled by quenching the fire of all other monarchs' prowess-' *anudivasama śastrābhyāsaśyāmikākalankitamaśēṣarājaka-pratāpāgninirvapaṇamalinamiva karatalamudvahantau*'- Harṣacarita, Chaturth Uchchhawas, page-234), hunting (at time of expedition of Rajya-Vardhana against Hunas, Harṣa spent several days away from camp on the skirts of the Himalaya, where lions, sarabhas, tigers, and boars are in plenty-' *kēsariśarabhaśārdūlavarāha bahulēṣu tuṣāraśailōpa-kanṭhēśūtkaṇṭhamānavadēvatākaṭākṣāśuśāritaśarīrakānti: kṛḍhmṛgayā mṛgalōcana: katipayānyahāni bahirēva vyalambata*'-Harṣacarita, Pancham Uchchhawas, page-258), eating betel leaf(pan) (there is mention of betel leaf bearer female attendant), taking Mukhwas to fragrant mouth (from Dadhicha's mouth breathing a fragrance of five materials- mangos, camphor, kakkola-fruit, cloves and coral trees-Harṣacarita, Pratham Uchchhawas, page-39), wearing different types of cloths and ornaments, drinking wine, for entertainment hearing song, music, story, poem etc. in court hall, giving shelter to specialists of different areas (Bāṇa Bhaṭṭa was poet, who lived in Harṣa's court) and having many queens in inner part of palace (Antahpur) in which there was one Patrani (Yashomati was patrani of Prabhakara-Vardhana).

There was special arrangement for protection of king and sons of king. Describing about childhood protection of Harṣa-Vardhana Bāṇa Bhaṭṭa has written- "the ministers of state preserved him like a state secret; the young nobles held fast to him as to virtue-'*mantra iva sacivamaṇḍalēna rakṣyamāṇē, vṛta iva kulaputrakalōkē nāmucyamānē*' (Harṣacarita, Chaturth Uchchhawas, page-229). After having reached years of discretion, there appointed youths related to noble family as attendant with sons of king. This is proved by appointment of Bhandi and Kumargupta & Madhavagupta, son of the Malwa king as attendant of Rajya-Vardhana and Harṣa-Vardhana. These youths of noble family were tried by every way and followed sons of kings like shadow and become adult. Probably they act like bodyguard along with them was appointed on posts like armychief.

Whole army of state and some special policemen were always ready to protect them. Along with that some special dogs were also protect kings. Describing use of dogs to protect king Chandrapid, Bāṇa Bhaṭṭa has written "Big dogs as size of asses were tightened in chain of gold and policemen were running ahead by dragging them and doubling enthusiasm of Chandrapid's travels by up roaring regularly-' *sahastraraśmāvārūhayēndrāyudhāmagratō bālēyapramāṇānākarṣayadbhiścāmōkara śṛṅkhalābhi:.*'"[60]

Bāṇa Bhaṭṭa has written in detail about special characteristics of Harṣa-Vardhana in Harṣacarita. Along with, in Harṣacarita and Kādambarī, there are many events from those light is thrown on merits and demerits of kings. Described demerits of kings of early half of seventh century are also seen in present rulers. This type of description presented by Bāṇa Bhaṭṭa develops perceptive vision of history in mind of common men. Different context, described by Bana, proves that in any time slot personal merits-demerits of rulers have important contribution in political change or disorder.

There was discussion about essential qualities for an ideal king in Shantiparva of the Mahabharata and Arthshastra of Kautilya. "It is said in the Mahabharata that Krit, Treta, Dwapar and Kali, these four eras are 'Rajvrit' i.e.kings are the maker or cause of these different eras. Because superiority and non-superiority or debased state of era is depends on righteousness or unrighteousness of king and so that kings were said man of era. '*yugamaṁ uccayatē*'-

kṛta trētā dvāparama ca kaliśca bharatarṣabha:.

rājavṛtāni sarvāṇī rājaiva yugamucyatē..

(śānti parva, chapter 91, ślōkā -6)

And Bana has written that Harṣa was cause of Krtiyuga-(karanamiv Krityugasya); i.e. there was effect, kingship or good governance of Harṣa so that even Kaliyuga has not dared to go near him- 'Durupsarp iti Kalina' and head of 'Kali' has made humble by Harṣa as after attacking, younger Krishna has humbled head of Kaliyanag-' *ākrāntakaliyaphaliyaphaṇācaṣkravālaṁ bālamiva puṇḍarīkākṣama*' (Dwitiya Uchchhawas, page-123 and 124).

That description of Bana, throws light that in Harṣa's government people feel comfort apart from bad governance and distress of Kalikal.

Kautilya has given name of 'Rajarshi' to king, who takes control on his genitals, intelligent, awakening for well-being of people, establishing people in their own work (swadharma) by discipline, do not touch other's thing or wife, follower of Dharma, do not accept money and do not have sex against Dharma, do not indulge in violence and always indulge in people's work.

Bana has also given noun of Rajarshi to Harṣa on account of these virtues (*avisaṁvādinama rājarṣima*). Throwing light on virtue of Rajarshi Harṣa , Bana has written- he had taken shelter of Dharma, to escape from slipping down from difficult Rajdharm or erring from Rajdharma, controlled his genitals, had not interest for addiction (i.e. to abstain from addiction), more illustrious for victory than Bhisma- *bhīṣmājjitakāśitamama* (Dwitiya Uchchhawas,page-130); calm in mind like Buddha himself(*sugata iva*) and carried out all the rules for the varna and ordered like manu- '*kartari varṇāśramavyavasthānāma......*') and bears the rod of punishment as visibly as Yama(impartial in punishment)-' *saṁvartiṇīva ca sākṣāddāṇḍabhṛti dēvē......*'(do, page-136)."[61]

Describing other virtues of king Harṣa-Vardhana, Bana has written "Thus his idea of jewels attaches to men of pure virtues, not to bits of rock,-his taste delights in pearl-like qualities, not in heaps of ornaments,- his judgement as to proper means is versed in deeds of bounty, not in the ichor-flowing temples of poor worms of elephants,-his highest love is for preeminent glory, not for the withering stubble of this life,- his magnificence is devoted to adorning the different quarters of the earth whose tribute he seizes, not the dolls which he calls his wives,-his notion of bosom friendship belongs to his well-strung bow, not to the courtiers who live on the crumbs of his board. His natural instinct is to help his friends, sovereignty means to him helping his dependants, learning at once suggests helping the learned and success helping his kinsfolk, power means helping the unfortunate and wealth helping the brahmans; his heart's main occupation is to remember benefits and his life's sole employment is to assist virtue, his body's one use is to carry out the dictates of courage, and the earth's to be an arena for his sword, attendant kings are wanted to amuse him, and enemies to help his majesty to shew itself. It could have been by no common merits in former births that he attained this glorious preeminence so that the shadow of his feet diffuses an all –excelling ambrosia of happiness round him."[62]

Light is thrown on other virtues of Harṣa-Vardhana from other contexts of Harṣacaritaa which are essential for success of a king. Harṣa-Vardhana was a steadfast person and did not act hastily on any incident. In any difficult situation he acted with wisdom after hearing suggestions of talented ministers. After murder of Rajya-Vardhana it was clear that angry Rajya-Vardhana attacked in hast on the Malwa king with only ten thousand cavalry. In spite of wining, he entangled in trap of the king of Gauda and he was murdered. Here it is to pay attention that according to description of Harṣacarita Rajya-Vardhana had taken his enemy lightly and forbidden Harṣa to not to go with him. Taking his enemy lightly and not to understand behavior of the king of Gauda showed Rajyavarthan's lack of foresight and foolishness. When Harṣa had to go on expedition against Gauda after murder of his brother then he took decision to go with his full army. That time he heard scholarly suggestion of elephant army chief Skandagupta in which he described cunningness of kings in detail.After that, arranging situation of state, he went on expedition. In the way, Bhandi met him and he got information about Rajyashri, then after sending Bhandi again against the Gauda, he himself went in search of Rajyashri. Doing so he showed his wisdom because it was essential to arrange anarchy situation of Kanauj. Expedition against the Gauda was possible in latter days. On request of Rajyashri to wore red garment he also said that 'At the end, when he would have accomplished his duties, she and he would assume the red garments together' (*iyama tu grahīṣyati mayaiva samama samāptkṛtyēna kāṣāyāṇī*- Harṣacarita, Ashtam Uchchhawas, page-459). From this context it is clear that Harṣa was wise, foresighted, and steadfast and true to one's promise.

From description of Harṣacarita it is clear that people were happy in the state of Harṣa. There was peace and prosperity every where in his state. He was a generous ruler and likes those people who had same qualities like him. He disliked those people who were crooked and licentious. That was the reason that in first meeting with Bana, when gatekeeper introduced Bana to him then Harṣa said "I will not see him (Bana) yet, as he has not as yet offered his tribute of respect" (Harṣacarita, Dwitiya Uchchhawas, page-134). And said to son of Malwa king, who was most beloved to him - 'He (Bana) is through petit-maitre (dissolute person or licentious)' (*'mahānayama bhujanga iti'*-Harṣacarita, Dwitiya uchchhawas, page-135).

Contemporary Chinese traveler Hiuen-Tsang has also praised administrative potential and virtues of Harṣa-Vardhana. Hiuen-Tsang has written "After thirty years his arms resposed, and he governed every where in peace. He then practiced to the utmost the rules of temperance, and sought to plant the tree of religious merit to such an extent that he forgot to sleep or to eat. He forbade the slaughter of any living thing or flesh as food throught the five Indies on pain of death without pardon. He built on the banks of the river Ganges several thousand stupas, each about 100 feet high; in all the highways of the towns and villages throughout India he erected hospices, provided with food and drink, and stationed there physicians, with medicines for travelers and poor persons round about, to be given without any stint. On all spots where there were holy traces (of Buddha) he raised sangharamas.

Once in five years he held the great assembly called Moksha. He emptied his treasuries to give all away in charity, only reserving the soldiers' arms, which were unfit to give as alms. Every year he assembled the Sramanas from all countries, and on the third and seventh days he bestowed on them in charity. The four kinds of alms (viz., food, drink, medicine, clothing). He decorated the throne of the law (the pulpit) and extensively ornamented (arranged) the oratories. He ordered the priests to carry on discussions, and he judged of their several arguments, whether they were weak or powerful. He rewarded the good and punished the wicked, degraded the evil and promoted the men of talent. If any one (of the priests) walked according to the moral precepts, and was distinguished in addition for purity in religion (reason), he himself conducted such a one to "the lion-throne" and received from him the precepts of the law. If any one, though distinguished for purity of life, had no distinction for learning. He was reverenced, but not highly honoured. It anyone disregarded the rules of morality and was notorious for his disregard of propriety, him he banished from the country, and would neither see him nor listen to him. If any of the neighbouring princes or their chief ministers lived religiously, with earnest purpose and aspired to a virtuous character without regarding labour, he led him by the hand to occupy the same seat with himself and called him 'illustrious friend"; but he disdained to look upon those of a different character. If it was necessary to transact state business, he employed couriers who continually went and returned. If there was any irregularity in the manners of the people of the cities, he went amongst them. Wherever he moved he dwelt in a readymade building during his sojourn. During the excessive rains of the three months of the rainy season he would not travel thus. Constantly in his traveling palace he would provide choice meats for men of all sorts of religion. The Buddhist priests would be perhaps a thousand; the Brahmans, five hundred. He divided each day into three portions. During the first he occupied himself on matters of government; during the second he practiced himself in religious devotion (merit) without interruption, so that the day was not sufficiently long."[63]

After thinking on different virtues of Harṣa-Vardhana, conclusion of Bāṇa Bhaṭṭa seems correct that 'the grave and gracious, the awe-inspiring and affable, at the same moment a holiday and a holy day, the universal Monarch' (*'gambhīrama ca, prasannama ca, trāsajananama ca, ramaṇīyama ca, kautukajananama ca, puṇyama ca, cakravartinama harṣamadrākṣīta'*-Harṣacarita, Dwitiya Uchchhawas, page-131)

From description of Bana it is clear that there was decreasing number of kings having virtue and spotless face like Harṣa in contemporary political scenario. He has attracted attention of readers on some demerits of kings. From this type of description it can infer that people had sharp reaction on demerits of kings. It is clear from description of Bana that general demerits of personalities of that time kings were tainted character, greedy about money and tendency of acquiring throne any-how.

In process of eagerness to hear the story of Harṣa, Shyamal, male cousin on the father's side of Bana, has mentioned tainted character of kings and said that "the king of the twiceborn ravished his preceptor's wife. Pururavas was severed from his beloved Ayus through greed for a Brahman's gold. Nahusa, lusting after another's wife, became a great sanke. Yayati took upon himself to win a Brahmani woman's hand and fell. Sudyumna actually became a woman. Somaka's cruelty in murdering Jantu is notorious. Through infatuation for the bow Mandhatri went with his sons and grandsons to hell. Even while an ascetic, Purukutsa wrought a deed of shame upon the daughter of Mekala. Kuvalayashva, through resorting to the world of snakes, avoided not the Naga-girl ashvatara. Prithu, that fine first of men, did violence to Prithivi. In Nriga's becoming a chameleon a confusion of castes was seen. By Saudasa the earth was not protected, but confounded. Nala, unable to control his passion for dicing, was overcome by Kali. Samvarana had a weakness for Mitra's daughter. Dasharatha came by his death through over fondness for his beloved Rama. Kartavirya was slain for persecuting cows and Brahmans. Marutta, though he performed the Bahusuvarna sacrifice, involving vast expenditure, was not highly honoured by gods and Brahmans. Shantanu, separated through infatuation from his (loved) river, wept all alone in the forest. Pandu in the midst of the woods lost his life, like a fish, in the heat of passion. Yudhisthira, downcast through fear of his guru, diverged from truth in the battle-front. Thus no reign has been stainless except that of this Harṣa, king of kings, sovereign of all continents."[64]

Praising Harṣa-Vardhana in Harṣacarita, Bana has written that 'wealth is but a remote consideration to your majesty, whose aim is to amass fame.'(*dēvasya hi yaśānsi sañcitcīṣatõ bahirangabhūtāni dhanāni* ’-Harṣacarita, Saptam Uchchhawas, page-393) Thinking wealth as bad thing and conferring all wealth for charity on interval of every five years was an ideal work and praiseworthy for that time. From this description it can infer that that time also kings had paid special attention to acquire wealth as present rulers are doing. Probably so, Bāṇa Bhaṭṭa has pointed out demerits of accumulating wealth by giving description about advice of ministers to king about demerits of wealth on many occasion in Harṣacarita and Kādambarī . In story of Kādambarī, on occasion of coronation of Chandrapid, indicating bad effect of accumulating wealth Mahamantri Shuknas has said “fortunately if this wicked Laxmi accepts kings any-how then they become restless by falling victim to it which included wickedness in their mind......., this corrupt Laxmi has made any person as villain even if he has however much qualities like scholar, attentive, powerful, person of good family, steadfast and diligent.”[65] These descriptions of Bana are important for any time slot and also imitative for present rulers.

In Harṣacarita it is described incidents about murder of kings by taking inappropriate manner by trustworthy people. When Harṣa-Vardhana ordered Gajsadhanakrit (elephant army chief) Skandagupta to prepare elephant army for marching against killer of his brother, then he requested king that “Thus do national types vary, like the dress, features, food, and pursuits of countries, village by village, town by town, district by district, continent by continent, and clime by clime. Dismiss therefore this universal confidingness, so agreeable to the habits of your own land and springing from innate frankness of spirit. O disasters due to mistaken carelessness frequent reports come daily to your majesty's hearing. In Padmavati there was the fall of Nagasena, heir to the Naga house, whose policy was published by a sarika bird. In Sravasti faded the glory of Srutavarman, whose secret a parrot heard. In Mrittikavati a disclosure of counsel in sleep was the death of Suvarnacuda. The fate of a Yavana king was encompassed by the holder of his golden chowrie, who read the letters of a document reflected in his crest jewel. By slashes of drawn swords Vidurath's army minced the avaricious Mathura king Brihadratha while he was digging treasure at dead of night. Vatsapati, who was wont to take his pleasure in elephant forests, was imprisoned by Mahasena's soldiers issuing from the belly of a sham elephant. Sumitra, son of Agnimitra, being over fond of the drama, was attacked by Mitradeva in the midst of actors, and with a scimitar shorn, like a lotus stalk, of his head. Sarabha, the Asmaka king, being attached to string music, his enemy's emissaries, disguised as students of music, cut off his head with sharp knives hidden in the space between the vind and its gourd. A base –born general, Puspamitra, pounded his foolish Maurya master Brihadratha, having displayed his whole army on the pretext of manifesting his power. Kakavarna, being curious of marvels, was carried away no one knows whither on an artificial aerial car made by a Yavana condemned to death. The son of Sisunaga had a dagger thrust into his throat in the vicinity of his city. In a frenzy of passion the over libidinous Sunga was at the instance of his minister Vasudeva reft of his life by a daughter of Devabhuti's slave woman disguised as his queen. By means of a mine in Mount Godhana, joyous with the tinkle of numerous women's jeweled anklets, the Magadha king, who had a penchant for treasure caves, was carried away by the king of Mekala's ministers to their own country. Kumarasena, the Paunika prince, younger brother to Pradyota, having an infatuation for stories about selling human flesh, was slain at the feast of Mahakala by the vampire Talajangha. By drugs whose virtues had been celebrated through many different individuals some professed physicians bought atrophy upon Ganapati, son of the king of Videha, who was mad for the elixir of life. Confiding in women, the Kalinga Bhadrasena met his death at the hands of his brother Virasena, who secretly found access to the wall of the chief queen's apartments. Lying on a mattress in his mother's bed, a son of Dadhra, lord of the Karusas, encompassed the death of his father, who purposed to anoint another son. Chandraketu, lord of Chakoras, being attached to his chamberlain, was with his minister deprived of life by an emissary of Sudraka. The life of the chase-loving Pushara, king of Chamundi, was sipped, while he was extirpating rhinoceroses, by the lord of Champa's soldiers ensconced in a grove of tall-stemmed reeds. Carried away by fondness for troubadours, the Maukhari fool Ksatravarman was cut down by bards, his enemy's emissaries, with the cry of 'Victory' echoing on their lips. In his enemy's city the king of the Sakas, while courting another's wife was butchered by Chandragupta concealed in his mistress' dress. The blunders of heedless men arising from women have been brought sufficiently to my lord's hearing. Thus, to secure her son's succession, Suprabha with poisoned groats killed Mahasena, the sweet-toothed king of Kasi. Ratnavati, pretending a frenzy of love, slew the victorious Jarutha of Ayodhya with a mirror having a razor edge. Devaki, being in love with a younger brother, employed against the Sauhmya Devasena an ear lotus whose juice was touched with poisoned powder. A jealous queen killed Rantideva of Virnti with a jeweled anklet emitting an infections of magic powder:

Vindumati the Vrisni Viduratha with a dagger hidden in her braided hair: Hamsavati the Sauvira king Virasena with a girdle ornament having a drug-poisoned centre: Pauravi the Paurava lord Somaka by making him drink a mouthful of poisoned wine, her own mouth being smeared with an invisible antidote."[66]

Facts described here would be helpful to understand facts related to ancient Indian clans. From this description it is proved that incidents of overthrow ruler are closely related to system of monarchy. About this account of twenty seven kings, presented by Bana, Dr. Vasudevsharan Agrawal has written – "Bana has presented this long list based on his earlier time historical gossip, those were in use in seventh century. It is to understand in content of this list that there is no place of imagination in it. Till now few names could identified due to lack of our limited knowledge about ancient history. Shishunagvansh, Vatsavansh, pradyotvansh, Mauryavansh, Shungvansh, Nagvansh, Guptavansh etc. are famous royal family of Indian history; those kings are described by Bana. The mention of murder of Shaka king by Chandragupta by the sword concaled in his mistress dress is more debated with historical point of view."[67]

Certainly above described demerits displeased kings from their main duty to serve subjects. There was flourished displeasure to king who viewed like faith and awe at one time. This type of demerits also seen in present time ruler and also in this modern era, selfish leaders managed to overthrow the rulers, by using public dissatisfaction, to satisfy their ambition. Certainly, due to these types of events, subjects have not benefited at all but their problems increased.

Bāṇa Bhaṭṭa has thrown light on work of kings, which were done in contemporary political scenario. According to Harṣacarita there was unbreakable relationship between king and subject. Kings considered all subjects as their relatives. In the situation of Prabhakara-Vardhana's illness, when Harṣa reached near him then he said to Harṣa that "Upon you my happiness, my sovereignty, my succession, and my life are set, and as mine, so those of all my people" (*'sukhama ca rājyama ca vaṁśaśca prāṇāśca paralōkaśca tvayi mē̃ sthitā:. yathā mama tathā sarvāsā̃ prajānāma'*-Harṣacarita, Pancham Uchchhawas, page-273). Again he had said "In their people, not in their kin, kings are rich in relatives" (*'prajābhistu bandhumantō̃ rājāna:, na jñātibhi:'*-do, page-274). As king loved his subject in the same way subject also showed respect to good and popular kings. After Prabhakara-Vardhana's death no one cooked food, no one bathed and no one took food in city.

It can be understood defined duties of kings from speech of Prabhakara-Vardhana, in which he had said to Harṣa before his death. He had said Harṣa to accept treasury, to make prize of the feudatory kings, to support the burden of royalty, to protect the people, to guard well your dependents, to practice yourself in arms, to check levity and to annihilate your foes. According to order of king Tarapid, army chief Balahak, gone for calling up prince, said to Chandrapid "now you have to respect kings. Pray to Brahmans. Take care of subject and give pleasure to your dependence."(' *sammānaya rājalōkama . pūjaya dvijātīna . paripālaya prajā:. ānandaya bandhu vargama.'*-Kādambarī , Poorvabhagah, page-164). So that, in Kādambarī , describing about travel for conquest of the world, Bana has written "So that slowly going around on earth-pressing down elevated people, elevating humble people, giving assurance to awful people, protecting displaced people, rooting up canning people, collecting gems, presenting different types of award, taking taxes to people, giving order related to administration, establishing memorial related to travel, dictating order letter, praying to Brahmans, bowing head to sants, keeping arrangement of Ashrams those were found in the way, giving his love to people, showing his valour, making his influence upon people, accumulating glory, expanding his virtues, to spreading good manner, crushing coastal forest and doing sea water dirty from flying dust of his big army's foot."[68]

Contemporary kings took special attention of expansion and development of agriculture. Describing work of Prabhakara-Vardhana in Harṣacarita, Bana has written that Prabhakara-Vardhana leveled on every side hills and hollows , clumps and forests, trees and grass, thickets and anthills, mountains and caves, the broad paths of his armies seemed to portion out the earth for the support of his dependents-*'yaśca sarvāsu dikṣu samīkṛtataṭāvaṭaviṭapāṭavītarutrinagulmavalmīka girigahanāirdandayātrāpathai: pṛthurbhirgutyōpayōgāya vyabhajatēva vasudhāma bahudhā'*(Harṣacarita, Chaturth Uchchhawas, page-204)

There is mention of events of giving alms by kings. There is description of giving alms by Harṣa-

Vardhana in Harṣacarita which is also proved by description of Hiuen-Tsang. Probably this tradition was inspired by thinking to uplift people economically, to determine economical equality and sense of people welfare. Every section of society was benefited from this tradition of giving alms. This was also proved by the description of Hiuen Tsandg. Describing the incident of giving alms by Harṣa-Vardhana, Hiuen-Tsang has written "At the present time Siladitya-raja, after the example of his ancestors, distributes here in one day the accumulated wealth of five years. Having collected in ;this space of the charity enclosure immense piles of wealth and jewels, on the first day he adorns in a very sumptuous way a statue of Buddha, and then offers to it the most costly jewels. Afterwards he offers his charity to the residentiary priests; afterwards to the priests(from a distance) who are present; afterwards to the men of distinguished talent; afterwards to the heretics who live in the place, following the ways of the world; and lastly, to the widows and bereaved, orphans and desolate, poor and mendicants."[69]

In Harṣacarita and Kādambarī there is mention of welfare works done by kings. In this type of welfare works important works were- to dig ponds, to plant saplings, to free prisoners from jail on special occasion and to give employment to handicapped, hunchbacked, eunuch and dwarf etc. Describing Ujjayini city in Madhyapradesh, it is written in Kādambarī that there were hundred of large pond (Kādambarī, poorvabhagah, page-106) and darkness was spread due to green gardens. (Do-page-105) Just so, in Kādambarī there is also mention about Chitrarath, ruler of Hemkut Mountain in north side of India. In that country of Gandharvas there is mention to cause to be made beautiful garden by Chitrarath and to cause to be dig a pond named Achchod. (Do-page-286)

There was provision to set free the prisoners on special occasions. Describing act of setting free the prisoners on occasion of birth of Harṣa-Vardhana, Bāṇa Bhaṭṭa has written "Away ran disorderly crowds of freed prisoners, their faces hairy with long matted beards, their bodies black with many a miry smirch, like the kindred of a waning Kali age."[70] Certainly this type of moderate behavior shows public welfare oriented character of contemporary monarchy.

There is mention of old persons, dwarf men, hunchbacked persons, deaf, eunuchs and dumb persons, those were present in palace. In process of describing Rajbhawan(palace), Bāṇa Bhaṭṭa has written that as in yagya of king Bali there was present ancient person 'Vaman Bhagawan', so that there were present old and dwarf men in that *Rājabhavana(palace)-baliyajñamiva purāṇapuruṣavāmānādhiṣṭhitābhyantarama*' (Kādambarī , Poorvabhagah, page-191). So that, describing arrival of queen to see her by hearing about illness of Mahashveta, Bana has written "Though, that time the gate was packed with Pratiharies, those were going forward to pave way of queen by holding gold sticks in their hands, with Kanchukies these were carrying betel, flower, powder and angaraga and with hunchbacked, deaf, dwarfs, eunuch and dumb persons those were going forward by taking Chamar in their hands."[71] From these descriptions it is clear that kings were taking notice also on old persons, dwarfs, hunchbacked, deaf, eunuch etc. and anxious about their welfare. They have given appropriate employment in court.

Along with people welfare works, contemporary kings were usually traveled in state to take actual condition of people. In story of Kādambarī, Bāṇa Bhaṭṭa has written about king Tarapid that "to praise people he met people time to time and also sited on throne to do special work."(Kādambarī, Poorvabhagah, page-127) The description of Bāṇa Bhaṭṭa is also proved by the description of Hiuen-Tsang. Hiuen-Tsang has written about Harṣa-Vardhana "If there was any irregularity in the manners of the people of the cities, he went amongst them. Wherever he moved he dwelt in a ready-made building during his sojourn. During the excessive rains of the three months of the rainy season he would not travel thus. Constantly in his travelling palace he would provide choice meats for men of all sorts of religion."[72]

Contemporary court remains packed with scholars. Scholars from every field were patronized by kings. Certainly, Indian culture was preserved by this system and kings were guided and motivated by those scholars to take care of their duties and welfare of state. In Kādambarī , describing palace of king Tarapid, Bāṇa Bhaṭṭa has written that painters had painted drawings on wall that presents different appearance of earth, there recite a tale of monkies (story of monkies or story of Hanumanji) like the Ramayana, there was put tomtom place to place like concert hall, there was obtaining pleasure from virtue of Bharat(or Natyashastra written by Bharat) like the family of Raghu, there were present so many wise officials those were efficient to capture wicked people and able to set free innocent people. They were able to devide appropriately according to sastras like dance song and materials. There was continued description of diplomacy like Narad purana. There was pervaded sweetness of different taste of word in palace and that palace was pleased to all by displaying extraordinary nature and emotion. From this description it is clear that there were present painter, singer, poet, story-teller, dramatic, song writers and other scholars. The role of scholars was important to make cheerful atmosphere of palace along with they also helped king to take appropriate decision.

From this description of Harṣacarita and Kādambarī it is concluded that king's main duty was to establish a welfare state. Expansion and development of agriculture, alms, people welfare oriented work, giving patronage to scholars in court, to know condition of subjects by frequent traveling and a special occasion set free the prisoners etc. works represents welfare character of contemporary polity. It is acknowledged that to think about internal and external safety of subjects was also considered as duty of kings. From context of giving employment to handicapped, hunchbacked and dwarf people in court it seems that kings had paid attention to every section of subjects and there was some provision of welfare for every one.

Cabinet and important officers/post holders :-

There is mention of different ministers and their work in Harṣacarita and Kādambarī. There is also given indication about appointment process and criteria for ministers in Bāṇa Bhaṭṭa's description. Contemporary kings consulted with cabinet members on different topics and took political decisions by considering their suggestions. It can be estimated about structure of cabinet on base of Bāṇa Bhaṭṭa's description.

Ministers were appointed on base of hereditary. Describing about ministers of King Shudrak Bāṇa Bhaṭṭa has written that "hereditary scholar ministers, who had to make fun of surguru Vrihaspati from their wisdom, were always with him to serve. They were well-wisher of state and free from greed. Their internal heart was got pure due to continued criticism of political science. He had spent his years of youth by pleasure seeking with princes those were loving and wise ministers and born in royal family. Wisdom of those princes was become very sharp due to careful study of all arts. Those all princes, brilliant and had knowledge of particular moment had respected effect of king Shudrak. Those princes, skilled in civilized laughter, specialist of disposition and bodily appearance, skilled in arts of poetry-drama-story-fable, painting-lecture etc., having very hard healthy shoulder, thighs and hands, were as visibly image of king Shudrak. Those princes, brave like cub, had tear to pieces the head of intoxicated enemy's elephants several time. They were humble besides lover of showing might."[73] In Harṣacarita Bana has written "At this season lord Harṣa, having on a certain occasion laid aside his occupations, saw himself unexpectedly surrounded by a great company of silent downcast noble headed by the whole assemblage of his aged maul ministers (hereditary ministers)-' *mahājanēna maulēnākāla ātmanama vēṣṭayamānamadrākṣīta*'." [74]

From above description it is clear that contemporary kings were accomplishing their work with help of cabinet. Hereditary was base for appointment of ministers and royal family members were appointed as minister those were called 'Maul ministers'. Only attachment to royal family was not criteria for their selection and appointment but there was provision to examine their virtue and talent also. Scholarly, devotion to state, creditability, not greedy, brave and expert in polity etc were basic criteria for selection of ministers. It is clear from context of sons of the Malwa king that they were beloved of Harṣa-Vardhana and always remain with him. Though Bāṇa Bhaṭṭa has not clearly mentioned about their portfolio but certainly they were important part of his cabinet. Sons of the Malwa king were princes who were captured in war, even so they were tested on talent, ability and credibility as Bāṇa Bhaṭṭa has written in their context that they were men founded by frequent trials untouched by any taint of vice, blameless, discreet, strong and comely('*bahudhōpadhābhi: parīkṣitau* -Harṣacarita, Chaturth Uchchhawas, page-235).

There was provision of promotion of ministers according to their talent and potential. From description of Harṣacarita it is clear that Bhandi, maternal brother of Harṣa-Vardhana, was appointed as attendant of Rajya-Vardhana and Harṣa-Vardhana. He was able to reach on post of army chief based on own talent and potential. Describing about valour of king Puṣyabhūti, Bāṇa Bhaṭṭa has mentioned Betal Sadhana performed by Bhairawacharya. Two disciples of Bhairawacharya, Patalswami and Karnatal (who was citizen of Dravid desh or South India), helped king Puṣyabhūti to defeat Shrikanth Nag. Latter, king Puṣyabhūti appointed Patalswami and Karnatal as army chief.

Bāṇa Bhaṭṭa has not written clearly about structure of cabinet. But based on Harṣacarita and Kādambarī's description it can be assumed about structure of cabinet. It is clear from description of Bāṇa Bhaṭṭa that king was supreme of administration. His decision was supreme on any matter related to state policy and system. But he consulted with ministers to reach on any conclusion. Kulputra's (associated with royal family) were appointed on post of ministers who were adorned the post of Aamatya.

It is clear from description of Kādambarī that in his old age king appointed his son on post of crown prince. Crown prince helped king in administrative work and also went out to march army if necessity. King Prabhakara-Vardhana had sent Rajya-Vardhana towards Uttarapath for war on time of Huna's attack.

In Kādambarī Bāṇa Bhaṭṭa has mentioned about prime minister who was probably a link between cabinet and king. Describing Kumarpalit, prime minister of king

Shudrak, Bāṇa Bhaṭṭa has written "old age barman, expert in all polity similar to Vrihaspati and head of all ministers, named Kumaramatya"(' *amaragurumīvāśēṣa nītiśāstrapāragama, ativayasama, agrajanmānama, akhilē mantrimaṇḍalē pradhānāmātyama kumārapālitanāma*'-Kādambarī , Poorvabhagah page-25-26). Again, also in Kādambarī mentioning Prime Minister named Shash, Bāṇa Bhaṭṭa has written that there were fast friends in large number and Shash was prime minister (Do-page-39).

Bāṇa Bhaṭṭa has addressed with word 'Kanchuki' or 'Mahakanchuki' which was a minister appointed to take care of inner palace or 'Rajmahal'. Old Brahmans were appointed on post of 'Kanchuki'. There is mention of Kanchuki who was present with other people around queen Yashomati at time of her lamentation.

In Harṣa period army chief had also an important place in cabinet. Army chief was head of entire army (infantry, cavalry and elephant army). Army chief was also called Mahabaladhikrit or Baladhikrit. Trusted person of king, experienced and person related to royal family (generally but not compulsory) was appointed as army chief. It is clear from description of Harṣacarita that in latter Harṣa's maternal brother Bhandi was appointed army chief. So that, there is mention of army chief Sihnad in Harṣacarita which has called fast friend of Prabhakara-Vardhana and he was old aged. Describing about appointment of Patalswami and Karnatal, both helped king Puṣyabhūti to defeat Shrikanth Nag, Bāṇa Bhaṭṭa has written "Patalasvamin and Karnatala; men of a warlike spirit, remained in the king's service. Elevated to a fortune beyond their wildest dreams; drawing their swords in the midst of the royal guard, occupying the front rank in battle."[75]

Describing the virtues of Sihnad, Bāṇa Bhaṭṭa has written that "Of fury's fire he was the rubbing stick, of valour the lordliness, of arrogance the arrogant quality, of pride the erysipelas, of violence the heart, of martial ardour the life, of enterprise the panting gasp: to the infuriate a hook, to noxious kings an elephant's goad, the colophon of chivalry, the family priest of martial companies, the scale-beam of the brave, the boundary over-seer of the village of swords, the performer of proud speeches, the sustainer of the routed, the executor of pledges, the authority on openings in great wars, the reveille drum of battle's devotees."[76] It is clear from this description that above mentioned virtues were considered essential to become army chief.

There was a minister appointed to establish relationship with neighboring states or foreign countries which was called 'Mahasandhivigrahadhikrit'. Probably this minister has status like present foreign ministers. This fact is proved by description of Harṣacarita. When Harṣa heard news of his brother Rajya-Vardhana's murder then he got angered. After that hearing after advice of Sihnad he vowed to free earth from the Gaudas. After this vow he gave instructions to Mahasandhivigrahadhikrit Avanti to dispatch letter to kings situated in four direction ordering to prepare their hands to give tribute, to bend their heads, to crown their heads with the dust of his feet, to join suppliant hands, to let go their lands and to take a good view of themselves in the nails of my feet or the mirrors of their swords. From this description it is clear that Mahasandhivigrahadhikrit was responsible to contact or made relationship with neighboring states.

On base of these descriptions, structure of Harṣa period cabinet can be shown as follows:-

King

↓

Crown King

↓

Prime minister	kanchuki	armychief	mahasandhivigrahadhikrit
(head of ministers and finance minister)	or mahakanchuki (minister of inner palace)	or mahabaladhikrit (defence minister)	(foreign minister)

<u>Important officers/post holders:-</u>

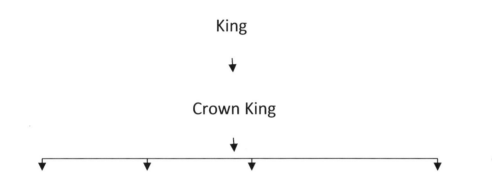

To handle successfully administration of Harṣa period, Amatyas, Adhyakshas, Sachivas and other officers and large number of employees were appointed. In description of Harṣacarita and Kādambarī there is mention of these types of officers/post holders.

Kulputras were appointed related to royal family, on top posts. In Harṣacarita and Kādambarī there is mention of following officers/post holders:-

Amatya –

Bāṇa Bhaṭṭa has mentioned Amatyas. Amatyas were also present in Maurya and Gupta period. There is mention in Arthshastra that those Amatyas were appointed on post of ministers who were beyond all attractions (*'sarvōpadhā śuddhāna mantriṇa: kuryāta'*- Arthshastra, tenth chapter). In Gupta period also Amatyas were appointed on post of ministers on the basis of their talent. Certainly this tradition was also present in Harṣa period. Describing the situation, after death of Harṣa's father, Bāṇa Bhaṭṭa has written that along with other people kings having possessing authority of Amatya post endowed with birth and character have surrounded Harṣa(*'śrutābhijanaśīlaśālinō̃ mūrdhābhiṣiktāścāmātyā rājanō '*- Harṣacarita, Pancham Uchchhawas, page-303).From this description it is clear that important persons related to royal family were appointed on post of Amatya. Like Gupta period, ministers were appointed amongst these Amatyas on base of talent. Harṣa's maternal brother Bhandi was appointed on post of army chief in latter period who was appointed as kumaramatya. Probably Amatya post of Harṣa period was similar to the post of Mansabdar of Mughal period.

Adhyaksha –

Bāṇa Bhaṭṭa has mentioned many 'Adhyaksha officers'. To take care of materials, that was captured after defeating the Malwa king, king Harṣa-Vardhana directed his different Adhyaksha officers to accept it according to rule(*'athālōcya tatsarvamavanipāla:svīkartu yathādhikāramadiśadadhyajñāna'*- Harṣacarita, Saptam Uchchhawas, page-406). "It is clear that there were separate Adhyakshas for different departments. Kautilya also specified separate Adhyakshas for different works or different department i.e.- Suvarnadhyaksha,Koshthagaradhyaksha, Ayudhagaradhya- ksha etc. (Arthshastra; 2 Adhikaran)."[77] "It is described in Harṣacarita that ruler Chet or servants ridiculed on kulputras that however the labour is ours, but when paytime comes some other rascals will appear. So it is clear that persons related to royal family, which were called 'Kulputa', were appointed on post of Adhyaksha of different department."[78]

Sachiva –

There is mention of Sachiva in Harṣacarita. Describing valour of King Puṣyabhūti Bāṇa Bhaṭṭa has written that "people, servants of state, Sachiva and defeated big Samantas who paid taxes were also present to serve him with gift and offering that were useful for worship of lord Shiva."[79] Describing situations, after death of Prabhakara-Vardhana, Bana has written that "on the same day the king's favourite servants, friends, and Sachivas, whose hearts were held tight by the bonds of his many virtues, went forth, and in spite of the remonstrances of tearful friends, abandoned their loved wives and children."[80] It is clear from these descriptions that post of Sachiva was separate. Probably, Sachivas were appointed to help Adhyakshas of different departments whose work was to counsel Adhyaksha.

Kumaramatya –

"Generally minister or Amatya of prince was called Kumaramatya. There is mention of Rajamatya and Kumaramatya named officers along with other officers in Devabarnark inscription of Jivitagupta second. It indicates that Amatya of king was called Rajamatya and Amatya of prince was called Kumaramatya in category of Amatyas.

There were different categories of Amatyas. Mahakumaramatya was above the Kumaramatya.

In Harṣacarita Kumargupta and Madhavagupta, son of the Malwa king, and Bhandi, son of Mahadevi Yashomati's brother, were appointed as attendant of Rajya-Vardhana and Harṣa-Vardhana in childhood –'*bhanḍi nāmānamanucarama kumārayōrarpitavāna - tathā*

- *kumāraguptamādhavagupta nāmānāvasmābhirbhava-tõranucaratvārthamimō nirdiśtau.'*(Chaturth Uchchhawas, page-231-35, page-236)

It seems that they were appointed as Amatya of prince or Kumaramatya."[81]

Lokpala –

There is mention of appointment of Lokpalas. Bāṇa Bhaṭṭa has written that "king Harṣa has appointed Prajapalakas in all directions for supervision."(*'atra lōkanāthēna diśāma mukhēṣū parikalpitā lōkapālā:'*-Harṣacarita, Tritiya Uchchhawas, page-154)

Again he has written that "with his long glances which penetrated space he (Harṣa) seemed to examine what the Lokpalas had done right or wrong." (' *dīrdhairḍigantapāttibhirdṛṣṭipaṭāirlōkapālānāma kṛtākṛtamivapratyāvēkṣamānama'*- Harṣacarita, Dwitiya Uchchhawas, page-120). Praising the virtues of king Narak, Hansavega had said to king Harṣa that from childhood, influence by his heroism, Lokpalas bowed their head in foot of king Narak.

From these contexts it is clear that protector or ruler of province were called Lokpala. Their main duties were to protect provinces.

Aayuktak –

"In Harṣacarita 'Adhikrant Aayukta' (praised Aayuktas) is mentioned. Yukta named officers are mentioned in Kautilya Arthshastra which was the officer of Arth department (*arthastaya*) or finance department. Kautilya has said that it is easy to know about activities of sky birds but it is difficult to know about stealing money secretly by Yuktas –

api śakyā gatirjñātuma patatāma khē patatrīṇāma .

na tu pracchnna bhāvānāma yuktānāma caratāma gati: ||3||

Probably Aayuktak or Yukta were officerof finance department. Kautilya has directed to appoint those persons on this post who have qualities like Amatya. From this, it is clear that Yukta-Aayukta were placed in higher category officers."[82] From Aayuktak related context, which is described in Harṣacarita, it is seemed that Aayuktak was tax collecting officer of district level.

Bhogapati –

Bāṇa Bhaṭṭa has mentioned Bhogapati named officer. In sequence of describing departure of king Harṣa's army, Bāṇa Bhaṭṭa has written that "They (people of village) were complaining false of Bhogpaties, praising hundreds of past officials, reporting ancient misdeeds of knaves."[83] In which relevant and context there mentioned Bhogapaties; it is seemed that Bhogapati was tax collecting officer of state level. Here 'Bhog' should be accepted as meaning of certain material or tax that was collected for king's treasury. That material or tax collecting officer was Bhogapati. It seems not correct to relate

'Bhoga' with Bhukti and infer meaning as ruler of state because it is not seemed any relation to call 'Lokpala' and 'Bhogapati' the ruler of state in one administrative structure.

Agraharik and Mahattar –

State level manager of agrahars (that land given in free to Brahmans called agrahar) were called Agraharik. Mahattar word is made from Mahatt. "According to Moniyar Viliyams Mahattar was head or old person of village. Village head was called Gramik in Arthashastra of Kautilya and directed that when Gramik gone out of village for village work then villagers should follow him. We found villagers with that Mahattar when they were going to meet king Harṣadeva. So Mahattar was head of village,main member of village or Gramik."[84]

Paripalaka –

Mentioning Paripalak named government servant, Bana has written that "some other people, satisfied with government servants (Paripalakas), were paparai raying as –'the king is Dharma incarnate' (*'aparāirādiṣṭaparipālaka puruṣaparituṣṭaī: 'dharma: pratyākṣō dēva:iti stutīrātaṁvadbhi:'* – Harṣacarita, Saptam Uchchhawas, page - 378). Probably Paripalak was village level officer worked for people welfare.

Sancharah and Sarvagata –

"In Pratham Uchchhawas (page-62) Bana has used phrase 'manōrathā: sarvagatā:' and 'raṇaraṇaka: sañcāraka:'. According to commentator sanchara means 'char' or 'guptachar' (*cārā: saṁsthā:,sañcārakāśca*)."[85]

Describing characteristics of Shukanash, minister of king Tarapid, Bāṇa Bhaṭṭa has written in Kādambarī that "his many spies were traveling till shore of four seas on earth. So even inhailing news of that very place king was not unknown to him like whole earth was his own home." ('*yasyacānēkacārapurusahastrasañcāranicitē caturudadhivalayaparidhipramāṇē dhāraṇītalē bhavana ivāviditamahara: samuckchasitamapi rājñāma nāsīta*' – Kādambarī, Poorvabhagah, page-122-23). It is clear from this description that spies those traveling everywhere without any hurdle was called sanchara.

Doot(messenger) and Lekhaharak(courier) –

In Harṣa period administration there was special importance of doots (messengers). It is clear from description of Harṣacharit that messengers were scholars, efficient in their work and skilled in conversation. From context of Hansveg it is clear that kings were trusted fully on their messengers even to establish relation with neighbouring states. Messengers were also responsible to deliver secret and oral message.

Bana has quoted as Lekhaharak for those messengers who deliver written messages. Dirghadhwaj named Lekhaharak delivered message of Krishan, brother of Harṣa, to Bāṇa Bhaṭṭa and Kurangak named Lekhaharak delivered message of Prabhakara-Vardhana's illness to Harṣa-Vardhana. So that, Lekhaharak work was not bounded only to deliver messages.

Lekhak and Pustakrit –

"Bana has mentioned both Lekhak and Pustakrit in Pratham Uchchhawas of Harṣacarita.

Lekhak means writer is clear. According to commentator Pustakrit means lipikar (writer). There is mention of Pustapal named officer in Damodarpur copper plate inscription of Gupta king Buddhagupta, who was responsible to preserb papers of government orders. Probably Gupta period Pustapal was called Pustakrit in Harṣa period. Probably Lekhak and Pustakrit were also officers & employees mentioned by Hiuen-Tsang who were responsible for preserving an archive and Nilpit and put in writing events. Writing events and preserving government orders was very important work for stability of government."[86]

Gram Akṣapaṭalika a and Karnika –

Mentioning Gram Akṣapaṭalika and Karnik Bāṇa Bhaṭṭa has written that in way of expedition against the Gauda "Gramakṣapaṭalika urged with his all Karanies, 'Let his majesty, whose edicts are never void, even now bestow upon us his commands for the day'. By saying so he gave a new-made golden seal with a bull for its emblem in Harṣa's hand."[87] In this regard Dr. Vasudavasharan Agrawal's view is absolutely correct that "Gramakṣapaṭalika was main finance officer of village, which can understand as present time Patwari. His assistant writers were called Karani. Government offices were called 'Adhikaran' in Gupta period. Writers related to that office were Karani. Till now a sub-caste of Kayasthas is named 'Karan' in Bihar."[88]

Dandi –

"Bana has mentioned terror of irate and savage Dandies from which, people who come to see king, were flying away (Saptam Uchchhawas, page-377). Main police officer was called Dandpashik (seal founded from Vaishali) in Gupta period. So it seems that Dandi (Danddhari) were police who worked under police officer."[89]

In Harṣacarita and Kādambarī there is mentioned other officers/employees along with these important officers. Following were important officers/employees who worked in palace –

Dwarpal - gate keeper, who guard on main gate.

Dauwarik – officer of Pratihar and Mahapratihar.

Pratihar – arranger of court, expert in rule and etiquette of royal Palace and was work to give suitable honour by identifying special guests coming in court.

Mahapratihar – officer or employee between Pratihar and Dauwarik.

Arm wearer Maul – Special bodyguard of king.

Var Vilasiniyan – Beautiful women attendants appointed in royal court or royal family.

Tambuldayak – male betel bearer for king or members of royal Family.

Tambulvahini – Female betel bearer for king or members of royal Family.

Achamanivahak – employee for bearing material of achaman (a ritual purification before religious ceremonies) for king.

Purohit – main Brahman who performed ceremonial acts or worship for royal family.

Mauhoortika – Scholar who calculates astrologically auspicious moment for auspicious work.

Jyotishi – Jyotishi has proclaimed merits/demerits of child, on occasion of child birth etc., by seeing his lines of palm and foots.

Shankhvadak – In Harṣacarita and Kādambarī there are mention of indicating timing of morning- afternoon-evening and denoting different works time as – time of meal, time of bath etc. by blowing conch shell. It is clear from this description that there appointed conch shell blower who alerts royal family with king about timing. There is also mentioned blowing conch shell on time of army eparture.

Working circumstances and mentality of government servants:

In Harṣacarita there is subtle tracing of working circumstances and mentality of government servants which were present in early half of seventh century. Hansvega, messenger of kamrupa's king Bhaskarvarma, had come to Harṣa with message of friendship. Harṣa-Vardhana accepted Hansvega's proposal of friendship and said him that he wanted to saw Bhaskarvarma soon. Then Hansvega responded to Harṣa that "what else remains? …………let your majesty consider:- When towards servitude inclined by overwhelming calamity, like a wicked mother, old in years; spurred on by greed like an unsatisfied wife; harassed by ill imaginings with their manifold cravings, begotten of youth, like bad children; beholding circumstances over-ripe, ……………, like aged servants, of long standing and not to be shaken off: when thus, cherishing in his heart in vain the desire of grasping the whole round of delights, as though the power of all his senses were blighted, a man makes up his mind to enter a palace, ……………, downbent through greed of wealth, like a tree branch over a treasure. Like an ape, he changes not colour when angrily reprimanded: ……………like a vampire, there is nothing he will not do under his master's spell: ……………avoided by self-esteem, as if stifled in a heart contracted by meanness: parted from magnanimity, as if angered by his condescension to low acts; through devotion to riches he heaps up troubles, …………..though learned, his speech is a blundering as a fool's: though capable, he folds his hands helplessly, like a leper. Roasted without fire at the elevation of his equals, dying without expiring at the rise of his inferiors, …………An eunuch whose love is but words, …………-if a wretch of a servant belongs to the world of men, then a *rājilā* snake is a cobra, and a withered stalk the best of rice."[90]

Here Bāṇa Bhaṭṭa has traced emotional feeling and working circumstances of government employees. From historical point of view Bāṇa Bhaṭṭa has pointed out important facts related to circumstances to get government services, difficulties to get jobs, feeling uneasy from burden of work, involvement of employees in blameworthy and unholy work and developing asceticism from service due to unpayment by mouth of king Bhaskarvarman's messenger Hansvega. From these facts it informed about joy and sorrow of an employee and it is also informed about his changing behavior according to time and circumstances. According to these facts and considering circumstances it can be also known about position of officers/employees of any time slot. Even present time officers (even I.A.S & I.P.S level) are also looked like performing dance on indication of politicians (present ruler) and probably they have no option apart from doing flattery of rulers. Bana has criticized behavior of employees as involving in blameworthy and unholy work. In present time also, officers and employees involving in this type of acts are promoting corruption by becoming subject of self interest.

First time in Indian History a survey has conducted for study of mental thinking of high level officers by Department of Administrative Reforms and Public Grievances (DARPG) of Indian government. This survey has carried out by the Centre for Good Governance, Hyderabad, on behalf of this department.4808 officers of ten central services (I.A.S., I.A. &A.S., I.P.S., Indian Forest Service, I.R.S. (custom and excise), I.R.S. (I.T.), I.P.S., I.R.P.S., I.R.T.S. and Indian Postal Service) have included in this survey.

According to finding of this survey 33 percent officers wanted to quit their job. Political interference, harassment and frustration along with huge wealth in private sector are included in those reasons which are responsible to bring in mental status of country's top level officers at this level. According to survey, government interference is only such reason which has agitated administration. "It appears that performance appraisals, posts and transfers, opportunities for deputation, political interference and timely promotion rank very high among the concerns of civil servants", Cabinet Secretary K.M.Chandrasekhar acknowledged in his foreword to the report.

It is revealed from report that 33 percent I.A.S. and 47 percent I.P.S. officers believe that majority of their colleagues pull strings to get a good posting. One in four civil servants believes very few officers had their integrity intact.Important findings of this survey are as follows:-

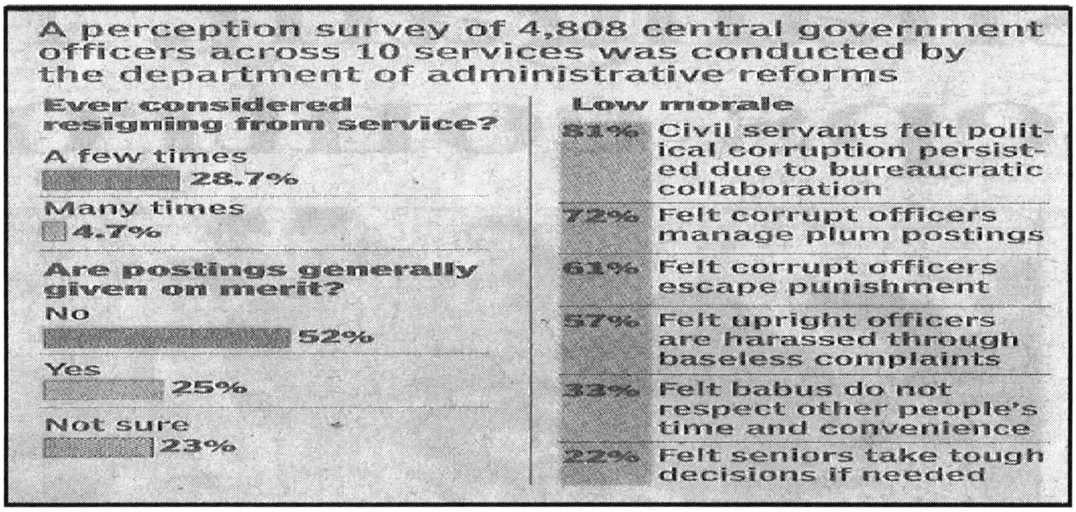
A perception survey of 4,808 central government officers across 10 services was conducted by the department of administrative reforms
Ever considered resigning from service?
A few times
28.7%
Many times
4.7%
Are postings generally given on merit?
No
52%
Yes
25%
Not sure
23%
Low morale
81% Civil servants felt political corruption persisted due to bureaucratic collaboration
72% Felt corrupt officers manage plum postings
61% Felt corrupt officers escape punishment
57% Felt upright officers are harassed through baseless complaints
33% Felt babus do not respect other people's time and convenience
22% Felt seniors take tough decisions if needed

(Source-Hindustan Times, Patna edition, dated-01.06.2010)

Time has changed but mental thinking of officers/employees is not changed so much. There is very similarity in this survey of twenty first century (year 2009) and conclusion of Harṣa period presented by Bāṇa Bhaṭṭa. From similarity of conclusions of Bāṇa Bhaṭṭa to findings of modern age survey it is proved that Bāṇa Bhaṭṭa was a sensitive historian who has modern thinking and determination to reveal truth.

Vision of Bāṇa Bhaṭṭa was acute and he has expressed his experience in Harṣacarita which has gained during living in Harṣa's court and contact with other contemporary kings. This type of description proved Bāṇa Bhaṭṭa as impartial historian along with stand him in line of modern historian. Certainly he has written history with point of view of common people.

Dr.Vasudevsaran Agrawal thinks this description of Bāṇa Bhaṭṭa as extraordinary for world literature. He has written "Bāṇa Bhaṭṭa has expressed different view in subject of people accepting government service, their different temperament about joy and sorrow, blameworthy work done by them, trickery, uncertain situation, flattery and sycophancy. This context is extraordinary in world literature. He has written "Bāṇa Bhaṭṭa has expressed different view in subject of people accepting government service, their different temperament about joy and sorrow, blameworthy work done by them, trickery, uncertain situation, flattery and sycophancy. This context is extraordinary in world literature. Till now, hardly ever any one had written this type of sharp remarks in fault or reproach of government service. These expressions are Bana's own those have told by him from mouth of Hansvega. By collecting his whole power of free personality he has done real criticism of flattery of royal palace, selfishness of servants and suffocating environment of self respected kings which has seen by him during wandering. Even he was not agree to accept government servants as man –" if a wretch of a servant belongs to the world of men, then a rājilā snake is a cobra, and a withered stalk the best of rice. Better for a manly man is a moment of manliness; at the price of bowing the wise deem not even the joy of a world-sovereignty worth a bow."[91]

Again he has written "witticism and severe scolding by Bana to people who were doing royal service or government service is unique in its own kind. Bana has presented acute analysis of mental thinking and blameworthy works done by government servants. It is possible that contemporary political writers have written about mental thinking and work done by royal servants and office workers and this description's colour was painted from those writings. But, there is no confusion that Bana's self personality was full of acute wisdom which is able to find reality by penetrating into every subject. He has closely inspected servants working in royal palace and studied their behavioural characteristics. Bana has not lost his own freedom of personality in comfort of royal service. As a neutral criticizer he was able to investigate demerits of royal families and government servants. It is suitable to give attention of his sentence 'Better for a manly man is a moment of manliness; at the price of bowing the wise deem not even the joy of a world-sovereignty worth a bow.'"[92]

Structure of Administration:-

Administration had divided on different levels in Harṣa period to run it successfully. From descriptions of Harṣacarita and Kādambarī it appears that generally Gupta period administrative structure was continued.

Generally administration was divided on central level, province level and district level. From description of Harṣacarita in which there is described about administrative control of Harṣa and power of king it is clear that administrative structure was centralized and there was given unlimited power to king. Even so there was provision of cabinet and before giving any administrative decision he consulted it. There was provision to appoint crown king who helped king in royal work and on very occasion when essential, he also led army. In Harṣacarita there is description about Rajya-Vardhana's attack against Huna. Central administration was divided in different important departments i.e. Finance, Foreign Affairs, Military and Internal management etc. and there were ministers appointed for each department. There were Sachivas, Officers and other employees appointed to assist ministers so that work could be completed as suitable manner.

There was important place of Samantas in central administration of Harṣa. Even kings were not able to defer from advice of Samantas. These Samantas were also helped kings with their army. Describing advice of Samantas to Rajya-Vardhana, consumed by sorrow after death of Prabhakara-Vardhana, Bāṇa Bhaṭṭa has written "At that hour, being solicited by the Samantas, who approached with inoffensive admonitions, Rajya-Vardhana reluctantly consented to take food."[93]

In a like manner, describing the palace of King Tarapid Bana has written that "In court of that palace there were seated thousand tilak marked Samantas on suitable sitting."[94] In Harṣacarita it is described that at time of expedition of king Harṣa, Samantas were also going with their belongings and there were kitchen appliances being carried on in front of the Mahasamantas. From these descriptions it is revealed that Harṣa period administrative structure was based on feudatory system.

In Harṣacarita there is mention of appointing Lokpalas for all directions by king Harṣa and monitoring them in order to overcome their wrong activity. It is clear from mention of Lokpalas that administrative work of province was completed through appointing Lokpalas at province level. Probably province was called as Janpad. Bāṇa Bhaṭṭa has mentioned Shrikanth Janpad which capital was Sthanishvar and Puṣyabhūti dynasty was arisen from there. Many officers and employees were also appointed to help Lokpalas. There is mention of Bhogapati named officer at province level. Dandi named police officer and Chat-Bhatt named police personnel were appointed to protect people and to punish guilty.

Bāṇa Bhaṭṭa has mentioned '*prativēśyaviṣayavāsinā*' (page-408) in Saptam Uchchhawas of Harṣacarita. From this description it is clear that provinces were also divided in Vishayas (districts) at time of Harṣa. Again Vishayas were also divided in village. There is mention of Gramakṣapaṭalika, officer responsible for tax collection at village level, which had presented a new- made golden seal with a bull for its emblem to king Harṣa.

Security Arrangement:-

It is clear from description of Harṣacarita and Kādambarī that there was extensive security arrangement to protect the state of Harṣa-Vardhana. There was permanent Army to protect the state along with policemen were also appointed for internal security. Army's main task was to suppress enemy, to protect king and royal palace and to give protection to feudatory princes. Security system of dynasty of Harṣa period can be understood by dividing it into two parts – (1) Army construction and external security and (2) Internal security. It is also known about security arrangement of king along with architecture of royal palace from description of royal palace which is described by Bāṇa Bhaṭṭa. To secure state frontier there was established camp of army men on border of state. In Kādambarī Bana has written "there was Gulmas or bushes here and there as Gulmas or camp of army was deployed here and there on border of state by kings who were attentive to security of their state-'*apramattapārthivairiva paryantavasthitabahugulmakai:.*'" [95]

(1) Construction of army and external security-

To protect vast of Puṣyabhūti state and to protect from external attacks, it was essential to have a huge army in north India. It was the reason that Harṣa had a huge army. So Bāṇa Bhaṭṭa has addressed him as 'Mahavahinipati'. Describing Harṣa's army Bana has written that "Thus the camp, exciting interest by manifold incidents, was like the doom's-day ocean gone abroad to swallow the world at a gulp."- ('*pralayajaladhimiva jagadagrāsagrahanāya pravṛttama*'- Harṣacarita, Saptam Uchchhawas, page-379)

Hiuen-Tsang has also mentioned that Harṣa had a huge army. He has written "After six years he had subdued the Five Indies. Having thus enlarged his territory, he increased his forces; he had 60,000 war elephants and 100000 cavalry."[96] King Harṣa had become 'Sakalottarpathaswami' due to this huge and strong army.

In Harṣa period army was called 'Katak'. There was tradition in Indian military system to construct army with elephant, horse, chariot and foot soldier. But Bana has mentioned elephant army, cavalry and foot soldiers at time of expedition of army but not mentioned about chariot army. From this it is concluded that, that time chariot army was not in use. Kings had directly appointed army men for military along with army of Samant kings was also attached with king's army at time of expedition of army. Bāṇa Bhaṭṭa has mentioned that kings of different countries were arriving, mounted on female elephants (Harṣacarita, Saptam Uchchhawas, page-367), calling up names of kings (Do, page-369) and king's residence became full of kings (Do, page-369). It is clear from these descriptions that army of Harṣa associated kings was also attached with Harṣa's army that was collected at time of special occasions.

People who were talented and specialist in war were appointed as soldier. Soldiers had to do regular exercise and practice of weapons. South Indian soldiers were also appointed in Harṣa's army. It is written in Saptam Uchchhawas of Harṣacarita that "Deckhan riders disconsolately contended with fallen mules."(Page- 367).

Success of Harṣa time army was depended on elephant army and horse army. Contemporary kings were confidence on these parts of army was according to their interest and faith. "According to description of Harṣacarita when Rajya-Vardhana had led army against the Malwa king then he gone with only cavalry (Shashth Uchchhawas, page -324) and when Harṣa had decided to go on expedition against the Gauda king then he ordered Gajsadhanadhikrit Skandagupta to prepare army of elephants – *śīghrama pravēśyantāma pracārnirgatānī gajasādhanānī* -(Shaptam Uchchhawas; page- 350).

So it seems that Harṣa had confidence mainly on elephant army. And it was also correct in position of that time. Because elephant, as Bana has said, are like 'moving hill fort', soldiers can fight with safety by mounting on them, along with ,elephant were effective in attacking on enemy's 'Durgas'(Forts) like present 'Tanks' – sañcāragiridurga rājasya- (Dwitiya Uchchhawas, page-116). Besides this they act like prakar of iron or wall to obstruct massive amount of arrows-*kṛtānēkabāṇavivarasahastrama lōhaprākārama pṛthivyā:;* (Do)."[97]

For army construction elephants and horses were selected on basis of their characteristics and potential. There were different type of horses, brought from different countries/foreign areas, in Harṣa's stable (Mandura). Describing those horses Bāṇa Bhaṭṭa has written that "There were some horses from Vanayuj (originated from Vanaghati Vajiristan); some horses from Arattaj (originated from Vahik or Panjab); some horses from Kamboja (originated from Pamir area of Bandhu river in middle Asia); some horses from Bhardvaja (originated from North Gadhaval); some horses from Sindhu desh (originated from Sindhsar or Doab of Thal); some horses from Parseek (originated from Sasani Iran)."[98]There were included large number of elephants in army like horses. It is described in Harṣacarita that intoxicated elephant and elephant found in charity were included in elephant army. That place was called 'Mandura' where horses were kept and that place was called 'Hathishal' where elephants were kept. "According to description of Harṣacarita probably army of camel and army of mule was also included in army of Harṣa (Saptam Uchchhawas, page-364-67). Describing camels along with elephants and horses, those were present at gate of royal palace, Bana has written "In another part it was tawny with troops of camels – having long tufts of hair and variegated threads of wool of five colours hanging near their ears; all tawny-red as monkeys' cheeks-'kapilakapola kapilaih kramelakakurauh kapilayamanam'-(Dwitiya Uchchhawas, page-100)."[99]

It is described about main officers and employees of army in Harṣacarita and Kādambarī. Final decision about marching of army was taken by king and he was the head of army. But army chiefs were appointed for different wings of army i.e. - elephant army, cavalry and foot army. There were many employees appointed to help these army chiefs.

Cavalry chief was called 'Brihadeshwar' by Bāṇa Bhaṭṭa. "In Harṣacarita there is mention of 'Kuntal' and 'Bhandi' named persons, those were trusted men of Rajya-Vardhana, who was appointed on this post. Bhandi was gone with Rajya-Vardhana, along with cavalry, to attack against the Malwa king.

Latter, Harṣa had also ordered him to march against the Gauda king (Shashth Uchchhawas, page-329 and Saptam Uchchhawas, page-404)."[100]

In Harṣacarita, describing dress of cavalry, Bāṇa Bhaṭṭa has written that "sheafs of javelins in cases under the charge of those who sat at the back, and saddles curving with scimitars and bristling with golden arrows. Girths, confining on either side the ends of the saddle, kept their cloth cushions motionless and gave a firm seat. The clash of their swaying foot-rests augmented the sound from the precious stones in their anklets. Their shanks were covered with their proper covering of delicate tinted silk. Their copper-coloured legs were chequered with mud-stained wraps, and a heightened white was produced by contrast with trousers soft and dark as bees. They wore tunics darkened by black diamonds glistening on bright forms; Chinese cuirasses thrown over them, coats and doublets showing clusters of bright pearls, bodices speckled with a mixture of various colours, and shawls of the shade of parrots' tales. Fine waistbands were wound about flanks made thin by exercise. Servants ran up to loose dangling earrings which had become entangled with pearl necklaces, tossed by their movements. Their ear-ornaments clashed as they struck against earrings budding with gold filigree work. The stalks of their ear-lotuses were fixed in their turbans. Their heads were wrapt in shawls of a soft saffron hue. They had linen turbans inlaid with bits of crest gems. Clouds of bees formed as it were peacocks' feathers in their topknots."[101]

Wearing different coloured dress by soldiers proves that armies of different Samant kings were included in Harṣa's army. Conjecture of Prof. Bhagawati Prasad Panthari is also similar to it. He has written "It is estimated from dress of different type and colour of cavalry that cavalry of different Mahasamantas and Samantas etc. had wore uniform of different types and colours. So uniform of Harṣa's cavalry is not in same colour mentioned as having different colours."[102] About this description Dr. Vasudevasharan Agrawal has thought that here described dresses are of different countries. He has written "It seems that Bana has described dresses of four different countries by these four words- Lajavardi, Kanchuk, Varban of Stavarak, Chincholak and Kurpasak. There was Iranian (South-west part of Iran) who were wore Kanchuk of lapis lazuli on their light-skinned body. Sasani or Pahalava, people of north-west Iran and Vahlik Kapisha (Afghanistan), were weared Varbana of Stavarak. Clearly dress of Chincholak was Chinese dress that was introduced to Indians on way of middle Asia and at junction of Chinese Turkistan and border of western China. Kurpasak dress had come to this country from Uigar Turka and Hunas who were situated in middle Asia and Chinese Turkistan."[103]

It is possible that Samantas who were placed at border areas or near border countries had accepted traditional dress of that area for uniform of their soldiers so uniform of their soldiers was different. Army of those king Samantas were present in their uniform to help Harṣa.

In Harṣacarita there is described about important employees those were appointed, to look after cavalry, are as follow-

Vallabhapal-Sthanapal – Ashvapal or servant who were responsible to look after horses

(Saptam Uchchhawas, page-365)

Parivardhak - Servants who were prepare horses with saddle for riding (Do.)"[104]

Servants responsible for shoeing a horse – There is mention about cone(equipment) for shoeing of horses (*khuradhōranī*- Kādambarī , Poorvabhag, page-43). From this description it is clear that there was vogue of shoeing of horses. Certainly there had appointed servants to do this work.

Probably these employees had worked under army chief of cavalry (vṛhadaśvāra).

In Harṣacarita army chief of elephant was called Gajasadhanadhikrit. Skandagupta was Gajasadhanadhikrit of Harṣa. In the morning Harṣa, after deciding to go on expedition against the Gauda, had called Gajasadhanadhikrit Skandagupta and told him to prepare elephant army.

Elephant army had special importance in Harṣa period. There was shelter near main gate of palace to keep elephants where elephants were kept. Bāṇa Bhaṭṭa has mentioned that there were many 'Achyut' elephants in army of Harṣa. "One 'Achyut' is equivalent to ten thousand. Accordingly there were certainly thirty thousand and above elephants in Harṣa's army. According to Chinese traveler Hiuen-Tsang there was sixty thousand elephants and one lakh cavalry in Harṣa's army so that he was able to rule thirty years peacefully. This means that king had prepared a huge army before year 618. Some time before this Bana had gone in king's court. Achyut Nagbal of Bana and sixty thousand elephant army of Hiuen-Tsang have supported each other. Bana has said Harṣa as 'Mahavahinipati'. This name is also correct as there is described about a huge army by Hiuen-Tsang. Presence of so many elephant in army reveals that Harṣa had special care about elephant army. Bana has also informed this fact in another way (*dānavatsu karmasu sādhanaśraddhā, na karikīṭēṣu*), which ironical meaning is derived that Harṣa's devotion or devotion to army was specially on elephants. When it was to prepare so huge army of elephants, so it was essential to give attention to catch and found elephants by every possible way. Bana has also thrown light on this. Followings are the source of elephants –

1. New catches (*abhinava baddha*).

2. Presented in tax (*vikṣēpōpārjita, vikṣēpa* = tax).

3. Presented in offering (*kauśalikāgata*).

4. Sent by officials of Nagavithi or Nagavan (*nāgavīthīpālaprēṣita)*.

5. Presented by those people who came to meet the king first time (*prathamadarśanakutūhalōpanīta*). It seems that it was mandatory to bring elephant to gift king when they had to meet with king first time.

6. Sent with group of ambassador.

7. Sent by chiefs of Shabar villages (*pallīparivṛḍhaḍhaukita*).

8. Given by self with or called for play of elephant-war and display sport.

9. Snatched by forcefully (*ācchidyamāna*).

There are some historical reasons behind preparation of huge elephant army. As kallidas has mentioned, in Gupta period army construction was depended on mainly horsemen. Probably Gupta's would learn this lesson from earlier Shakas. Shakas love for horse was well-known in world. Reaction is essential because horse power had reached on its supreme level. Use of elephants had proved successful to break attack of cavalry from front. Its second reason could be, after dispersion of Gupta empire there increased number of Samant, Mahasamant and Mandalik kings in country and every king had construct forts for self. Horses were not as effective as elephants to crack forts. Actually institution of Kottapala had emerged approximately at that time. Bana has indicated about dual use of elephants. He had said elephants as steely wall that had capability to endure rain of arrow that came from army of enemy: *kṛtānēkabāṇavivarasahastrama lōhaprākārama*. This fact came in mind of contemporary army chiefs that attack of cavalry's arrow could be successfully discharged by steely wall of elephants. Second use of elephant was to crack fort. Elephants were like moving hill-forts. Soldiers sat in high wooden Attal or Burja that were put on back of elephants and cracked mountain forts in similar way as soldiers seated in Attal or Burja of fort attacked with arrow from there. Bana has called this type of Burjas as kutattalaka: *uccakūṭāṭṭālakavikaṭama sañcārigiridurgama* . Elephants were used in similar way in war technique of Gupta period and Indian elephants were carried away to Iran. Characteristics of Sasani war technique was to put down Burja or soldier of enemies by pulling them who were attacked by throwing Kamand from travelling Attalakas. It is known that this art was developed separately in India or it was accepted like other things from contact of Sasani Iran. In army, elephants were used for these work and there used arātisaṁvēṣṭana word for these with help of Hastapāśākṛṣṭi and Vāgurā. Moving kutyantra of enemies was trapped by 'Hastapāśākṛṣṭi' and soldiers who were seated on horses or elephants were dragged by 'Vāgurā'. Bana has described elephant's army asthe means of churning enemy's army (vāhinīkṣōbha) and means of suddenly search or attack (avaskanda). Rounding in circle (maṇḍalabhrānti) and moving truculently were main techniques among techniques to train elephants. Elephants were also used to guard army (yāmasthāpita). New elephants were caught with the help of kumaki elephants (nāgōddhṛtī). Elephants were also used in royal possession. Elephants decorated like kotal horses were moved ahead without any rider. There was tightened Patbandh on their head: Paṭṭabandhārthamupasthāpita. There were kettledrums carried on back of elephants (ḍiṇḍimādhirōhaṇa) as procession of camels, by putting kettledrums on their back, were moved off in medieval time. Elephants were decorated with (śṛngārābharaṇa) flag, chawar, shankh, bell, angaraga and nakshatramala etc. There is several times mention of ornament made from conch shell had been hanged near both ears (*karikarṇaśaṁkha* or *avataṁsaśaṁkha*). Gold rings were fitted on teeth of elephants."[105]

Processed leather was on the back of elephants, prepared for war and then put hawdah full of essential weapons (bow, sword, spear etc.). Those hawdahs were decorated with different coloured colloq.

It is mentioned in Harṣacarita about different employees worked under elephant army. According to description of Harṣacarita Prof. Bhagawati Prasad Panthari has prepared list of these employees which is as follow:-

"**Under chief of elephant army** – To care elephants there

Appointed ev-bhishagvar (elephant doctor, *ibhabhiṣagvārānvaravāraṇānāma* -Shashth Uchchh-awas, page-347).

Ganikadhikari – (Do., page-347-48). Ganikadhikaries have knowledge about characteristics of elephants and specialist of activities(or trainer).

Karpati – Servants who care elephants.

Mahamatra – These officials are responsible to train elephants for war with help of puppet made from skin of dead elephants-'*mahāmātrapēṭakaiśca prakaṭita karīkarmacarmaputāī:* – (Do., page-347).

'For all officers and attendants in the elephant wing of the army and Mahamatras were of the highest rank'-(The Deeds of Harṣa, p. 159).

Nagavan Bithipal – (Do., page- 347 Dwitiya Uchchhawas, Page -99), Guard of elephant forest.

Adhorana- Elephant- driver (Mahavat), according to Commentator Shankar. Probably, Adhorana were officials who trained elephant of army to move slowly(The Deeds of Harṣa, p. 159 – Harṣa-

Charita, Dwitiya Uchchhawas, page – 111, Saptam

Uchchhawas, page – 364).

Lesik and Nalivahak – Responsible tobring grass for elephants

– (Do; Dwitiya Uchchhawas and Saptam Uchchhawas).

Hastipak – Mahavat (Saptam Uchchhawas, page – 375).

Mentha – Attendants responsible to bath elephants – (Do.)."[106]

There is also mention about other officers/employees in Harṣacarita beside these officers and employees of cavalry and elephant army. Probably these officers were general for whole army. About their work Prof. Bhagawati Prasad Panthari has written –

"**Baladhikrit** – High level officer of army, whose work was to organize army. Certainly his post was equivalent to army chief (Saptam Uchchhawas, page – 362). In Gupta period Baladhikrit and Mahabaladhikrit were called Senapati and Mahasenapati.

Patipati – Supervisor of army (Do., page -363)

Bhandagarini – They were head of store-room and who were manage to send goods and ration for army. They also manage to convey tent materials of Samantas on elephants – *sambhāṇḍāyamānabhāṇḍāgāriṇi, bhāṇḍāgāravahanasaṁvāhyamānabahunālīvāhikē* (Saptam Uchchhawas, page -364)."[107]

Iron was produced from mines to prepare weapon for army. Bana has mentioned about producing iron from mines to prepare a weapon named Paridh (*paridhapraharaṇahētōrūdagiranti girayōpi lōhāni tē* – Harṣacarita, Shashth Uchchhawas, page-336). Armour was made from iron which was weared on body to save from attack of weapons. It is mentioned in Kādambarī that the whole body was covered with black iron made armour leaving hand, foot and eyes."(*karacaraṇalōcanavarjayasitalōhajala kāvṛtaśarīrairalānastambhēriva* – Kādambarī , poorvabhagah, page-196) and "That place was ever covered with armour like large black bee as bodies of soldiers were covered with black armours like flock of large black bee"(*daṁśitairiva bhramarasanghātakavacāvṛtakāyai:* – Do., page -266). Prepared weapons were kept in special underground room that was called 'Aayudhashala' or 'Shastrashala'. In Kādambarī describing royal palace of king Tarapid, Bana has written "There was a underground cave full of snakes like a heavy shastrashala in that royal palace"(*antargatāyudh anivahābhirāśīviṣakulasankulābhi: pātālaguhābhirivāti gambhīrāyudhaśālā bhīrupētama* - (Kādambarī , Poorvabhag, page-182).

"In Harṣacarita Bana has described, in short but not detailed, about different weapons used by soldiers. Bana has mentioned those weapons (aggressive and defensive). Whose names are given below:-

Asi – (Pratham Uchchhawas, page – 37) Asi is called a type of sword in Arthshastra of Kautilya. Kautilya has said 'Asiyashti' a sword or scimitar has long and narrow size-(Adhikaran 2, Chapter- 18)

Khadga – (Pratham Uchchhawas, page – 37, Tritiya Uchchhawas, page- 352).

Kripana – (Pratham Uchchhawas, page- 37, Tritiya Uchchhawas, page- 192). This was also a type of Khadga (or sword). Kripana was in both sizes – big and small. Bana has mentioned 'Kripanya' which was probably small sized Kripana and trucked into waistband – '*kṛpāṇyā karalitaviśankaṭakaṭipradēśama*'-(Ashtam Uchchhawas page- 415).

Attahas Kripana – It was a long sword or Kripana, which has sharp edge and lightning to flash, called 'Maha Asi' (

Tritiya Uchchhawas, page- 182-83).

Nistrinsh – (*śaiśunāgiścanagarōpakaṇṭhēkaṇṭhē nicakṛtē niśtriśēna* - (Shashth Uchchhawas, page – 353 and Tritiya Uchchhawas,page – 187). Kautilya had given a sword name nistrinsh in different types of swords. This scimitar or sword (Asi) front was curved (Adhikaran 2, Chapter – 18).

Bhindipal – (Saptam Uchchhawas, page -367). This weapon was also mentioned in Arthashastra of Kautilya (Adhikaran 2, Chapter -18). There is also mention of Bhindipal in Prayag inscription of Samudragupta. Bana has described Bhindipal in 'puls'(*Bhindipāla pulikai*), that were put in quivers by attendants which were seated behind soldier who were seated on back of elephants. According to Dr. Fleet these were arrows of iron (Iron arrows, C.I.I. Vol. iii ,p.12).

Iron arrows are called Dandasan and Narak in Arthashastra (Kautilya) (Adhikaran 2, Chapter- 18).

So it is not correct to understand

Bhindipal as iron arrows. This type of arrows were not used traditionally. These were probably short lance(*laghu Pras*), whose front was sharp like arrow and that was used to attack on nearby enemies with hand like modern 'grenade'.

Kona- Mungari or Mudgar (Harṣacarita, Pratham Uchchhawas, page- 37).

Weapons of Khur-dhar (sharp-edge) – (Shashth Uchchhawas, page-355); Bana has mentioned Kshur-dhar (sharp- edge) mirror by that queen Ratnavali had killed king Jaruthya, the king of Ayodhya (Harṣa-Charita, Saptam Uchchhawas, page- 408). In Arthashastra, Kuthar, Pattatis (that both edge were pointed like trishula) and spade etc. are called 'Kshurkalpo' (Adhikaran 2, Chapter -18).

Bhallee – Short lance which were kept in quiver like arrow. Probably that were used to throw from near or used as 'Sangines' in near war (Ashtam Uchchhawas, page – 415).

Dhanush – (Saptam Uchchhawas, page- 359, Ashtam Uchchhawas, page – 415). Bana has mentioned bow from names of 'chap'(*chapavanatnilankaranad......*), 'Karmuk'(*cāpavanāṭaniṭānkāranāda , kārmukakarmaṇyavaṁśaviṭapasankaṭai:*) and 'Kodand'(Shashth Uchchhawas, page- 341, Saptam Uchchhawas, page- 410 and Ashtam Uchchhawas, page- 414).

Kautilya has given name of three type of bows – Karmuk, Kodand and Druna. Chap, Karmuk and Kodand were made from bamboo and Daroo(wood) etc.

Bana has also mentioned a bow named 'Sharanga' (Saptam Uchchhawas; page – 367). This was made from horn. Lord Rama's bow 'Sharanga' was well-known, so he called 'Sharangik'.

Bhastra-Bharan – A quiver to kept bunch of arrow, Bhallee and Bhindipala. In Harṣacarita there is mention of Bhastra-Bharanas (quivers) full of Bhallee, Sharas and

Bhindipalas – '*bhāllīprāyaprabhūtaśarabhṛtā ... bhastrābharanēna ...*' Do. Page -415, and '*bhastrābharaṇabhiṇḍipālapūlikai:*', page – 367).

Shara – Teer or arrow (Harṣacarita, Ashtam Uchchhawas, page- 415); In Arthashastra Kautilya has mentioned Venu, Shara, Shalaka, Naracha (*vēṇuśaraśalākā daṇḍāsannaracāśca iṣava:* – Adhikaran 2, Chapter- 18) etc. type arrows. Venu, Shara and Shalaka were made from wood. Arrows were also used by poisoning their needle in poison – *viṣamaviṣadūṣitavadanēna ca ...*(Ashtam Uchchhawas, page – 416).

Jya – (*guñjajjyājālajanitajagajjvarama* -Shashth Uchchhawas,page- 341), cord of bow. According to Arthashastra of Kautilya jya, murva, arka, shana, gavedhu, benuva were made from sinew (leather strap) ('*mūrvārkaśaṇagavē dhuvēṇusnāyūni jyā:*' – Adhikaran 2, Chapter – 18).

Parivar – Scabbard, in which Asi and Kripana was kept. This was covered with leather. Bana has mentioned scabbard covered with decorated skin of Chitrak(Leopard) – *citracitrakatvaktārakitaparivārayā* – (Harṣacarita, Ashtam Uchchhawas, page – 414).

Pattika – A cloth strip for tightening waist in which Asithem (short sword) and kripanya(khunkhari) were thrust into – *dviguṇapaṭṭapaṭṭikāgāṛha granthigrathitā sidhēnunā* – (Pratham Uchchhawas, page – 37).

Bana has also mentioned strip made from skin of snake beside cloth strip- *ahōramanīcarmanirmitapaṭṭikayā* – (Ashtam Uchchhawas, page – 414).

Leather of Kardaranga (shield, charmaphalak, Tritiya Uchchhawas, page -187) – Bana has mentioned shield made from leather of kardranga (Saptam Uchchhawas, page- 368). Probably, leather of kardaranga was importaed from outer-island (country). It is clear from this that foreign made shields were imported.

The king of Kamarupa had also sent leather of kardaranga by Hansavega in gift (Do; page – 386).

Shirastran – Ushnisha, Shikhand Khandika, Dookoolpattika were curtain to cover head (Pratham Uchchhawas, page – 43, Shashth Uchchhawas, page – 344, Saptam Uchchhawas, page – 368).

Kanchuk – (Pratham Uchchhawas, page – 34; Saptam Uchchhawas, page – 368). According to Kautilya Kanchuk was Varma or shield (Adhikaran 2, Chapter – 18).

Probably Kanchuk was soldier's dress or iron overcoat long up to knee. Bana has also mentioned Kanchukmade in china – *kañcukakaiścāpacitacīnacōlakaiśca* – (Saptam Uchchhawas, page – 368).

Varbana – Bana has mentioned Varbana stitched with pearl like stars – *tāramuktāstabakitastavaraka vārabānaiśca* –(Do.) Varbana was also iron varma (shield). Probably this was wear below up to ankle.

Kurpas – Bana has mentioned different coloured variegated Kurpasas (Do.).

This was also Varma (shield). Probably this was weared to safeguard shoulders.

In Arthashastra of Kautilya Charm (shield) , Shirastran, Kanchuk, Varbana and Kurpas etc. were called 'Aavaranani' (curtain to cover body) (Adhikaran 2, Chapter -18).

Hiuen-Tsang had also mentioned weapons used by soldiers mainly – spear, bow, arrow, sword, khadga and shield etc. (Watters, Vol. I, p. 171)." [108]

There is actual description of ascertain an auspicious moment for departure of army, preparation of army, supervision of army parade by king, blowing conch shell for starting of army's march in Harṣacarita. Along with there is actual description, touching the inner heart, of people inconvenient during march of army.

It is clear from this description, presented by Bana, that there was tradition to ascertain an auspicious moment for departure of army. That certain day the king performed worship after bathing and gave charity to people. After that the kings smeared on his weapon and then rub sandle ointment on his body up to head to foot. Happy Purohit sprayed water of peace on king's head. After that letters were sent to call associated kings. In Harṣacarita Bana has written "on a day with care calculated and approved by a troop of astronomers numbering hundreds, was fixed an hour of marching suitable for the subjugation of all the four quarters. The king bathed in golden and silvern vessels, like autumn clouds which were skilled in pouring water; had with deep devotion offered worship to the adorable Nilalohita; fed the up-flaming fire, whose masses of blaze formed a rightward whorl; bestowed upon Brahmans sesamum vessels of precious stones, silver, and gold in thousands, myriads also of cows having hoofs and horn tips adorned with creepers of gold-work."[109] It is mentioned that on this occasion Harṣa bestowed upon the Brahmans a hundred villages delimited by a thousand ploughs along with honoured kings. Probably this type of vast convening was organized to cause enthusiasm in people, Brahmans and kings.

It is mentioned in Harṣacarita that on day of army march Baladhikritas mustered crowds of Patipaties after the drums rattled and the horn blared. "In Gupta period Baladhikrit was important post in construction of army. Probably head of a Vahini was called Baladhyaksha. Cowell had inferred meaning of Patipati as superintendents of barracks, which seems correct, because it was correct to give order for preparation of army to Baladhikrit for

Patipaties. It was said panchadhikaranoparik patyuparika to Mahasamant Vijaysena in Ganaidhar-copper plate of Vainyagupta. There is also known this meaning of Pati i.e. long barracks for stay soldiers. When Baladhikrit ordered Patipaties then thousands of torches lighted."[110]

After that describing, about preparation of army to march, Bana has written that horses and elephants had to prepare for war. Servants of house-builders (Grih Chintak) rolled up awnings and cloth screens belonging to tents and marquees. Scraper of grass also became active. Cluster of utensils from Samanta's store-rooms were lifted on elephants. Helpless corpulent bawds lagged as they were with difficulty dragged along with hands and legs sprawling sideways. The carriages of the high born nobles' wives were thronged with roguish emissaries sent by princes of rank. Utensils, food materials and other goods were loaded on cart and oxen. A troop of seraglio elephants advanced where the press of people gave way before the glare of their runners' torches. Kings also reached there mounted on elephants and their names were proclaimed aloud. Thus the front of king's residence became full of kings. From this description it is clear that on occasion of army march whole royal family was marched in which female members of inner palace were also included. "This tradition was not vogue in Gupta period wars which were battled up to Vahlik-Sindhu. War discipline of that time was very hard. In latter days, probably at time of Kumaragupta, people of inner palace stayed together at time of march."[111] Latter this tradition was accepted in Mughal military system. There were managed splendid material states of camps at time of departure of Mughal army. "It was resulted that roughly Mughal army became like a moving city. In personnel materials of royal court, which were moving on elephants and camels along with army, was a part of inner palace and servants. That was a moving court in which musicians, painters, office, workshop and market were included. Treasury was traveled on elephants and camels. Materials of army were departed through hundreds of ox-cart. Royal furniture and many other goods were carried on by mules."[112]

In Harṣacarita there is mention of blowing conch shell denoting preparation of Samayoga Grahan (presentation of arraying the army) of Harṣa period army. After information of Samayoga Grahana Harṣa came out from royal house and supervised army of kings and divided them according to their several deserts. After doing so he saw Skandhavar passing through gate of royal palace and at last dismissed samayoga (the assembly) from Bahya Aasthanamandap after reaching at living place. From this description it is clear that there were organized assembly of army before march, conducted supervision and made announcement of dismissing assembly by king.

Soldiers went ahead with army by taking war indicating flags in their hands at time of army's march and along with king proceeded by thousand of ushers, like rays, heralding his appearance (word Jay) and clearing the way. During this march general people had to meet very inconvenience. Describing inconvenience of people Bana has written "Hundreds of friends were spectators of the men's exits from the interior of their somewhat constructed huts. Elephants keepers, assaulted with clods by people starting from hovels which had been crushed by animals' feet, called the bystanders to witness the assaults. Wretched families fled from grass cabins ruined by collisions."[113]

"Thus people had to suffer loss also in crowd during march of army. Bana has depicted true picture of destruction at both places- city and countryside during movement of that heavy assembly of people."[114]

Describing people's expression during march of Harṣa's army Bana has written that "demanding the protection of the crops: flying before their terror of irate and savage chamberlains, they yet in spite of distance, tripping, and falling, kept their eyes fixed upon the king, bringing to light imaginary wrongs of former governors, louding hundreds of past officials, reporting ancient misdeeds of knaves. Others, contented with the appointed overseers, were bawling their eulogies:- 'The king is Dharma incarnate'; others, despondent at the plunder of their ripe grain, had come forth wives and all to bemoan their estates, and to the imminent risk of their lives, grief dismissing fear, had begun to censure their sovereign, crying 'Where's the king?' 'What right has he to be king?' 'What a king!'"(The Harṣacarita of Bana-Trans.by E.B.Cowell & F.W.Thomas, Chapter-vii, page-208-09). Mentioning expression of Agrahari Brahmans Bana has written "There shrieking quarrelsome Brahmans, mounted on tops of trees were being expelled by the rods of chamberlains standing on the ground (Do., page – 209).

It is clear from this description that "Villagers had not any medium to convey their feelings to king in spite of having wished to complain about wrong-doing of old Bhogapaties and Chat soldiers. Thus Bana has given true glimpse of subject's pain. Not only on time of army march but at time of hunting people were caught to drive away elephants. At time of illness of Prabhakara-Vardhana when Harṣa-Vardhana had to come back suddenly then neighbouring caught villagers had to stand day-night to denote his way of journey."[115]

(2) Internal Security –

We see a glimpse of internal security from description of Harṣacarita and Kādambarī. Internal security includes security of king, internal law and order of state and security arrangement of royal palace under management of internal security system.

Bodyguards were always accompanied king for his security. Mentioning security of Harṣa, Bana has written that "the swords of guards caged him in like a lion's whelp" (*mṛgapatipōta iva rakṣipuruṣaśastrapañjaramadhyagatē* – Harṣacarita, Chaturth Uchchhawas, page – 229). Foot soldiers were also with horsemen along with king, when he came out from royal palace. In Kādambarī, describing about soldiers accompanied king Chandrapeed with their dogs to protect him, Bana has written "Chandrapeed ride on Indrayudh (his favourite horse) before sunrise and went towards forest along with many elephants-horses and foot soldiers. His guards were running ahead and making noise of festivities by dragging big dogs sized like donkeys tightened with golden chain and making travel zeal of

Chandrapeed soubled."[116] In Harṣacarita, at time of army's march, it is mentioned about shouting by horsemen to dogs tied behind them (*hayārōhāhūyamānalambita śunī* -Harṣacarita, Saptam Uchchhaas, page- 366). It is clear from this description that there were dogs used for security work at that time.

The king was aware every time about status of state with help of spies. There is mention of spies in Harṣacarita and Kādambarī. In Harṣacarita Bana has written that "Even as a conqueror, Death gathers his troop of heroes, Assembling them from this place and that on the earth, sending forth his own secret emissaries to bring them in" (The Harṣacarita of Bana –Trans.by E.B.Cowell & F.W.Thomas, Chapter-iv, page- 164). Accordingly in Kādambarī there is mention of collecting news of whole earth by Shukanas, minister of king Tarapeed, with help of his spies (Kādambarī , Poorvabhagah, page- 122-23). From these descriptions it is clear that informations of spies were used for internal security for expansion of state.

There is mention of Chat-Bhatt police and Dandi or Dandadhar in Harṣacarita and Kādambarī. Probably police officers were called Dandi and general policemen were called Chat-Bhatt. Bāṇa Bhaṭṭa has mentioned flying away of people by terror of Dandadhars. Probably there were police officers appointed to conduct administration satisfactorily and to give protection to people. In this concern Prof. Bhagawati Prasad Panthari has written that "Probably Chat were policemen. According to Dr. Fleet Chat were irregular soldiers."[117] From description of Bana it is clear that internal security of Harṣa's state was good and people lived with peace and prosperity.

Royal palace was controlling centre of state in Harṣa period. There was also special arrangement for security of royal palace. It is mentioned in Harṣacarita and Kādambarī about deployment of security persons for security of royal palace. In Kādambarī, describing security position of royal palace, Bāṇa Bhaṭṭa has written "It is difficult to enter into inner palace because dwarpalas (gatekeepers) stood at dyodhies (gates) holding cane stick in hands."[118]

It is clear from description of Bāṇa Bhaṭṭa, which is given about architecture of royal palace, which paid attention to provide every happiness while construction of royal palace. It is described in Kādambarī that one can meet to king after passing seven dyodhies (gates). Certainly contemporary architects were constructed this type of structured royal palace to provide security to king and royal palace.

It can be understood the structure of Skandhavar and royal palace of Harṣa period from description of Harṣacarita and Kādambarī.

In Harṣa period Skandhavar was spread in wide area in front of royal palace. Structure of Skandhavar was like army camp in which tents of elephants, horses, Samantas came from home and abroad, kings, group of ambassadors, Acharyas and hermits were situated. There was also a market in Skandhavar.

First time Bāṇa Bhaṭṭa went to meet Harṣa in Skandhavar situated near Manipur village. He had given lively drawing of Skandhavar that he saw during going to main gate of royal palace. Bāṇa Bhaṭṭa has written that the royal gate was all dark with crowds of elephands, the place seemed all in waves with the plunging horses, it was tawny with troops of camels and the camp was filled on every side with conquered hostile Mahasamantas. Again he has written that "Other kings too were there, came from the desire of seeing his glory, native of various countries, who were waiting for the time when he would be visible. There were also Jains, Arhatas, Pashupatas, medicants of the school of Parasharya, Brahman students, natives of every land, and savages from every forest that fringes the ocean-shore, and ambassadors from every foreign country were seated there."[119]

Along with people of these camps there was also market in Skandhavar. Bāṇa Bhaṭṭa has written that when Harṣa returned at noon in Skandhavar after hearing illness of his father Prabhakara-Vardhana then no merchandise was exposed for sale in the shops (*aprasāritāpaṇapaṇyama* - Harṣacarita, Pancham Uchchhawas, page – 262). Again there is mention in Harṣacarita that Harṣa had seen Yamapattika passing through market.

Skandhavar was spread in large area and people could pass to and fro there freely. There was arrangement of market to supply essential commodities in Skandhavar along with camp of kings, samants etc. Probably this market also completed requirements of near people (neighbouring villages) along with requirements of royal palace guests, kings, samantas who came from different countries. Regarding this Dr. Vasudevasharan Agrawal has written " Vipanivartma or street of main market was considered as a part of Skandhavar.Large ground in front of Red Fort of Delhi was called Urdu market i.e. market of Chavani(camp). This was the medieval structure of Vipanivartma."[120]

After Skandhavar there was royal palace or Rajkul. Entering in royal palace was difficult because there were deployed Pratihar to guard it. It is mentioned in Harṣacarita that different Samantas, Kings, Ambassadors etc. had to spent the day in the hope of meeting the king. Bāṇa Bhaṭṭa had also waited on gate of royal palace to meet Harṣa and Pariyatra named Dauwarik had caused to meet him to Harṣa after permission of king.

It is clear from description of Harṣacarita that there were four parts in royal palace which were called Kakshya. In first kakshya there was horse shelter (Mandura) in right side and elephant shelter (dhishnyagar) in left side. Height of elephant shelter was high. Beloved horses and elephants were kept in horse shelter and elephant shelter. Bāṇa Bhaṭṭa had seen elephant Darpashat 'beloved elephant of Harṣa' in the elephant shelter of first kakshya.

In second kakshya there was Bahya Aasthanmandapa. In Bahya Aasthanmandapa there was a posture and in front of this there was an open courtyard. In Bahya Aasthanmandapa there was performed work related to organizing court, audience with people, for discussion with ministers and giving information about dismissing of Samayoga (parade pf army). In Harṣacarita Bana has written that "At the door of his lodgings Harṣa graciously dismissed the chiefs on either side by motions of his brows; then entering, he dismounted and retired to a seat in the outer audience tent, where, after dismissing the assembly, he remained for a short time."[121] In Kādambarī, Chandrapeed had also called meeting with kings in Bahya Aasthanmandapa and departed with kings for expedition from there.

In third kakshya there was living place for royal family. It was called Dhavalagriha. It was two-storeyed and there made steps to climb on it. Security arrangement of Dhavalagriha was tight and talented & experienced were deployed to guard it.

"There was a courtyard in middle of Dhavalagriha and there constructed shalas or rooms on all sides so it was called Chatushshal. In language of Gupta period synonym of Chatushshal was Sanjavan. Bana has used the word Sanjavan by describing Dhavalagriha of Prabhakara-Vardhana. Prabhakara-Vardhana was on first floor but his perturbed servants were mourn below by assembling in Sanjavan or Chatushshal. It is known that rooms of Chatushshal were for vastragar, kashthagar, granthagar etc. and were used to stay guests. There were open gallery in front of rooms of Chatushshal and there were constructed long corridor between pillars which is called Suveethi by Bana."[122]

Kings lived with their queens on upper floor of Dhavalagriha. "In upper floor of Dhavalagriha in front of that was Pragreevak in middle, Sauth in one side and Vasabhavan or Vasagriha in other side. Shayangriha was a part of Vasagriha. Pictures were painted on wall in Vasabhavan. So this place was called Chitrashalika. Derived from this, the word chitrasari is used in language. Queen Yashovati has slept in Vasabhavan. Sleeping room of Harṣa was also there. Saudh was only to get up and sit down for queens. Yashovati sat on that roof in moonlight by putting off Anshuk from her breast. Middle room was called Pragrivaka because that was constructed on griva (the neck) place of Dhavalagriha. There is mention of Pragreeva room constructed in kumareeshala in Arthashastra of Kautilya (Arthashastra, 2/31). Women of relatives came by hearing Prabhakara-Vardhana's illnesses were seated in Pragrivaka room of upper floor which was screened around or covered: *bāndhavānganāvargagṛhītapracchannapragrīvakē*.

As there was Pragrivaka or Mukhashala in front part, so that, there was Chandrashalika in back part of upper floor. There were only roofs and pillars in it and king-queen had pleasure of moonlight by sitting there. In pregnancy Yashovati had to see shalabhanjikas (women figures carved on pillars), that were carved on that pillars, by sitting there.

Right and left long corridors, which had attached Chandrashalika and Pragrivaka, are called Prasadakukshi in which there were constructed Vatayans. In which king had enjoyment of festivals of dance and music with selected loving guests."[123]

Bāṇa Bhaṭṭa has mentioned Vyayamashala, Snanagar, Jaladroni, Devalaya and Vilepanabhumi in sequence of describing daily routine of king Shudrak in Kādambarī. It is clear from this description that there was arrangement of gymnasium for exercise of king; there was Jaladroni (like modern swimingpool) in bathroom for bathing, temple for worship and Vilepanagriha for rubbing ointment on body in royal palace. At departure time of Harṣa's army there is also mentioned carrying droni for bath (bath tub) by servants in Harṣacarita. Probably rooms related to these works were part of Dhavalagriha and situated at third part of royal palace. In description of Bana there is also mention of Grihodyan (royal garden), Grihadeerghika (stream of water in which there produced lotus and made arrangement of water-sport for swan), Mahanasa (place for kitchen) and Aaharmandap (place for taking food) etc. Probably these all were part of Dhavalagriha.

Fourth kakshya of royal palace was called Bhuktasthanamandapa. King had discussion with ministers and their special people at that place. First meeting of Bana to Harṣa was held in Bhuktasthanamandapa.

"To understand description of Bana about Skandhavar and royal palace it is essential to put in front of eyes the remains of royal palaces and mansions of medieval Hindu and

Muslim kings. Requirements of royal families are same to much extent; so that similarity in different parts of royal palace of different communities is natural.

If we see palace of Shahjahan constructed in Red Fort of Delhi then similarity of that in many facts is clear from palace of Harṣa. The reason for the similarities is that the Mughal emperors added many things in construction from outside but adopted many characteristics from old royal palaces. For example, there are found similarities in following things –

Palace of Bana (7th Century) -	Mughal period palace of Red Fort Delhi -	Hampton Court palace in London ($16-17^{th}$ Century)
1.Big assembly of Skandhavar in Front of royal Palace and way of Market.	Spread ground in front of Red Fort which was called Urdu bajar.	
2.Parikha an Prakar	ditch and wall of Fort.	Moat and Bridge.
3.Royal gate.	Sadar gate of Fort, from which Starts guarding.(comp. Darsadar In Kirtilata.	The Great Gate House.
4.Alinda or room of	Line of both side constructed	Barracks and Porter's

Outer gate.	rooms in Sadar gate where at Present stablished shops.	Lodge in the Entrance.
5.First Kakshya- Shelter of elephants And horses	open ground.	Base court.
6.Bahya Aasthanamandap And courtyand in front Of that.	Deevan Aam and open courtyard in front of that.	Great Hall and Great Hall court.
7.Stairs to climb up from Courtyard to Aasthana-Mandapa.	Stairs in front of Deevane Aam.	Grand Stair-case (king's Staircase).
8.Kings seat puted in Aasthanamandapa	Special place to seat king in Deevane Aam.	Clock court.
9.Abhyantarakakshya.		
10.Dhavalagriha.	Inner palace.	Principal Floor.
11.Grihodyan, Kreedavapi Kamalavan.	Nazar bag and pond constructed There(compa. Chatussama palval And there puted Chandrakantmani Of Kirtilata.	Privy Garden, Pond Garden (Vinery, Orangery, Etc.)
12.Grihadeerghika	Nahare- bahisht	Long canal, 'Long water'
13.Snanagriha, Yantradhara, Snanadroni, Mahanasa, Aaharamandapa.	Hammam, Hauj and Fountains.	Bathing Closet, King's Kitchen, Banquesting Hall, Private Dining Room.
14.Devagriha.	Masjid or Namajagah	Royal Chapet.

	(Moti Masjid).	
15.Chatuhshala.		Cellers on the Ground Floor.
16.Veethiyan.	Khurramgah Rangamal, (Khurramgah of Kirtilata and Sukh Mandir of Aamer palace).	Galleries.
17.Bhuktasthanamandapa	Darbar Khas	Audience Chamber.
18.Pragreevak, Gavaksha Mukhashala attached with Vatayanas(view of Padataditakam).	Musammam Burja (Suhaga Mandir of Aamer palaces, from where queens had looked outer view by sitting in Small barred window).	Queen's Gallery, Great Watching Chamber.
19.Darpan Bhavan or Aadarsh Bhavan.	Sheeshamahal[ther is also mention Aadarsh Bhavan in Tilakamanjari by Dhanpala(11th century)] .	
20.Shayangriha, Vasagriha (Chitrashalika),Saudh, Nivasaprasada made from Pillar of elephant teeth and Muktashail(white stone), Room of Heera made from Arched gateway of elephant Teeth(sadantatoran vrajamandir.	Personal rooms of Badshah and Begums(Khvabagah where roof and wall were painted).	King's Drawing room Queen's Drawing room King's Bed-room Queen's Bed-room.
21.Sangeetagriha.		
22.Chandrashala.		
23.Prasad-kukshies.		Presence

		Chambers.
24.Prateeharagriha.	Palace of khvajasara.	Lord Chamberlains Court , where He and his Officials had Their lodging.

It is clear from this list that there was continuity in literature from former times to subsequent times about the architecture of palaces mentioned by Bana. Actually the continuity in the palaces of the seventh century was not only in the artitecture but also in the utilities such as servants, entertainment and royal works. In the same way their spendour continued in the forth coming eras. It is the actual historical sequence. We shall have to fill beauty and colour in these hazy pictures of Bana. The figure of Indian royal palaces would be clearer from the study of royal palaces of later kings of Gurjar-Pratihar, Pala, Parmar, Chalukya, Yadav, Kakati, Ganga and Vijay Nagar and architecture and literature of Muslim Period."[124]

Judiciary System –

In Harṣacarita and Kādambarī there is analysis of different aspects of Judiciary system of Harṣa period. It could be understood about base of judiciary system, nature of guilt and process of justice and law of punishment from description presented by Bāṇa Bhaṭṭa.

In Harṣa period king was super decisive in field of judiciary. Decision was taken on base of dharmashastra and neetishastra while giving sentence to punishment for different guilt. On the whole there were inducted liberal laws for judgment. In Kādambarī Bāṇa Bhaṭṭa has criticized hardness of Chanakya Neeti. Criticizing kings, who were tainted and strayed from the path, Bāṇa Bhaṭṭa has written that "how far say about those kings. They regard as authentic the spiritual instructions of Chanakyaneeti filled with excessive cruelty."(*kĩ vē tēṣã sāmpratama yēṣāmatinṛśaṁsaprāyōpadēśanirghṛṇaṁ kauṭilyaśāstrama pramāṇama* – Kādambarī , Poorvabhagah, page-229). It is clear from this description that Arthashastra of Kautilya was also used for giving justice but hard rules, which were described in that, were not liked.

There is mention of court which is called Adhikarana by Bana. Dharmadhikaries were gave justice by occupying high seats in these courts. Decisions of these courts were written by clerks. In Kādambarī describing about court, which was situated in royal palace of king Shudraka, Bana has written "There were present big Dharmadhikaries (judges), having image of incarnate dharma, weared costly dresses and occupied lofty seats in Nyayalaya (court). Writers of judges (clerks) were writing thousand order letters, presenting splendid work by experience of writing whole worlds activities and by remembering every village and city name and looking whole world like a house, in comparison of city of Dharmaraj."[125]

According to nature of guilt courts were divided in two parts – (i) Criminal court and (ii) Civil court. It is mentioned in Harṣacarita that "the followers of Mimamsa alone have to ponder problems in administering justice (adhikarana) while they examine the several adhikaranas or 'cases for discussion' in their system"(The Harṣacarita of Bana – Trans.by E.B.Cowell & F.W.Thomas, Chapter-2, page- 65). In Kādambarī, mentioning about collected wealth by justice in palace of Shudrak, Bāṇa Bhaṭṭa has written "As Hiranyagarva was born to decide behaviour of creature in universe, in similar way there is collected wealth in that palace by taking fee on occasion of giving justice to people."[126] It is clear from this description that there was arrangement of civil court to give wealth punishment.

There are also mentioned contemporary offences in Harṣacarita and Kādambarī. Some main offences were – struggle, sin, enmity, trickery, not to take order of gurus or disrespect of gurus, sexual intercourse with other's wife, divorce, telling a lie and kill some one by poisoning. Offences were divided in small and big according to their seriousness. Punishment was given according to offences.

There were determined different punishments for different offences in seventh century. Along with there was tradition of Divya Priksha (ordeal). In Harṣacarita, describing administration of Harṣa, Bana has written "only bees quarrel in collecting dews (dues); the only feet ever cut off are those in metre; only chess boards teach the positions of the four 'members', there is no cutting off the four principal limbs of condemned criminals; only snakes hate Garuda the king of birds (dvija-guru), no one hates Brahmans or gurus."[127] There was good-governance in Harṣa's state so it was not necessary to give this type of punishments. But it can infer from these mentions that these types of punishments were certainly used in other states of Harṣa period. In similar way there was praised administrative system of king Tarapeed in Kādambarī. In Kādambarī Bana has written "only controlled organs there was no punishmnent for subjects; only elephants had to go in vari i. e. in place of confine subjects had not to take oath in varipradesh i.e. standing in water; only fire was hold by people taken vow of Agnihotra etc.; people had not to hold fire on their palm to take oath. Only sun-moon etc. planets had to mount on pair of seals; people had not to take oath by mounting on pair of scales. Purification was conducted by poison after rise of Agastya; one had not to prove purified oneself by consuming poison."[128] Consequently again it is written "Salvation of Tarak (Tarakasur) was completed at time of praising Shadanana; not put out the eye ball of one for punishment."[129]

Although these sentences were written to praise administrative system of king Tarapeed though it can infer that methods of entering into water, taking fire on palm, mounting on pair of scales and consuming poison were used to prove guilt. Some other main methods of punishment, those are described in

Harṣacarita and Kādambarī, are imprisonment, punishment of wealth and punishment of whip.

These descriptions of Bāṇa Bhaṭṭa are also proved by description of contemporary Chinese traveler Hiuen-Tsang. Hiuen-Tsang has written "when the laws are broken or the power of the ruler violated, then the matter is clearly sifted and the offenders imprisoned. There is no infliction of corporal punishment; they are simply left to live or die, and are not counted among men. When the rules of propriety or justice are violated, or when a man fails in fidelity or filial piety, then they cut his nose or his ears off, or his hand and feet, or expel him from the country or drive him out into the desert wilds. For other faults, except these, a small payment of money will redeem the punishment. In the investigation of criminal cases there is no use of rod or staff to obtain proofs (of guilt). In questioning an accused person, if he replies with frankness the punishment is proportioned accordingly; but if the accused obstinately denies his fault, or in despite of it attempts to excuse himself, then in searching out the truth to the bottom, when it is necessary ordeal used – (1) by water (2) by fire (3) by weighting (4) by poison."[130]

Revenue System –

There is thrown light on Harṣa period revenue system from description of Harṣacarita and Kādambarī. There is mention of taken out pitchers of huge treasury hoards from underground tightened with golden chains. This type of treasure proves vogue a systematic tax system. Along with a generous tax system is indicated in description of Bana. In Kādambarī, praising the state of king Shudrak, Bana has written that taking the hand ritual performed only in wedding; there is not given pain to any one for tax. In similar way mentioning Sthanvishvar Janapad, in Harṣacarita, Bana has written that people were not familiar with searching of people by king to pay tax. It is clear from descriptions that royal tax was collected liberally.

In revenue sources for state, tax on agriculture, tax collected from Samantas, revenue from forest, tax collected from businessmen, income from mines, captured wealth of defeated kings and tax collected from defeated kings etc. were main sources. Pieces of land were distributed after developing unfertile land and leaning forest, to Samantas to increase income of state. These Samantas were regularly paid taxes to kings. Describing valour of King Prabhakara-Vardhana Bana has written "Leveling on every side hills and hollows, clumps and forests, trees and grass, thickets and anthills, mountains and caves, the broad paths of his armies seemed to portion out the earth for the support of his dependents."[131] In Kādambarī there is description of materials obtained from forest. Describing group of Bheels, those were going with army chief of Shabars by holding these materials in their hands. Bana has written "entire flocks of Bheels were going along with army chief. Many of them were holding hairs of Chamaramriga and bundle of elephant teeth. Many Bheels were going with leaf-cup full with honey. Some Bheels, brave like lion, were going by take pearls taken out from skull of elephants. Many Bheels, similar to demon, were taken load of meat. Many Bheels, having peculiar image like gana of Lord Shiva, were holding skin of lion. Some Bheels, like Buddhist, were taken peacock's wing. Some Bheels, like child, were holding crow-feather. Some Bheels were representing Lord Krishna's character by holding teeth of naturally dead elephants (Lord Krishna had rooted out teeth of Kuvalayapeed elephant by killing him)."[132] These goods, obtained from forest, would sell in market and certainly tax would impose on them by state. In Kādambarī, describing about selling goods on street of Ujjayini city, Bāṇa Bhaṭṭa has written "In that city streets of market are spread like ocean given by MaHarṣai Agastya. Golden sand was spread in them. There are hoards of conch sell, mother-of-pearl, pearl, coral and emerald to sell."[133] It is clear from description of this type of developed markets that there would be special arrangement by state to regulate and conduct markets. Probably taxes were imposed on goods that were sold in these markets.

"It is mentioned in Harṣacarita that gifts and presents were offered to the king Puṣyabhūti by citizens, Padopajeevi(employees), Sachivas and Mahasamants, whom his arm's might had conquered and made tributary for worship of Lord Shiva (Tritiya Uchchhawas, page-171)

Deva Harṣa had collected tax by defeating state of Tushar-Shailabhu. (Do.-page-154)

Royal reasury and Jewellery was captured by Rajyavardhan after defeating Malwa king. And that accumulated wealth was presented to Harṣa by Bhandi after returning from expedition. (Saptam Uchchhawas, page-405-06).

So Bana has written about Prabhakara-Vardhana that he counted a host of enemies the acme of prosperity and the fall of sword strokes a shower of wealth (sense is about happiness by capturing accumulated wealth of killed enemy)- *śatru nidhidarśanama diṣṭavṛddhima śastraprahārapatanama* - (Chaturth Uchchhawas, page-204-05)

Gifts received from friend Samant kings were huge source of income. Bhaskarvarman, king of Kamarupa, had sent different precious and useful goods by his ambassador Hansavega to king Harṣa wishing his friendship (Saptam Uchchhawas, page-386-88).

States had got elephants from kings as tax and gift. Bana has written that gate was all dark with crowds of elephants. These mountain like elephants look as collected to make a bridge over the ocean. Some elephants were collected in tax and some were presented in gift and some were taken (from state of enemies) by force.(Dwitiya Uchchhawas, page-99) Collection of elephants was necessary because they were part of military."[134]

Probably Gupta period taxation system was also continued in Harṣa period. There is not any mention, in Harṣacarita and Kādambarī, about any type and amount of tax. It is informed, from description of Bana, that taxes were collected from people in form of goods and coins. He has mentioned gold and silver coins. There is mention, at time of Harṣa's expedition, about presenting of curds, molasses, candid sugar, and flowers in baskets by elders of village. Probably people paid a part of their production to king as Bhag-Bhoga. From presence of huge hoards of wealth and people had unlimited gold coins, mentioned in Harṣacarita and Kādambarī, it is clear that tax was collected in form of coin.

There were appointed employees on every stage to collect tax. Grāmākṣapaṭalika at village level and officers named Bhogapati at province level were responsible to collect tax.

Revenue, collected from whole state, was used for strengthening military, enjoyment of royal family and welfare oriented works (digging canal, pond, plantation, gardening, providing employment etc.). On every five year Harṣa distributed accumulated wealth of treasury in people to ascertain similarity and improve economic condition of people. This was the reason that people were happy in Harṣa's state and good governance was spread everywhere. Drawing of state's prosperity and happiness of people which is sketched by Bana is also proved by description of Hiuen-Tsang.

It can be concluded that political situation of seventh century is known from descriptions of Bana. There are described political events related to Puṣyabhūti dynasty in Harṣacarita. There is thrown light on events of establishment of Puṣyabhūti clan to expedition of Harṣa for conquest of world from these descriptions. It seems that Bana had not completed Harṣacarita and Kādambarī due to unfortunate death. He has thrown light on duties of contemporary kings. It is known from his description that kings work with sense of people welfare. Kings were traveled personally to know joy and sorrow of subjects as it is mentioned about king Harṣa. There was cabinet that helped king to conduct administration. There were several officers and employees apointed to conduct administration successfully. There is also drawn sketch of mental condition of state's employees in Harṣacarita. Impartial analysis of mental status of employees proves that Bana was a sensitive historian having modern thinking. He has also given authentic information about administrative structure, architect, security arrangement and revenue system of seventh century. Descriptions of Bana are also proved by other contemporary historical sources.

References:-

1. Harṣa Charitam- Chowkhamba Vidyabhawan Varanasi-
   Page-202.

2. Rajvansh: Maukhari aur Puṣyabhūti- Prof. Bhagwati Prasad
   Panthari- Bihar Hindi Granth Akadamy Patna- page-26.

3 . Harṣa Charitam- Chowkhamba Vidyabhawan Varanasi-

Page-203.

4. Do - Page-203.
5. The Harṣacarita of Bana- Trans. By- E.B.Cowell & F.W.Thomas –Motilal Banarsidass Pvt.Ltd.Delhi- Page-101-102.
6. Do - Page-110.
7. Harṣa Charitam- Chowkhamba Vidyabhawan Varanasi- Page-229.
8. Rajvansh: Maukhari aur Puṣyabhūti- Prof. Bhagwati Prasad Panthari- Bihar Hindi Granth Akadamy Patna-28-29.
9. Buddhist Records of The Western World- Samuel Beal- Low Price Publication Delhi- Page- 209-10.
10. Harṣa Charitam- Chowkhamba Vidyabhawan Varanasi- Page-168-69.
11. The Harṣacarita of Bana- Trans. By- E.B.Cowell & F.W.Thomas –Motilal Banarsidass Pvt.Ltd.Delhi- Page-89.
12. Harṣa Charitam- Chowkhamba Vidyabhawan Varanasi- Page-183.

13. Rajvansh: Maukhari aur Puṣyabhūti- Prof. Bhagwati Prasad Panthari- Bihar Hindi Granth Akadamy Patna-26-27.

14. Do - Page-30-31.

15. The Harṣacarita of Bana- Trans. By- E.B.Cowell & F.W.Thomas –Motilal Banarsidass Pvt.Ltd.Delhi- Page-119.

16. Rajvansh: Maukhari aur Puṣyabhūti- Prof. Bhagwati Prasad Panthari- Bihar Hindi Granth Akadamy Patna-31-32.

17. Kādambarī -Poorvabhagah- Chowkhamba Vidyabhawan Varanasi- Page- 214.

18. The Harṣacarita of Bana- Trans. By- E.B.Cowell & F.W.Thomas –Motilal Banarsidass Pvt.Ltd.Delhi- Page-122-23.

19. Rajvansh: Maukhari aur Puṣyabhūti-Prof. Bhagwati Prasad Panthari- Bihar Hindi Granth Akadamy Patna-Page- 33.

20. The Harṣacarita of Bana- Trans. By- E.B.Cowell & F.W.Thomas –Motilal Banarsidass Pvt.Ltd.Delhi- Page-132.

21. Rajvansh: Maukhari aur Puṣyabhūti- Prof. Bhagwati Prasad Panthari- Bihar Hindi Granth Akadamy Patna- Page-

34.

22. The Harṣacarita of Bana- Trans. By- E.B.Cowell & F.W.Thomas –Motilal Banarsidass Pvt.Ltd.Delhi- Page-142-43.

23. Rajvansh: Maukhari aur Puṣyabhūti- Prof. Bhagwati Prasad Panthari- Bihar Hindi Granth Akadamy Patna- Page-36-37.

24. Do - Page- 37-39.

25. The Harṣacarita of Bana- Trans. By- E.B.Cowell & F.W.Thomas –Motilal Banarsidass Pvt.Ltd.Delhi- Page-178.

26. Rajvansh: Maukhari aur Puṣyabhūti- Prof. Bhagwati Prasad Panthari- Bihar Hindi Granth Akadamy Patna- Page-42.

27. Do - Page-42-43.

28. The Harṣacarita of Bana- Trans. By- E.B.Cowell & F.W.Thomas –Motilal Banarsidass Pvt.Ltd.Delhi- Page-viii.

29. Buddhist Records of The Western World- Samuel Beal- Low Price Publication Delhi- Page-210.

30. The Harṣacarita of Bana- Trans. By- E.B.Cowell & F.W.Thomas –Motilal Banarsidass Pvt.Ltd.Delhi- Page-224.

31. Rajvansh: Maukhari aur Puṣyabhūti- Prof. Bhagwati Prasad Panthari- Bihar Hindi Granth Akadamy Patna- Page-46.

32. Harṣa Charitam- Chowkhamba Vidyabhawan Varanasi- Page-329.

33. Rajvansh: Maukhari aur Puṣyabhūti- Prof. Bhagwati Prasad Panthari- Bihar Hindi Granth Akadamy Patna- Page-47.

34. Do - Page-51-52.

35.The Harṣacarita of Bana- Trans. By- E.B.Cowell & F.W. Thomas –Motilal Banarsidass Pvt.Ltd.Delhi- Page-218-19.

36. Do - Page-217-18.

37. Buddhist Records of The Western World- Samuel Beal- Low Price Publication Delhi- Page-198.

38. Rajvansh: Maukhari aur Puṣyabhūti- Prof. Bhagwati Prasad Panthari- Bihar Hindi Granth Akadamy Patna-65-67.

39. The Harṣacarita of Bana- Trans. By- E.B.Cowell & F.W.Thomas –Motilal Banarsidass Pvt.Ltd.Delhi- Page-224.

40. Buddhist Records of The Western World- Samuel Beal- Low Price Publication Delhi- Page-210-11.

41. On Yuan Chwang's Travels in India- Thomas Watters- Low Price Publications Delhi- Vol.-1, Page- 343.

42. Harṣa Charitam- Chowkhamba Vidyabhawan Varanasi- Page-447.

43. Rajvansh: Maukhari aur Puṣyabhūti- Prof. Bhagwati Prasad Panthari- Bihar Hindi Granth Akadamy Patna-69-70.

44. The Harṣacarita of Bana- Trans. By- E.B.Cowell & F.W.Thomas –Motilal Banarsidass Pvt.Ltd.Delhi- Page-258.

45. Harṣa Charitam- Chowkhamba Vidyabhawan Varanasi- Page-124.

46. Buddhist Records of The Western World- Samuel Beal- Low Price Publication Delhi- Book-v, Page- 233.

47.Harṣacarita: Ek Sanskritik Adhyayan- Dr. Vasudevasarana Agrawal- Bihar Rastrabhasha Parishad

Patna- Page- 46.

48. Harṣa Charitam- Chowkhamba Vidyabhawan Varanasi- Page-203.

49. Rajvansh: Maukhari aur Puṣyabhūti- Prof. Bhagwati Prasad Panthari- Bihar Hindi Granth Akadamy Patna- Page-31.

50. Do - Page-84.

51. Buddhist Records of The Western World- Samuel Beal- Low Price Publication Delhi- Book-11, Page- 272.

52. Rajvansh: Maukhari aur Puṣyabhūti- Prof. Bhagwati Prasad Panthari- Bihar Hindi Granth Akadamy Patna- Page-86-87.

53. Do - Page-90.

54. The Harṣacarita of Bana- Trans. By- E.B.Cowell & F.W.Thomas –Motilal Banarsidass Pvt.Ltd.Delhi- Page-210-211.

55. Harṣacarita: Ek Sanskritik Adhyayan- Dr. Vasudevasarana Agrawal- Bihar Rastrabhasha Parishad

Patna- Page- 168-70.

56. Kādambarī -Poorvabhagah- Chowkhamba Vidyabhawan Varanasi- Page-232.

57. Harṣa Charitam- Chowkhamba Vidyabhawan Varanasi- Page-89.

58. Kādambarī -Poorvabhagah- Chowkhamba Vidyabhawan Varanasi- Page- 5.

59. Adbhut Bharat- A.L.Basham- Shivlal Agrawal and company Agra- Page- 67.

60. Kādambarī -Poorvabhagah- Chowkhamba Vidyabhawan Varanasi- Page- 207.

61. Rajvansh: Maukhari aur Puṣyabhūti- Prof. Bhagwati Prasad Panthari- Bihar Hindi Granth Akadamy Patna- Page- 124-25.

62. The Harṣacarita of Bana- Trans. By- E.B.Cowell & F.W.Thomas –Motilal Banarsidass Pvt.Ltd.Delhi- Page-42-43.

63. Buddhist Records of The Western World- Samuel Beal- Low Price Publication Delhi- Book- v, Page- 213-15.

64. The Harṣacarita of Bana- Trans. By- E.B.Cowell & F.W.Thomas –Motilal Banarsidass Pvt.Ltd.Delhi- Page- 74-75.

65. Kādambarī -Poorvabhagah- Chowkhamba Vidyabhawan Varanasi- Page-224-31.

66. The Harṣacarita of Bana- Trans. By- E.B.Cowell & F.W.Thomas –Motilal Banarsidass Pvt.Ltd.Delhi- Page-192-94.

67. Harṣacarita: Ek Sanskritik Adhyayan- Dr. Vasudevasarana Agrawal- Bihar Rastrabhasha Parishad Patna- Page-135-36.

68. Kādambarī -Poorvabhagah- Chowkhamba Vidyabhawan Varanasi- Page-248-49.

69. Buddhist Records of The Western World- Samuel Beal- Low Price Publication Delhi- Book- v, Page- 233.

70. Harṣa Charitam- Chowkhamba Vidyabhawan Varanasi- Page-220.

71. Kādambarī -Poorvabhagah- Chowkhamba Vidyabhawan Varanasi- Page-328-29.

72. Buddhist Records of The Western World- Samuel Beal- Low Price Publication Delhi- Book- v, Page- 215.

73. Kādambarī -Poorvabhagah- Chowkhamba Vidyabhawan Varanasi- Page-11-12.

74. Harṣa Charitam- Chowkhamba Vidyabhawan Varanasi- Page-308.

75. The Harṣacarita of Bana- Trans. By- E.B.Cowell & F.W.Thomas –Motilal Banarsidass Pvt.Ltd.Delhi- Page- 99.

76. Do - Page- 181-82.

77. Rajvansh: Maukhari aur Puṣyabhūti- Prof. Bhagwati Prasad Panthari- Bihar Hindi Granth Akadamy Patna- Page- 147.

78. Do - Page- 146.

79. Harṣa Charitam- Chowkhamba Vidyabhawan Varanasi- Page- 170-71.

80. Do - Page- 301.

81. Rajvansh: Maukhari aur Puṣyabhūti- Prof. Bhagwati Prasad Panthari- Bihar Hindi Granth Akadamy Patna- Page- 151.

82. Do - Page- 145.

83. Harṣa Charitam- Chowkhamba Vidyabhawan Varanasi- Page-378.

84. Rajvansh: Maukhari aur Puṣyabhūti- Prof. Bhagwati Prasad Panthari- Bihar Hindi Granth Akadamy Patna- Page- 143-44.

85. Do - Page- 148.

86. Do - Page- 142.

87. Harṣa Charitam- Chowkhamba Vidyabhawan Varanasi- Page- 361.

88. Harṣacarita: Ek Sanskritik Adhyayan- Dr. Vasudevasarana Agrawal- Bihar Rastrabhasha Parishad Patna- Page- 140-41.

89. Rajvansh: Maukhari aur Puṣyabhūti- Prof. Bhagwati Prasad Panthari- Bihar Hindi Granth Akadamy Patna- Page-146-47.

90. The Harṣacarita of Bana- Trans. By- E.B.Cowell & F.W.Thomas –Motilal Banarsidass Pvt.Ltd.Delhi- Page-219-23.

91. Harṣacarita: Ek Sanskritik Adhyayan- Dr. Vasudevasarana Agrawal- Bihar Rastrabhasha Parishad Patna- Page- 176.

92. Do - Page- 179-80.

93. Harṣa Charitam- Chowkhamba Vidyabhawan Varanasi- Page- 314.

94. Kādambarī -Poorvabhagah- Chowkhamba Vidyabhawan Varanasi- Page- 185.

95. Do - Page- 266.

96. Buddhist Records of The Western World- Samuel Beal- Low Price Publication Delhi- Book- v, Page- 213.

97. Rajvansh: Maukhari aur Puṣyabhūti- Prof. Bhagwati

Prasad Panthari- Bihar Hindi Granth Akadamy Patna- Page-110-111.

98. Harṣa Charitam- Chowkhamba Vidyabhawan Varanasi- Page-106.

99. Rajvansh: Maukhari aur Puṣyabhūti- Prof. Bhagwati Prasad Panthari- Bihar Hindi Granth Akadamy Patna- Page-110.

100. Do - Page-113-14.

101. The Harṣacarita of Bana- Trans. By- E.B.Cowell & F.W.Thomas –Motilal Banarsidass Pvt.Ltd.Delhi- Page-202-03.

102. Rajvansh: Maukhari aur Puṣyabhūti- Prof. Bhagwati Prasad Panthari- Bihar Hindi Granth Akadamy Patna- Page- 117.

103. Harṣacarita: Ek Sanskritik Adhyayan- Dr. Vasudevasarana Agrawal- Bihar Rastrabhasha Parishad Patna- Page- 157.

104. Rajvansh: Maukhari aur Puṣyabhūti- Prof. Bhagwati

Prasad Panthari- Bihar Hindi Granth Akadamy Patna- Page-115.

105. Harṣacarita: Ek Sanskritik Adhyayan- Dr. Vasudevasarana Agrawal- Bihar Rastrabhasha Parishad Patna- 38-40.

106. Rajvansh: Maukhari aur Puṣyabhūti- Prof. Bhagwati Prasad Panthari- Bihar Hindi Granth Akadamy Patna- Page-114-15.

107. Do - Page- 115, 117.

108. Do - Page- 118-21.

109. The Harṣacarita of Bana- Trans. By- E.B.Cowell & F.W.Thomas –Motilal Banarsidass Pvt.Ltd.Delhi- Page- 197.

110. Harṣacarita: Ek Sanskritik Adhyayan- Dr. Vasudevasarana Agrawal- Bihar Rastrabhasha Parishad Patna- 143-44.

111. Do - Page- 149.

112. Madhyakaleen Bharat- V.D.Mahajan- S. Chand And Company Ltd. New Delhi- Page- 305.

113. The Harṣacarita of Bana- Trans. By- E.B.Cowell & F.W.Thomas –Motilal Banarsidass Pvt.Ltd.Delhi- Page- 201.

114. Harṣacarita: Ek Sanskritik Adhyayan- Dr. Vasudevasarana Agrawal- Bihar Rastrabhasha Parishad Patna- 148.

115. Do - Page- 167.

116. Kādambarī -Poorvabhagah- Chowkhamba Vidyabhawan Varanasi- Page- 207.

117. Rajvansh: Maukhari aur Puṣyabhūti- Prof. Bhagwati Prasad Panthari- Bihar Hindi Granth Akadamy Patna- Page- 145.

118. Kādambarī -Poorvabhagah- Chowkhamba Vidyabhawan Varanasi- Page- 41.

119. The Harṣacarita of Bana- Trans. By- E.B.Cowell & F.W.Thomas –Motilal Banarsidass Pvt.Ltd.Delhi- Page- 49.

120. Harṣacarita: Ek Sanskritik Adhyayan- Dr. Vasudevasarana Agrawal- Bihar Rastrabhasha Parishad Patna- 207.

121. The Harṣacarita of Bana- Trans. By- E.B.Cowell & F.W.Thomas –Motilal Banarsidass Pvt.Ltd.Delhi- Page- 211.

122. Harṣacarita: Ek Sanskritik Adhyayan- Dr. Vasudevasarana Agrawal- Bihar Rastrabhasha Parishad Patna- 212.

123. Do - Page- 212-13.

124. Do - Page- 216-19.

125. Kādambarī -Poorvabhagah- Chowkhamba Vidyabhawan Varanasi- Page- 185.

126. Do - Page- 190.

127. The Harṣacarita of Bana- Trans. By- E.B.Cowell & F.W.Thomas –Motilal Banarsidass Pvt.Ltd.Delhi- Page- 65.

128. Kādambarī -Poorvabhagah- Chowkhamba Vidyabhawan Varanasi- Page- 119-20.

129. Do - Page- 120.

130. Buddhist Records of The Western World- Samuel Beal- Low Price Publication Delhi- Book- 2, Page- 83-84.

131. The Harṣacarita of Bana- Trans. By- E.B.Cowell & F.W.Thomas –Motilal Banarsidass Pvt.Ltd.Delhi- Page- 101.

132. Kādambarī -Poorvabhagah- Chowkhamba Vidyabhawan Varanasi- Page- 64.

133. Do - Page- 105.

134. Rajvansh: Maukhari aur Puṣyabhūti- Prof. Bhagwati Prasad Panthari- Bihar Hindi Granth Akadamy Patna- Page- 167-68.

Chapter-3

Bāṇa Bhaṭṭa and Indian Society during Seventh Century

We have different sources to know social condition of early half of Seventh century in which there is important place of Harṣacarita and Kādambarī written by Bāṇa Bhaṭṭa. Bāṇa Bhaṭṭa has given interesting description of contemporary society. We cannot understand social condition in the whole without description of Bāṇa Bhaṭṭa. Through his description he has thrown light on different aspects of contemporary society as- arrangement of Varna, caste, women position in society, dress and ornament of that time, food and beverage, condition of health and manner of living etc.

Classification of society and caste:-

It is clear from description of Harṣacarita and Kādambarī that society of Harsha-period was based on arrangement of Varna. He has written in Pratham Uchchhawas of Harṣacarita that Vatsyayana named Brahamans had taken purified food to separate from three Varnas (apart from Brahmans of own gotra, Kshatriya and Vaishya)- *varṇatrayavyāvṛttiviśuddhāndhasa:* (page-69-70).

Brahmans had top position in all castes in society. They were provided special benefits due to this type of position. In some matters they had liberty from social restrictions. Bāṇa Bhaṭṭa has not mentioned about shudra varna. But there is mention of many castes/sub-castes in Harṣacarita and Kādambarī and some are mentioned as related to low castes or untouchable. People related to these castes were do different types of work. Probably these castes were come under Shudra Varna in contemporary classification of society. In description of Hiuen-Tsang Indian society is also divided in four classes. He has written "with respect to the division of families, there are four classifications. The first is called the Brahman (Po-lo-men), men of pure conduct. They guard themselves in religion, live purely, and observe the most correct principles. The second is called Kshattriya (Tsa-ti-li), the royal caste. For ages they had been the governing class: they apply themselves to virtue (humanity) and kindness. The third is called Vaisyas (fei-she-li), the merchant class: they engage in commercial exchange, and they follow profit at home and abroad. The fourth is called Sudra (shu-t'o-lo), the agricultural class: they labour in plaughing and tillage. In these four classes purity or impurity of caste assigns to every one his place."[1]

According to Bāṇa Bhaṭṭa, Brahman Varna was considered as best from other Varnas due to his wisdom, consciousness, practicability, humble and knowledge.

Accepting the importance of Brahmans in society Hiuen-Tsang had written "The families of India are divided into castes, the Brahmans particularly (are noted) on account of their purity and nobility. Custom has so hallowed the name of this tribe that there is no question as to difference of place, but the people generally speak of India as the country of the Brahmans (Po-lo-men)."[2]

It is also clear from description of Bana that Brahmans were considered honourable in that time. When Durvasa cursed Saraswati then Savitri became angry with him and became ready to curse him but Saraswati hindered her saying –"Dear friend, restrain thy wrath: even to Brahmans by birth merely, uninitiated in heart, respect is due- *sakhi, saṁhara śēṣama asaṁskṛtamatayōpī jatyaiva dvijanmānō̃ mānanīyā:.*"[3] But it is also clear from this description that deficiency in instinct of Brahmans was perceptible. There is mention of shrieking quarrelsome Brahmans, mounted on the tops of trees, frightened by police in Saptam Uchchhawas of Harṣacarita.

Kshatriyas were placed in society after Brahmans. People of Kshatriya caste were worked to handle royal-work and it was considered their main work to ready every time for war to protect country. In Kādambarī, describing king Shudraka, Bāṇa Bhaṭṭa has written "hereditary scholar ministers were ever active to serve him. They were without greed and well-wisher of state. Their internal hearts had become pure due to regular criticism of ethics. He had spent his most time of the years of youth with same age group princes, those were loving and scholar minister, born in clan of Kshatriya kings and well jewelled, with ecstasy by pleasure seeking."[4] It is clear from this description that people of Kshatriya caste were responsible to take care of royal-work. According to Bana king Harsha was also related to Kshatriya caste.

People of Vaishya caste were having important place in society. It can be easily estimated the importance and prosperity of Vaishya caste by mention of trade activities that is mentioned in sequence of describing Ujjayini city. Resident of Ujjayini city were called as Kotisar (possessor of a crore of rupees). Probably these were businessmen and related to Vaishya caste. Regarding this Dr. Vasudevsarana Aggrawal has written "Mahakavi has drawn many pictures, like picture taken by camera, from his power of illustration regularly in style of compound words. It is suitable to give attention on scenes of Ujjayini's architecture. Long and wide spread vast Ujjayini had seemed like second earth. There was huge dig full of water around city. After dig there was white painted high wall. Inside wall architectures, responsible for making drawing of city, were divided that place in many part by developing wide roads. These roads were called as Mahavipanipath or wide roads of markets. There were shops in both sides of roads in markets and behind markets there were constructed buildings. In medieval Indian cities the numbers of markets were counted upto eighty four. Names of these eighty four markets have been given in Prithvichandra Charita. It can conjecture similar to that type of custom in Gupta-Period. Svarna-hatt or markets of jewellery was considered as main in all markets. In latter that was also called as Sarrafa. In Gupta-Period special title of famous businessman of Svarnahatti was Naigam or Mahajan. This main market was situated at middle of the city in most safe place. Poet had thought sufficient to give only one picture of main Svarna-bajar as a sample by drawing picture of Ujjayini's market. In shops of Naigames there were hoards of conch shell, shellfish, pearl, coral, emerald, beads of precious stone and crystal gold (*cāmīkaracūrṇavālukānikaranicita*). It seems that sea had poured out jewel and precious stones in markets of Ujjayini."[5]

In Pancham Uchchhawas of Harṣacarita, mentioning distressed people due to illness of king Prabhakara-Vardhana, Bana has written that the favourites saw the accomplishment of their wishes fade away.(*kṣīyamāṇa prasādavittakamanōrathasampadī*, page-267) In a like manner, Rajya-Vardhana, consumed by sorrow after father's death, had told Harsha that his sorrow increases daily, like moneys employed by an usurer.(*vārdhuṣikaprayuktānīvadhanānīva pratidivasama vardhantē*, Shashth Uchchhawas, page-316). It is clear from these descriptions that people of Vaishya caste were done their business without any restriction in Harsha-Period. There were also supports by administration.

In addition to Brahman, Kshatriya and Vaishya caste there is mention of Chandal, Das, Bheel, Baheliya, Kinnar, Gandharva, Vanamanush etc castes in Harṣacarita and Kādambarī. Existence of these castes was merely based on their work. Their acceptance in society was also based on their work. Daughter of Chandal was said to be, in Kādambarī, as untouchable because she was contaminated and belongs to low-caste.

There is mention of Dasas (slaves), in Harṣacarita and Kādambarī; those were worked in royal court. Hansavega, messenger of the king of Pragyajyotish, had said "this dreadful name of Dasa, like a torrent of mud, lays everything low-*prabalapanka iva sarva madhāstānnayati dāruṇō dāsaśabda:.*"[6] In context of old dravid worshipper it is mentioned, in Kādambarī , about picking up old aged Dasi(women servant) on cot and bringing near to old dravid worshipper and to act out ritual of wedding to him. It is clear from this description that merely servants were also called by word 'Dasa'. These servants were considered as low in other servants so those were addressed by special word 'Dasa'. Probably these types of servants were persons those were confined in a prison during war. Certainly they could not compare to Dasas of western civilization because they were able to avail all convenience similar to other servants.

Bana has also mentioned Bheel, Baheliya and Nishad (a boatman). People who live in forests were called Bheel or Shabar. They depend on forest resources. Life style of Bheels or Shabars was special type that is described detailed in Kādambarī. Earning means of Baheliyas were catching and selling of birds and animals. Nishads lived with army chief of Shabar.

There is mention of kinnar and Gandharva, in Kādambarī, who lived in mountain areas. Kādambarī was daughter of Chitraratha, the king of Gandharva.

Mentioning Gandhi and Tamoli, Bāṇa Bhaṭṭa has written "The royal palace was decorated with useful bathing materials, incense, Ubatan (paste) and sandal etc fragranced materials like the house of Tamoli, the seller of fragrance. Like Tamoli's house there were collected Lavalee (fragmented creeper specially) clove, cardamom, Kankol and mace etc materials."[7] Probably Tamoli and Gandhi were sub-castes which came under Vaishya caste.

In addition to these castes there were different special names were in vogue for people who did different works (as Kumhar for pot maker, Rajak for washer man etc) those were latter accepted as separate caste.

"There was not restriction in mutual social contact in different sections and Varnas of society. Vyaghraketu, son of Atvik-Pradesh (Forest-Pradesh) king Sharabhaketu, met in Vindhyatavi to Dev Harsha along with Shabar youth Nirghata, nephew of Shabar army chief Bhukampa. Nirghata bowed his head on the ground and made his obeisance to the king and offered the patridge and hare (Shasha) as his present. King had accepted the present of Shabar youth and addressed him as Anga (=brother, Thomas-Cowell has taken meaning as 'sir') with respectfully and inquired about his sister. Nirghat stayed along with king till Rajyashri met and at last when king had to return from Vindhyatavi after searching out sister then he allowed Nirghat to leave after Satisfying with cloth, jewell etc

Bana was self related to high clan of veda-specialist Brahmans but we find names of his childhood friends as Parshava brothers Chandrasena and Matrisena (child of Brahman father and mother of Sudra caste were called Parshava), Jangulik (Garudhi-poison-remover), Mayuraka, Tamboli (betel-seller), Chandak, drummer of dhol (double-drum) Jimuta, Kalad (*svarṇakāra:*=goldsmith),Chamikar Hairik (head of goldsmiths= '*svarṇakāra: kalāda: syāttadādhyakṣstu hairika:*= commentator) Sindhushena, toy maker from clay Kumaradatta, Sairandhri, Kurangika (Shampooer), Samvahika (women tasked to press down foot) Keralika, dancer Harina, Parashar saint Sumati, Kshapanaka (Jain-monk) Veerdeva, Shaiva Vakaraghosha, juggler Chakoraksha, Maskari (traveller sage) Tamrachuda etc. It is obvious that these people were from different castes, works (peshas) and religious but all stay together."[8]

Position of women-

In sequence of tracing Harsha-Period society Bana has demarcated the social status of women. He has described in detailed about their rights, responsibilities and works, intention of society towards them, their educational arrangement and different aspects related to their life.

From descriptions of Bana it is known about privileges of women. It is clear from his descriptions that women had importance in society. But he has also written about discrimination to women in man-oriented Harsha-Period society. Mentioning about cause to be plundered everything on birth of Rajya-Vardhana and Harsha-Vardhana by king, Bana has written "The king gave away all his fortune. Heaps of wealth, like Kuvera's treasuries, was plundered by the folk on every side."[9] But on the birth of Rajyashri Bana has not mentioned any special festival celebrated there which indicate that there was discrimination between son and daughter.

Main reason behind difference or discrimination between son and daughter was revealed in context of mentioning discussion of Rajyashri's wedding. In Chaturth Uchchhawas of Harṣacarita Bāṇa Bhaṭṭa has written "the queen with tearful eyes and a heart alarmed by love for her daughter replied: - 'Mothers, your majesty, are to their daughters no more indeed than nurses, useful only in rearing them. In their bestowal the father is the judge. Love for a daughter however far exceeds love for a son, pity causing the difference."[9] Regarding this Prabhakara-Vardhana also thinks so. In sequence of discussion of Rajyashri's wedding he had said "It is a law of right, by whosoever framed not with my consent, which children born of our body, dandled at our breasts, never to be abandoned, are taken from us by the unexpected arrival of some one unknown to us. Truly, these indeed are the brandamarks of this transient life. Herein has sorrow's fire more than in aught else a power to burn, that whereas both are our offspring good men grieve at a daughter's birth. Hence is it that to their daughters noble men offer water even at birth in their tears. For this fear sages, neglecting marriage, dispensing with domestic life, take refuge in desolate forests. Who indeed can bear to part with a child?"[10]

Similar care was taken to teach women as men in Harsha time though in society there was discrimination between men and women. By the descriptions of Harṣacarita and Kādambarī it can be said that women were trained in different arts. In Chaturth Uchchhawas of Harṣacarita Bana has written about Rajyashri "Meanwhile Rajyashri gradually grew up in daily increasing familiarity with friend's expert in song, dance & etc and with all accomplishments and in a comparatively limited period she came to maturity (Page-239)." In a like manner describing life-story of Kādambarī, Mahashveta had said to Chandrapeed "We both had trained simultaneously in dance, song etc all arts and our childhood days were spent in joy with full freedom."[11] Describing palace of Chandrapeed Bāṇa Bhaṭṭa has written about elephants, standing there, that like women of noble family that female elephants standing at one place due to training and courtesy. It is clear from these descriptions that there was arrangement to educate women related to royal family and they became expert in different arts after education. Women were given training in those arts which were as follow – training of horse-riding (in Harṣacarita it is mentioned that Malati was mounted on horse), dance, song, music (training to operate different type of instruments as vina, Vasuri, Tabala etc), drawing, training to play different sports, training for gambling, education of telling an aphorism and training for Shishiropachara or health related training etc.

Along with these arts there was provision to give education of religion and philosophy to women. Harsha has told Shramanacharya Divakaramitra that "From this day forth, while I discharge my vow, and console my subjects in their sorrow for my father's death, I desire that she should remain at my side and be comforted with your righteous discourses, and your passionless instruction which produces salutary knowledge, and your advice which calms the disposition, and your Buddhist doctrines which drive away wordly passions. At the end, when I have accomplished my design, she and I will assume the red garments together."[12]

Bāṇa Bhaṭṭa had also thrown light on wedding system of women. It is clear from his descriptions that child-marriage was in vogue, that time. Generally in age of eight to nine girls were married. Wedding of Rajyashri was concluded before maturity. In Harṣacarita, Prabhakara-Vardhana had told to his Maharani that "Our darling Rajyashri, my queen, is now grown a young women. The thought of her, like her noble qualities, never for a moment leaves my heart. As soon as girls near maturity, their fathers became fuel to the flame of pain."

It is known from descriptions of Harṣacarita and Kādambarī that inner palace of kings were full of queens. It is clear from this description that system of polygamy was in vogue that time. One queen had dignity as main queen among queens who was called as Patarani. "'Mahadevi' word was used for Mahishi or Pattapradhan queen (=Patrani). Hemapatta was tightened on her head. According to Vrihatsanhita, Patta was made from gold (*śuddhakāñcana vinirmita:*). Only king, crown king, Rajamahishi and army chief- these four have right to tie up Hemapatta on head. Fifth type of Patta was called Prasadapatta which was indicator of king's grace and it could be given by king to his any recipient of favour. In Harṣacarita Patta of Yashovati had called as Mahadevi Patta."[13] Other queens who lived in inner palace had to obey orders of Patarani. In other word, Patarani had supremacy on other queens. When Harsha tried to restrain his mother from becoming Sati then his mother Yashovati had said that "Upon the heads of rival wives have these feet been set; they have been adored with diamond-wreaths of diadems by the bending matrons of a whole capital."[14]

From this description it is known that queens of inner palace were divided in two groups. One was main queen who had all privileges and other queens whose position was after main queen. Due to this division there was tension in inner palace. In Harṣacarita and Kādambarī there is mention of rival wife and anger caused by rival wives. In Harṣacarita, describing position before birth of Rajya-

Vardhana, it is mentioned about queen Yashovati that resigning her form to her friends' bosoms, she (Yashovati) set her feet on the laps of her handmaids, on the heads of her co-wives. Like present, that time also, existence of co-wives was main reason of anger in women. Bana has written in Kādambarī "existence of co-wives is the main reason of anger in women. In future it becomes main reason of aversion because it is the big situation of defeat."[15]

There are two incidents of becoming Sati mentioned in Harṣacarita. This type of first incident was the incident of becoming Sati by Yashovati, mother of Harsha, after death of Prabhakara-Vardhana. Though Harsha had restrained her, Yashovati became Sati in wish to die before her husband was alive. Second incident was preparation of Rajyashri to become Sati that was stopped by interference of Harsha. It is not reasonable to conclude from mention of these events that Sati-custom was in vogue in Harsha-Period. Thinking on circumstances of these events it is clear that self wish of women, to get free from distress of widow and wish to die before husband's death like facts were behind these events. On other side probably salvation by becoming Sati and obtaining so-called supernatural pleasure like facts were motivated these types of events.

Women at first take bath, after that gave away all her wealth, garments and assumed the vestments of death. Queen Yashovati had worn two saffron-brown robes and the tokens of her unwidowed death. "That time widows were wore red silken strip as the tokens of unwidowed death. Red neck-cord was hanged in their neck. Their limbs being all aglow with moist saffron paste. Filled the bosom of robe with flower offerings to its blaze. From neck down to instep hung wreaths of strung flowers. Her hand carried a picture representing her husband with steadfast. She clasped her lord's speal-haft. In this spear-haft or spear there tied on waving string and hanged a garland of flowers for worship. Spear with waving string was characteristics of medieval Rajput horsemen. It is known from statue of horse-ridden coins. It is known that imagination of this purport was started in seventh century."[16]

Sati custom was not in vogue in Harsha –Period but contemporary scholars were certainly anxious from these types of incidents. Bāṇa Bhaṭṭa has thought this work as work of fools. Criticizing this, in Kādambarī, he has written "It is senseless to die self after death of any beloved person. This is way of fools. It is foolish, stupidity, work of imprudence, poor point of view, very big intoxication and great decline due to foolishness to end life after death of own father, brother, friend or husband. It should not end breath to insist if breath not end naturally. On considering it is clear that end of breath is also selfishness because it is not a way to give away intolerable sorrow and pain. Dead person did not be benefited from this work. He was no alive again from this work, his religion not grow from this work, not gained auspicious world, he not escape from going in hell, not able to see dead person and not met dual after death because he had gone at suitable place to obtain the fruits of his works. In this manner dead person is able to share only sin of his suicide. If he was alive then by offering of water in the cupped hands etc he can able to bring about dead person and self well-being. But after death he can not able to benefit none of both."[17]

Giving credit, to oppose Sati custom in manner of cute, stable and judicious, to Bana A.S.Altekar has written " It is clear that Bana was struck with horror by the tendency to eulogise the Sati custom, shown in some quarters in his days, and was anxious to offer the most determined opposition to it. Tantra writers also joined him in the crusade. They pointed out that women was the embodiment of Supreme Goddess, and boldly declared that if a person burnt her with her husband, he would be condemned to eternal hell."[18]

From historical point of view actually thinking of Bāṇa Bhaṭṭa against Sati custom is important of all times. It is praiseworthy as he has firmly criticized this inhuman work. This thinking of Bana is also useful in context to prevent incidents which have happened sometimes (which are rare) also in modern time.

There is mention of keeping in purdah as conduct by women at many places in Harṣacarita and Kādambarī. It is mentioned about Malati in Harṣacarita that "A thick swarm of bees, settling eagerly upon the blooming blue lotuses of her eyes, covered half her face like a veil of dark blue silk."(Pratham Uchchhawas, page-57) Again in Chaturth Uchchhawas of Harṣacarita it is written about Rajyashri "Her face, hidden, like the morning twilight, by its roseate veil, dulled the gleaming lamps by its radiance."(Page-251) In this manner it is mentioned in Kādambarī that "When Abhisarikas were running here and there by covering their face with veil made from black cloths then it seems that Laxmi of Kamalvana, covered with rays of blue lotus, is wandering with covered face by frightened from rays of moon."[19] Particularly in Kādambarī quoting Mahashveta, it is mentioned "I had covered with veil, made from red cloth like rays of coloured lotus. I had adopted such a manner that my relatives also can not able to saw me."[20] From mention of women, covering face with veil on special circumstances as conduct, purda-system is not proved. In this context Prof. Bhagavati Prasad Panthari has written correctly that "This veil should be taken as conduct or adornment of women, not a sign of purda-system. Malati had weared silk –veil at time of wandering outside and Rajyashri had weared veil as bride-dress." [21] In this context A.S.Altekar has expressed similar opinion and denied from vogue of purda-custom. He has written "In the Malti-Madhava the heroine and her numerous friends go out to the temple without any veil whatsoever; the hero is thus able to perceive the maddening beauty of the heroine and falls in love with her. Similarly in the Kādambarī of Bana, neither Mahasveta or Kādambarī, nor any of their numerous friends and attendants are observed in any Purda. From the Meghaduta (I, 26) we learn that women of Ujjayini used to go to the Sipra for sportin water at the time of bath. This would not have been possible if the Purda were in vogue there. Yuan Chuang has given an intimate picture of the Hindu society of the 7th century A.D., but he nowhere refers to the Purda system. We learn from him that Rajyasri, the widowed sister of Harsha, used to come out without a veil in her brother's court."[22]

From descriptions of Bāṇa Bhaṭṭa it is also thrown light on condition of widows in society. It is written in Kādambarī that widows were deprived of Talapatra (ear ornament)- '*kvacidvidhavēvōnmuktālapatrā*' (Poorvabhaga, page-41). In this manner, mentioning condition of widow Rajyashri, in Harṣacarita it has written "I saw her with her kindred and her graces all gone, her ears and her soul left bare, her ornaments and her aims abandoned, her bracelets and her hopes broken."(The Harsa Charita of Bana-Trans.by-E.B.Cowell & F.W.Thomas, Chapter-VIII, page-243). Again, In Harṣacarita it is written "with braided locks and eyes not from collyrium lustrous, appeared in the wine of their goblets the reflections of the lotus faces of warriors' wives."(The Harsa Charita of Bana-Trans.by-E.B.Cowell & F.W.Thomas, Chapter-VI, page-195). It is clear from these descriptions that widows were prohibited from wearing ornaments. Widows were also not used toilet items (i.e. not applying collyrium lustrous in eyes) and prohibited to comb the hair. Only braided hair was indicator of widows.

Social condition of widows was accomplished with difficulty so they prefer death rather than remain alive. Probably, they can not able to remarriage and they have to spent life alone and neglected. In Harṣacarita and Kādambarī nowhere is mention of remarriage of widows.

Prostitutes were also part of Harsha-Period society. Mentioning the festival at time of Harsha's birth, it is written in Harṣacarita that there was not remained separation between women of royal family and prostitutes (Chaturth Uchchhawas, page-220). Again it is mention about dancing of prostitutes for entertainment of people at several places during festival. From descriptions of Harṣacarita it seems that prostitution was means of subsistence for some women. These prostitutes have separate identity. These were expert in dance and music and on special occasion they entertain people by taking payment. They were called on occasion of festival that was performed in royal court.

In Harṣacarita and Kādambarī , there is mention of Chamaragrahini (women who take Chamara), Tambulavahini (Betel bearer women), women who entertain king by dancing and singing, women who pressing down feet and women those were ready every time to do several works were called as Varavilasiniyan. These Varavilasinies were permanent payable women servants who work in inner palace. These Varavilasinies were skilled in several works of royal-court and inner palace. Along with these work they were also expert in dancing and singing and also entertain people of royal court by dancing and singing. There is similarity in Varavilasinies and Rupajeevies mentioned in Arthashastra.

In Harsha-Period society there was a group of women who spend their life like saints. In Harṣacarita and Kādambarī these women were called as women wearing reddish-brown cloth, women who kept a vow and old aged women saint. These women were observer of principle of different religion and religious sects. It is mentioned, in Kādambarī, that Mahashveta was surrounded by female ascetic of different religious sects. "In those female saints were-

1. Weared reddish-brown cloth and related to religious sect of Pashupat Shaiva whose foreheads were decorated with white ashes and those were telling Akshamala beads.
2. Buddhist nun (*raktapaṭa vratavāhinī :*) those were wore dress of same coloured like ripen fruit of the palm tree.
3. White pata or nuns related to religious sect of Shvetambar Jain those were tightened their breast with white nipple strap.
4. Faithful chaste and virtuous female ascetic women those were endowed with matted hair, the hide of a tiger, the brahmanical sacred thread, bark garment and foliage.

These wandering female ascetics were reciting sacred eulogy of lord Shiva, Ambika, Kartikeya, Vishnu, Jin (=Buddha); Arya Avalokiteshvar and Arhata."[23]

Female ascetics were related to high clan families because in Kādambarī they have said to born in pure clan (*śuddhāntarvaśikai:*, page-198). Female ascetics told story of Puranas, history and spiritual instructions by having books. Probably, women became ascetic in search of calmness by dispirited with social difficulties. When effort of Rajyashri, to die, became unsuccessful then she requested to Harsha through Patralata that "A husband or a son is a woman's true support; but to those who are deprived of both, it is immodesty even to continue to live, as mere fuel for the fire of misery. Your highness' coming stopped my resolution to die, even on the point of accomplishment; let me therefore in my misfortunes be allowed to assume the red robe."[24]

Importance and place of women in society:-

Though the society of seventh century was male dominated but there was not lack of opportunity for all-round development of women. There was appropriate arrangement of education for women of royal family. Probably, women of general community had no this type of opportunity. In Harṣacarita and Kādambarī there is mention of different works done by women. It is known, the social status and opportunity they got, from variety of these works. Following were important works performed by women- to mount guard, horse-riding, work of message-bearer, to swing fly-whisk (Chamar), to work as betel-bearer, to perform treatment of coolness, to play pipe, to play vina, to water creeper of home garden, to prepare garland of flower, to play different indoor games (i.e. dice, ball, chess etc),to sing a song, to dance, to paint, to orate an aphorism and to deliver spiritual instructions etc

Women were free to live according to their own style. This was the reason that many women were become ascetic by accepting different religious sects.

If we see in the whole the condition of women in Harsha-Period was satisfactory. They had important place in society. Inner-palace of kings was full of women who were appointed as worker.

In Kādambarī, Bāṇa Bhaṭṭa has imagined women-era. Attaching his imagine to inner-palace of the king of Gandharva (where there was a free world of women) Bana presented it as a fifth era. Mentioning inner-palace of the king of Gandharva, that was situated on mountain of Hemakuta, Bana has written "Chandrapeed saw, by entering the gate, and felt that filled with lakh of women that was a free world of women. As if, women of whole world were collected there for counting. As if, that was a world where any man was not present. As if, that was an uncommon island of women. As if, fifth incarnation of women-era. Eras are four but it was fifth the era of women. As if, by hating males Prajapati had created a new world or as if, it was treasury of women that was prepared together and put to create many eras. It was the situation of daughter's (Kādambarī) inner-palace."[25]

This description, presented by Bana, is an imagination of poet according to literature. But it presents revolutionary thinking according to women-oriented writing. Actually Bana is the first historian who has this type of thinking. This imagination is of seventh century but today, in twenty-first century, his thinking is more relevant. Men have ruled on women in four eras. Like a long-sighted historian he had concluded in seventh century that one era would come in which women would have supremacy on administration. He has told that fifth era as women-era in which women have supremacy. To step out its first step, in direction of converting imagination of women era in reality, Indian government has reserved fifty percent seats in panchayat and municipality for women. In near future parliamentary bill related to reservation of thirty three percent seats for women will be certainly an important and revolutionary step in direction of converting imagination of women-era in reality.

In whole writing of Bāṇa Bhaṭṭa has inclination towards women. He has highlighted matters related to women through his writing. It seems that he was hurt by discrimination which was done with women and supremacy of men. It is clearly reflected state of floundering, in his writing, to raise the voice for rights of women. It was the reason that he has imagined the fifth era as women era. In his childhood his friend circle, which was formed during his wandering life, consisted of women friends like dancer Harinika, Katyayanika Chakravakika, Sairandhri Kurangika and Samvahika Keralika. It can be said, in term of these facts, that name of Bāṇa Bhaṭṭa is at leading position among women-oriented writers those have raised the voice for rights of women.

Condition of living:-

Clothing-

It is known, about clothing of seventh century, from descriptions of Harṣacarita and Kādambarī. There is light thrown on clothing that was in vogue in Harsha-Period, types of garments and their characteristics, colouring of cloths and painting on those cloths etc in these books.

Bāṇa Bhaṭṭa has divided garments worn by male, in two parts – 'Adhovastra' and 'Uttariya'. Garment that was worn below waist called 'Adhovastra'. Generally present time dhoti (a piece of cloth worn around the lower body) was particularly called 'Adhovastra'. Adhovastra (dhoti) was made from a piece of fine and white silk cloth named 'Netra'. Describing adhovastra of the king Harsha Bana has written "He shone, like the mountain Mandara with Vasuki's skin at the churning of the ocean, with his lower garment which was radiant with shot silk-threads, washed in pure water, clinging closely to his loins, ornamented with the rays of the jewels of his girdle, and white like a mass of ambrosial foam."[26]

Bana has thrown light on style of wearing dhoti. Describing the dhoti of Dadhicha it is said in Harṣacarita that "His slim waist was marked off by a tight-drawn lower garment of Harita green, of which one corner was gracefully set in front a little below the navel and the hem hung over the girdle behind, and which on both sides was so girt up as to display a third of his thigh."[27]

Beside dhoti, main garments that worn below waist were Chandatak, Svasthan, Pinga and Satula. These garments were mainly trousers that were in vogue in that time. "In this country tradition of trousers has started in first century B.C. at time of Shakas. Its many proofs are found in Mathura-art of first century. After Shaka-Kushana-era dress of salvar-trousers for soldiers dress would continue by the Gupta-kings. On some coins of Samudragupta and Chandragupta the king himself had marked in this dress which was considered as 'Udeechyavesha' (high profile dress)."[28]

It is mentioned in Harṣacarita that Mekhalak named messenger of Krishna's, brother of Shri Harsha deva, tunic girt up tightly by a mud-stained Chandatak (*kārdamikacēlacīrikāniyamitō ccaṇḍacaṇḍātakama*). In this manner describing Shrikantha nag Bana has written that above a Chandataka white as the ketaki petal his flank was drawn tight by a scarf (*kētakīgarbhayatrapāṇḍurasya caṇḍātakasyōpari kṣāmatarīkṛtakukṣi:*). From these descriptions it is estimated that Chandataka was a short garment, long to knee, that was worn in waist.

Describing kings those had worn svasthan or Soothana Bana has written that their shanks were covered with their svasthana of delicate tinted silk (*uccitranētrasukumārasvasthāsthagitajanghākānḍaiśca*). "It is indication in word svasthana that this type of trouser was tightened on its own place or on calf of the leg. This was made from silk-cloth named Netra and on which painted flower-leaf (*Uchchinetra*). A female dancer had worn this type of trouser of narrow cuff and flower-painted is drawned in temple of Devagarha."[29]

There is mention of Pinga named trouser or salvar (loose cotton trousers worn by women). Some kings had worn chequered with mud-stained copper-coloured long salvar or pinga (*kārdamikapaṭaka lmāṣitapiṣangapingē*). Pinga was a slack salvar long to calf of the leg so Shankara had said it as Janghika or Janghala (Jangha= part of calf of the leg). How the name of Pinga is created? It is known that answer of this question is that Pringa named silk cloth was imported from middle-Asia. Many times this cloth is mentioned in inscriptions of Middle-Asia. Pringa cloth is also mentioned in descent book of Bauddhas. Salvar made from Pringa cloth would be known as named Pringa. Prakrit form of Pringa is Pinga. By explaining garments, mentioned in context of wedding of Rajyashri, Shankara had said Pringa as synonym of Netra. Netra and Pringa, both were silk cloth in which flowers-leafs were weaved. But Netra was generally of white coloured and Pringa was coloured. Net, Prakrit form of Netra, is today also a type of fine cloth which is made in Bengal. How this word is used for cloth? In Deeghanikaya twisted rope of horse neck is called Netra (*sārathiriva nēttāni gahētvā*). In the Mahabharata word Netra is used for rope of a churn which has called Neti or Neta in Hindi. Use of word Netra is natural for silk strip which was rolled around body as twisted Neti. Kushana-Period strip were flat and Gupta-Period were twisted and circular. Silk cloth that was used to made strip was called Netra in latter period. It is possible that the cloth named Pringa was also used for strip and on base of this Netra and Pringa were considered as synonym.

Describing Pinga Bana has said it Pishanga or Unnabi (copper-coloured). 'Kardamika patakalmashit' adjective which is added before Pishanga Pinga is special cousiderable. Kardamik coloured means coloured from colour of kardama. In a vartik (4/2/2) of Katyayan it is mentioned colouring cloth from shakal (a potsherd of mud) and kardama (mud). Mud-stained strip or ash-coloured strip was worn above calf of the leg and end part of salvar, probably that is mentioned hear by Bana. A male idol found from Ahichhatra has worn coat and salvar. There is wraped a strip in lower part of salvar and above calf of the leg. Meaning of Bana is known from that type of wearing."[30]

There is mention of garments named Satula, that was long upto knee and worn by kings, in Harṣacarita. "According to Shankar Satula was Ardhajanghika or Ardhajanghala or was garment long upto knee which can be called today as Ghutanna or shorts. Bana has described Satula in following words – *alinīlamasṛṇasatulāsamutpāditasita samāyōga parabhāgai:* i.e. dark blue coloured janghikas, which were worn by kings, radiant was increased due to stitched white strip of cloth. According to Shankara Samayaga was defined word for craftsman of sewing. Generally this means uniform. Parabhaga means decoration of second colour on background of one colour. Many examples of Satula or Ghutanna is found in cave-painting of Ajanta and Gupta-Period art. Fortunately a painting of male idol, in cave No. 17 of Ajanta, has worn that type of dark blue coloured Satula added with white strips as Bana has described."[31]

Garment worn by man on upper part of body is called 'Uttariya Vastra' in Harṣacarita and Kādambarī. There was two type of Uttariya garment- First, garment without stitch i.e. shawl and long towel like Uttariya. And Second, stitched garment i.e. different types of coat in which main were- Kanchuk, Cheencholak, Varabana, Kurpasaka and Aachchhadanaka.

Describing Uttariya of the king Harsha, Bana has written that his thin upper garment (Uttariya) spangled with worked stars like the round world with its surrounding ether cloudless and full of stars (*aghanēna satārāgaṇēnōmparikṛtēna*). Again it is mentioned in Saptam

Uchchhawas of Harṣacarita that Harsha had, at time of his expedition to conquer the world, put on two seemly robes of bark silk marked with pairs of flamingos (*pāridhāya rājahammithunalakṣmaṇī sadṛśē dukūlē*). Also in Kādambarī, king Shudraka had worn two seemly robes as fine as skin of a snake and washed in pure water (*dhavalajaladharacchēda śucinā dukūlapaṭṭapallavēna)*. It is concluded from two seemly robes, worn by kings, that two pieces of cloths were used to wear. One piece of cloth was worn like Adhovastra (dhoti) and second piece of cloth was put on upper body as Uttariya (shawl). Probably, upper part of body was fully covered from this type of Uttariya.

Beside shawl there is mention of different types of without stitched Uttariya garments in Harṣacarita. In these garments main were- Tarangita Uttariya, Bhangur Uttariya and hanging Cheevar garment from shoulder. This type of Uttariya was made from long and narrow pieces of cloths. These Uttariya were waved by wind because those were made from light and fine cloths.

"Tarangita Uttariya means that type of Uttariya structure in which thin wrinkle was displayed in Uttariya in front on chest. This distinguishing feature is found in idols of stone and bronze. Making of this type of idols was started in seventh century. It is known from extract of Bana."[32] Yashovati, mother of Harsha, was also worn tarangita breast-Uttariya.

Describing preparation of Rajyashri's wedding there is mention that the fragile stuffs were torn, while grasped by servitors, who lifted their arms to clutch them (*kacchuraṇēraparairūdbhuja bhujiṣyabhajyam ānabhangurōttarīyai :*). "Till now word bhanjana is used for putting on wrinkle. Twisted shawl is not folded like other cloths but placed as ringlet after twisting. So here 'bhangur' word is used. Fortunately exact sample of Bhangutar Uttariya is found from neck of a clay idol which is found from Ahichchhatra and it is understood by help of that. There is description of 'kshaum vastras' in presents sent by Bhaskaravarma, which were kept in baskets of reeds as ringlet. Those cloths were that type of cloths which were kept in baskets as ringlet."[33]

Medicants wore very soft red cloth or cheevar (arunen cheevarapatalena mradeeyasa samveetam) as Uttariya. Giving context of Harsha's welcome by Divakaramitra Bana has written that Divakaramitra gathered together his robe which was somewhat disordered by his sudden movement as it hung from his left shoulder. In fact, most idols of Gupta-Period has robe of both shoulder i.e. their both shoulders has shown as clad in robe or upper cloth. Tradition of left shoulder cloth has found in many Kushana-Period Buddha idols of Mathura. Both shoulder tradition was also continued in Mathura from effect of Gandhara-art. In Gupta-Period most idols have both shoulders cloth but in some idols old system was continued. As idols represent that thing were also in actual life of medicants i.e. some medicants throw on cloth on their both shoulder and some throw on only left shoulder. Wearing of Divakarmitra was like former type. Wearing style of cloths was associated with kind of religious sects- just so Chinese traveler I-Ching has written. It is known that follower of the raved or old tradition, which was related to Buddhist sect, had continued to throw on cloth on both shoulders."[34]

Bāṇa Bhaṭṭa has also mentioned that type of Uttariya that was like coat to cover whole body. These coats were stitched and made from different kind of cloths. Four type of coats were mentioned in Harṣacarita and Kādambarī, those are- Kanchuk, Varbana, Chinacholaka, Kurpasaka. Along with these there is mention of Aachchhadanaka named Uttariya cloth which was put on shouler.

It is mentioned in Saptam Uchchhawas of Harṣacarita that some kings wore Kanchuk darkened by black diamond's glistening (lapis lazuli) on light-skinned body (*avadātadēhavirājamānarājāvarttamēcakai: kañcukai:*). "In Kādambarī daughter of chandal had worn blue kanchuka; which was long up to calf of the leg: *āgulphāvalambinā nīlakañcukēnāvacchinnaśarīrāma.* In cave 1 of Ajanta chamaragrahini, who has stood left side of Padmapani Avalokiteshvar, has worn blue kanchuka long up to foot. Malati had worn kanchuk of white fine silk hanging down to her toes. There is shown a man, in a scene of Vishvantarajataka, has worn white coloured kanchuka long up to foot in Ajanta cave 17. It is known from this that kanchuka was a long sleeved coat which collar was closed from front."[35]

Describing Varbana named kanchuka Bana has written that some kings had worn Varbana named kanchuk like garments which showing clusters of bright pearls. "Varbana was also kanchuk like garment but it was short in comparison of kanchuka long upto knee. As it is clear from name, it was dress of war. It was adopted in India from dress of Sasani Iran. A marble Sun idol of fourth century is found from Khairakhana, about 20 miles north from Kabul. He is dressed a coat long up to knee which is a form of Varbana. A toy of male idole, who has worn absolutely that type of coat, is found from Ahichchhatra. It was also a sleeve coat long up to knee. Upper coat of Sun, guard behind him and Pingal's garment found in Mathura-art is particularly known as varbana. It is doubtful that varbana is origionally a Sanskrit word. This is known as a sankrit form of any Pahlava word. It's Persian form 'Baravan', 'Varpanaka' in Aramaik language, 'Guramaika' similar like form in Serian language and 'Juramanakaha' form are found in Arabian, those all should extracted from any main word of Pahlavi.

According to Bana Varbana was made from a special cloth named Stavaraka. Stavaraka is mentioned two times by Bana: one is here Varbana made from stavaraka and second in context of wedding of Rajyashri, where ceiling of shed are said to erected from stavaraka cloths. Shankar has said it a type of cloth. There is not thrown any light on stavaraka from any proof of Sanskrit literature. First time particularly Bana has used this word. Main form of Sanskrit stavaraka was 'stavraka' of Pahlavi, from which 'istabraka' of Arabi and 'istavraka' of Pharasi was produced. This cloth was carried, prepared in Iran of Sasan-era, to India in east and Arab in west. Bana was introduced to it in palace of Harsha. Embroidered and decorated coat of idols of Sun God is a sample of stavaraka. Generally dress of these idols is similar like royal dress of Sasani. Generally there is shown stitched pearls in these coats. Bana has also written that clusters of bright pearls were stitched on stavaraka: *tāramuktāstabakita*. There are two toys of clay found from digging of Ahichchhatra whose garmentrs were stitched with clusters of pearls. In these one is Sun idole as Sasani form and second is a dancer worn low voluminous skirt. In these there is stitched a star below each clusters of pearls, which can be identified from 'tarmukta' of Bana."[36]

Describing Kanchuka of China Bana has written that some kings had worn Chinacholaka Kanchuka (*kañcukaiścāpacitacīnacōlakai :*). "Certainly this garment, as it is clear from name, is adopted from country China. It is also known that Chinacholaka was worn upon Kanchuka and all type of other garments. In idol of Kanishka there is shown under a long Kanchuka and upon a long coat like cloak open from front that may be Chinacholaka. This type of open neck upper garment is also found in many idols of Sun from Mathura. This dress was brought by Shakas of middle Asia and spread by them and this was continued in vogue in Indian garment in Gupta-Period and till the time of Harsha. It is true that this dress was understood as honourable and respectful. So practice of this dress for bridegrooms was everywhere in north-west India till present which is called 'Chola'. Chola is a loose open collar garment long upto Gulphas which was worn above all. It is in vogue till now in wedding. Long upper garment of Chashtan idol, dug out from Mathura, is also known as Chincholaka which collar is open as triangle from front. Chinacholaka of Kanishka was likely to open from middle and that of Chashtan's having two folds in which upper fold is likely to open in left side and triangular part of collar was to open in middle of neck. Chinacholaka of Kanishka style is still clearer in D-46 named idole of Mathura museum, only difference in cutting of cloth. A similar cholaka of about seventh century is found from Middle Asia. The main text of that place was '*apacitacīnacōlaka*' which had corrected '*upacita....*' To make it simple. In commentary of Shankara and copies of Kashmir particulary '*apacita*' text is present which meaning is, according to dictionaries, honoured, adored and distinguished. Meaning of Bana is that some kings had worn distinguished Chinacholaka garment."[37]

Kurpasaka is said variegated cloth. Bana has written in Harṣacarita that some kings had worn variegated, due to coloured with different colours, Kurpasaka (*nānākāṣāyakarbūrakūrpāsakai :*). "Garment of Kurpasaka was famous in Gupta-Period. In Amarakosha meaning of kurpasaka is chola. Kurpasaka was garment of man and woman with miner difference. For woman it was like blouse and for man it was like short quilted waistcoat or mirjai. It has two characteristics – first, it was high from waist and second, it was generally without sleeve. Actually its name was kurpasaka because sleeve was above elbow in this. Origionally kurpasaka was also in use in dress of middle-Asia like chinacholaka and it adopted in this country from there. Kurpasaka like modern garment is vaskata but according to conduct of Asia it is considered as upper garment whereas in west civilization it is inner garment. In whole-Mangolian, China, Turkistana and Pakhtoonistan it was custom to wear short quilted waistcoat was universal and it was considered as perfect and distinguished garment. Phatui or Phituri, Banda, Kabja, Choli are names and types of one main garment. That garment was famous from name of Kurpasaka in Gupta-Period."[38]

Describing Achchhadanaka nemed clothe Bana has written that some kings had worn Achchhadanaka of the shade of 'parrots' tails (*śukapicchacchāyācchādanakai :*). "Recognition of Achchhadanaka is comparatively simple in some idols of Mathura museum, which are of Sun and servants of his back side, integral part of sasani dress a small light shawl has covered both shoulders and shown as tightend in front of chest. This is Achchhadanaka which called 'Apron' in English. Outlining of Achchhadanaka in idol number D-1 and 513 is absolutely clear and certainly known. Achchhadanaka has also shown in paintings of Ajanta. There is depicted lapis lazuli Achchhadanaka on shoulder and back of sword holding Sasani soldier who is standing between painting of Nagraj and Dravidaraj in cave number one."[39]

Along with Adhovastra and Uttariya people wore turban and strip of cloth to cover head. Thin silk cloth made of Anshuk, was used to put on a turban. Generally people liked turban of white cloth. Pearl, emerald and ruby were sticked on turbans of kings. Turbans of general people were made of cheap cloth. Strip of cloth (*paṭṭa cīrikā*) was also tightend on head which is called 'Sapha' in Kādambarī.

Vikukshi is described as tightened strip of washed dukula cloth (*dhautadukūlapaṭṭikāparivēṣṭita*).

There is also description of dress of Mahashiva religious sect in Harṣacarita. A glimpse of male garment of this type of sects in contemporary society is known from this description. In process of describing Betal-Sadhana of king Pushyabhuti, describing garment of disciple of Bhairavacharya, Bana has written "A red ascetic's scarf hanging from his shoulder formed his vaikaksaka wrap; his upper robe, consisting of a tattered rag knotted above his heart and stained with red chalk, seemed to be token the knotted passions of his heart, which he had rent in pieces. In one hand he grasped his bamboo stool. There was a yoke pole resting on his left shoulder, where its motionless point of support was tied with a complicated fastening of hair rope; to this were attached his dirt-scraper and sieve of bamboo bark, his loin cloth at the end, his alms bowl contained in its receptacle, namely a cavity of Kharjura wood, his waterpot fixed in a triangular support made of three sticks, his slippers disposed outside, and a bundle of manuscript bound by a string of stout cord."[40]

In Kādambarī describing garment of Harita, son of Jabali and his friends, sons of sages, Bana has written that there was hanged blue and yellow mix coloured krishnajin as if they were discharging smoke absorbed during ascetic fervor. "Hanging krishnajin on shoulder is shown generally in idols of sages and Brahma etc gods of Gupta-Period. It is also in Nar-Narayana idol of Devagarh temple."[41]

Women garment was also divided in two pats like men –'Adhovastra' and 'Uttariya'. Women wore petticoat (=caṇḍātaka) as Adhovastra. It is written in Harṣacarita about adhovastra of Malati that underneath gleamed a petticoat of safflower tint and variegated with spots of different colours, as if she was a crystal ground enclosing a treasure of jewels (*kusumbharāgapāṭalama pulakabandha citrama caṇḍātakamanta: sphuṭama sphaṭikabhūmiriva ratnanidhānamāmādadhānā* -Harṣacarita, Pratham Uchchhawas, page-56). Besides chandataka women wore Svasthana, Pinga and Satula named trousers as adhovastra.

Women mainly wore Anshuka and Varbana as Uttariya garment. Along with they also wore Chinacholaka, Kurpasaka and Aachchhadanaka named Uttariya garment like men.

Anshuk cloth was two types. One Anshuk was long up to foot. Describing garment of Malati Bana has written that her body was concealed with white bleached silk, lighter than a snake's slough, hanging down to her toes. But other side "describing women of Sthanishvar it is said that they had worn kanchuka or short blouse. This dress was not in Gupta-Period. Tradition to wore blouse or brassiere was started about sixth century after invasion of Hunas. There are idols of women, worn blouse, found in excavation of Ahichchhatra period of which is between 550AD to 750AD."[42]

Bana has also mentioned wearing sheet by women. In Kādambarī, describing garment of daughter of Chandala, Bāṇa Bhaṭṭa has written that her body was covered with blue labada (overcoat) reached up to joint of foot. She was covered with a red sheet over that – '*gulphāvalambi nīlakañcukēnāvācchnnaśarīrāma upariraktānśukaracitāva guṇṭhanāma*' (Kādambarī, Poorvabhagah, page-20). Again also in Kādambarī, describing garment of Patralekha, it is written that she had covered with a red sheet like the red-velvet insect – '*śakragōpakālōhita rāgēṇāmaśukēna rācatāvaguṇṭhanayā*' (page-212-213). It is clear from these descriptions that women put on woman's sheet to cover own breast. These women's sheet was also used as veil on special occasions. Describing Rajyashri, in dress of bride, it is written that her face, hidden, like the morning twilight, by its roseate veil, dulled the gleaming lamps by its radiance- '*aruṇānśukāvaguṇṭhitamukhī prabhātasandhyāmiva svaprabhayā- niṣprabhānpradīpa kānkurvānāma*' (Harṣacaritam, Chaturth Uchchhawas, page-251).

Women also put on Gatrika-Granthi (a cloth garment worn over shoulders and tied) and Yogapatta. "On upper part of Savitri's body a Gatrika Granthi of lotus filament was tied in a svastika knot between her bosoms: *stanamdhyabaddhagātrikā granthi*. Hindi word 'Gatee' is derieved from Gatrika. Till present time practicenor of brahmacharya or an ascetic are knot gatees of Uttariya."[43] "there was hanging kundalikrit Yogapatt from Savitri's left shoulder which was downwards to waist through right side. In this description kundalikrit, yogapatta and vaikakshya are technical. Vaikakshya is appeared several times in Bana's books.When string of beads, garland and cloth was worn from left shoulder towards right armpit then that was called Vaikakshya. Yogapatta was that cloth which was put on by an ascetic to cover upper part of body. This word is used at several places in literature. In 'Yashodhar Charita', poetry of Apbhransha language it's Jogavahu form is appeared: *galajōgavaṭṭaṭṭu sajjīu vicitu*. Jayasi has used that's Jogavata form in old Avadhi. This writing of Bana that Yogapatta was wore as ringlet or roll up can be understood merely from seeing of idols of Gupta-Period in which yogapatta is throw on by doubling and downwards from left shoulder."[44]

At several places, in Kādambarī, there is description of female ascetic worn reddish-brown cloth. These female ascetics were female beggar initiated in different religion. They wore different types of garments according to principles of own sects i.e. female beggar of Pashupat sect worn ochre-coloured cloth, Buddhist nun worn red coloured cheevar similar to the palm tree fruit, female beggar of Svetambar Jain sect worn white cloth and brahmacharini women endowed with bark garment of foliage.

Along with these cloths there is mention of other types of cloths in Harṣacarita and Kādambarī. King Harsha had worn adhovastra made from a cloth named kshirodaka (*kṣīrōdaghēnapaṭaladhavalāmbaravāhī*). There is description of cloth made from Kush (sacred grass) and bark of mythol (*kalpatarulatāvalkalēna*) in Kādambarī. Cleaned leather of tiger and deer was used as cloth. There is mention of cleaning leather of deer by sons of saints to make it suitable to wear (*upasaṁsakriyamāṇakṛṣṇājinama*). "It was not possible to wear skin of deer in natural form, by ascetics and it was not acceptable for self dependent ascetics to send them out of abode to prepare that. So they self, curry leather by collecting bark of the babul tree (work to prepare raw leather is called kamana or jhavana)."[45] Cloth was also made from inner skin of banana. In Kādambarī, there is mention of attractive cloth made from inner skin of banana (*āsāvasaktakadalīgarbha patracārucīrama* -Kādambarī , page-341).

From descriptions of Bana it seems that white cloths were liked in Harsha-Period. Along with people were also wore coloured cloths. Blue, red, black and yellow colours were used for colouring cloths. Turmeric was used for colouring cloths in yellow colour. King Tarapeed was thinking, distressed from grief of childless, that whom I should glad to see queen as wore yellow cloth coloured with colour of turmeric like sky of dazzling light from childhood penance and attached with new risen Sun and coming by holding son in her lap-‘*kadā hārindravasanadhāriṇī sutasanāthōtsaṅgā dyōrivōditaravimaṇḍlā sabālātapāmā bhanāndyiṣyati dēvī*’ (Kādambarī , Poorvabhagah, page-134). Nowadays these types of cloths are called peeliya. Some cloths were coloured in different colours so that cloths colour was variegated. Variegated Kurpasaka named garment coloured with different colours (*nānā kaṣāya karbūra kūrpāsakai :*), was made from this type of cloths. A dyer of cloth was called Rajaka in Harṣacarita. Describing preparation of Rajyashri’s wedding Bana has written that some were being dyed by Rajaks, who beamed with respect for the courtly old ladies of the harem-‘*ācāracaturānta:purajaratījanitapūjārājamānarājakarājyamānai:*’ (Harṣacaritam, Chaturth Uchchhawas, page-244).

Different pictures and diagrams were made on cloths to make them attractive. It is clear from description of wrapped painted netra cloth on pillars of royal palace (*uccitranētrasukumārasvasthānasthagitajaṅgākānḍaiśca*) and covered thighs of kings from flower leaf painted trousers made from netra named silk cloth that picture was made on cloths. Dr. Vasudevasharna Aggrawal has written “uchchita related to those cloths in which various diagrams were casted at time of wearing. Several samples, contemporary to Bana, were found from middle-Asia. These diagrams were two types-one are those on which pictures are made by connecting line-sub-line and dots and second were those on which pictures of fish etc were made.”[46] Different diagrams were made on borders of cloths to make attractive. It is mentioned in Kādambarī that two swans were made on border of two cloths by gorochana-‘*amṛtaphēnadhavalē gōrōcanālikhita haṁsamithunasanāthaparyantē*' (Kādambarī, Poorvabhagah, page-16-17). "Bana has mentioned one other type of cloths which is prepared specially for bridegroom. White cloth is made auspicious by making hand spot with wet kumkum (wet turmeric in liquid of lemon) on that: *ārabdhakunkumapankasthāsākchuranai*. Till now it was tradition, in Punjab, that the bridegroom went on for riding on horseback in a marriage procession after wearing this type of wedding robe."[47]

Other objects of garment:-

It is known from descriptions of Harṣacarita and Kādambarī that people wore sacred thread or Yagyopaveeta which considered auspicious. In Harṣacarita there is mention of white sacrificial thread (*dhavalayajñōmpavītinīma*) put on Lord Brahma's body. In this manner in Kādambarī there is description of hanged Yagyopaveeta from shoulder (*āsāvalambiyajñōpavītama*) of great ascetic Jabali. Shoes, socks along with wooden soled sandal were in vogue to wear in feet. In Kādambarī Bana has written that one side there was put pairs of shoes on fresh shikahar made from matted hair of coconut-' *baddhanālikērīphalabalkala mayadhautōpāna dyugōpōtāna*'(Kādambarī , Poorvabhagah, page-280). Again describing old aged south Indian virtuous (worshipper) he has written that silk sock of his foot was torn. So that his toe of foot was cracked and in which wound was appeared place to place-'*kauṣēyakakōśāvaraṇakṣativranitacaraṇāmaguṣṭhakēna*' (Kādambarī, Poorvabhagah,page-459-60).

Handkerchief was also used by people in Harsha-Period society. Rajya-Vardhana had wiped his face, which the hot tears had scorched, with a piece of moonlight in shape of handkerchief presented by the betel-bearer-'*tāmbūlikōpasthāpitēna ca vāsasā candrātapa śakalēnēvōṣṇōṣṇavāṣpadagdhama vadanamunmamārga*' (Harṣacaritam, Shashtha Uchchhawas, page-312).

Ornaments:-

In every era ornaments have been used by people to decorate body. It is known about social status, prosperity, development of art & craft and desire of people of that era from ornament-jewellery of any era that is in vogue. Tradition to wear ornaments also continued in seventh century with some changing. It is thrown light on ornament-jewellery of seventh century, which was in vogue, from description of Harṣacarita and Kādambarī.

In seventh century man and women had similar desire of ornament. According to Bana, ivory, gold, silver, pearl, lac, conch shell, pewter and different precious stones (i.e. quartz, indraneelamani (sapphire), and marakatamani (an emerald) etc) were used to make ornaments. People also wore different precious stones. Describing people of Ujjayini Bana has written that people of Ujjayini had worn all precious stones taken away from sea – '*mandarēnēvōdadhṛtasamagrasāgararatnasārēṇa*'. Probably that time people have also faith in wonderful astonishment of precious stones and wore them on suggestion of astrologers. Contemporary kings and queens had so desire of ornaments that boxes of ivory (patalaka ratna manjusha) were full of ornaments which were used by them. Very attractive box of ivory to contain ornaments is found from ancient Kapisha (modern Begram, Afghanistan). Along with, ornaments were listed for accounting. In Kādambarī, maintaining of garments, and ornaments by Chandrapeed, Bana has written that "after worship he (Chandrapeed) has entered in angaragashala. As soon as he was seated the royal servants along with pratiharas sent by the king and female servants along with Kulavandhana sent by queen Vilasavatee and female servants of inner palace were present that time in front of him with boxes full of many necklaces, ointments and cloths. They handed over all materials to Chandrapeed."[48] Describing royal palace of king Tarapeed, also in Kādambarī, Bana has written that "In that royal palace hundred of precious stones and thousand of jewelleries which were given queens to wore, list was prepared- '*dīpamānamaṇiratasahastrālankaranakṛtalēkhyapatrasañcayama*'."[49]

Rich people wore ornaments made from expensive metals and precious stones. Poor and simple people wore ornaments made from less expensive metals, wood and flower-leaf. Describing Shabar youth, in Ashtam Uchchhawas of Harṣacaritam, Bana has written that "his ear had an ear-ring of glass-like crystal fastened in it and it assumed a green hue from a parrot's wing which ornamented it, he wore a tin armlet, decorated with white godanta beads, which was placed on his fore-arm, the back of which was covered with a bundle of the rootlets of Nagadamana fastened together by the bristles of boars and the top of the arm was gay with a blue jay's tail fastened on the upper one third part. In this manner, in Kādambarī , daughter of Chandal had worn ornament made from black leaf of sandle and ornament made from sandal-wood were tightened on muscular arm of servants who were present in court of Tarapeed.

Following ornaments of different parts of body were described in Harṣacarita.

Head ornament-

Main ornament was shikhmani or chudamani makarika that was worn on the top of head. Chudamani was worn in the same way by men and women. Malati had worn chudamani makaritka on her head. "Makarika named gold ornament was made by jointing two Capricorn mouths, taken out in both sides, which was worn in hair from front or on head."[50]

Crown had been worn on head by kings. Crown was made from expensive metals and precious stones. A synonym of crown was Kireet. By praying his teacher, in Kādambarī, Bana has written that "I pray that foot of my teacher which was worshipped by clan of crown helder Maukharies of ancient India and fingers of that foot were turned red by touch of upper point of kireets of all feudatory princes."

Bana has also mentioned an ornament named 'Balapasha' which was worn on head. This ornament was helpful to stable hair at its proper place. "Balapasha was long leaf of gold in which bunch of pearl and muktajal (tangle of pearl or santanaka) were hung. Generally this type of Balapasha is found in paintings of Ajanta. Balapashas were tightened on head of Nagaraja and Dravidaraja (cave-1) in which bunch and tangles of pearls are clearly shown. In this painting golden strip were also shown on head of other characters but bunch and tangles of pearl are not present only a bunch is shown hanging from the parting of a women's hair. According to Amarakosha synonyms of

Balapasha or Balapashya (ornament for stable hair at its proper place) was also Paritathya Balapasha. It was named Paritathya Balpasha because it encircles around head. It was new word for Gupta-Period as new word sanjavan was in use for chatuhshal. Tradition to fasten hair with thin gold leaf was also in Sindhu civilization. Many ornaments, of this type, are found in excavation of Mohanjodaro which are ten to twelve inches long and holes are present on both ends to fasten it. Nowadays it is in use in south-east Punjab; this ornament was called 'Pat' in local language. Bana has written that Karnapoor of ear and Balapash of head were colliding mutually from departure. Actually Balapasha ornament was fastened on hair but its hanging bunch of pearls sounded by attaching with Karnapoor: *cāmīkarapatrānkarakarṇapura kavighatu mānavācālabālapaśē:*"[51]

Women wore a precious stone fitted ornament hung on forehead. Describing the ornament of Malati Bana has written that dancing upon her forehead and kissing her hair-parting was chatula tilaka named precious stone. This type of Chatula tilaka is generally shown in Gupta-Period female idols. This ornament was similar to recently used jewellery named Mangatika.

Ear ornament-

Main ear ornaments of seventh century were-Patrankura Karnapoora, Karnapasha (large ear-ring) and Trikantaka jewellery. Men and women wore these ornaments in similar way. Structure of flower with petals was made in Patrankura-Karnapoora ornament. Karnapoora was similar like present Karnaphula jewellery. Hanging ear-jewellery was called Kundala. Kundala was also called Karnapasha. Leaf like structure had been hung in Kundala which can sway by mild wave of wind. In description of Bana emerald and precious stone fitted Kundals are mentioned. Describing ornament of Kādambarī Bana has written that "She had worn talleepatt jewellery like Karnapasha made from gold in her ears which leaves were swinging by wave of wind. Emerald and precious stone fitted such Kundala made splendid in her ear-'*utkṛṣṭahēmatālīpaṭṭābharaṇabhāramāyuktakarṇōtpalacyutamadhudhārāsandēhakārinama karṇapāśama dōlāyamānapatramarakatamaṇikyakuṇḍalama dādhatī.*"[52]

It seems from description of Harṣacarita that ear jewellery named Trikantaka was popular in men and women. Describing Dadhicha Bana has written that he wore Trikantaka which was made by fitting an emerald between two bulky pearls. Bhandi's (first cousin of Harsha on mother's side) ear-ornament was also made from pearl fitted in indraneelamani and trikantaka. Royal women had also worn trikantaka in ears on occasion of Harsha's birth festival. Dr. Vasudevasharana Aggrawal has written about recognition of trikantaka "fortunately I found a ear-ornament, ear-ring size gold jewellery made by fitting an emerald between two pearls, similar to description of Bana; that is now well-protected in New Delhi museum. That can be recognised as trikantaka."[53]

Neck ornament-

Main ornaments of neck were string of beads and necklace those were worn in Harsha–Period. Men and women wore these ornaments in similar way.

String of beads was made from quartz,pearl and Rudra-eyed. It is known from descriptions of Harṣacarita and Kādambarī that string of pearl beads was very popular that time. In Harsha Charit there is description of a special string of beads named Ekavali. This string of beads was made from beads of pearl and has one string so its name was Ekavali. This string of beads has endowed with many features. Medicant Nagarjuna had given it to a king Satavahana. In course of time it came into Divakaramitra hands by the regular succession of pupil-hood which he gave to Harsha. "This description of Bana is based on mixture of contemporary hearsays. Medicant Nagarjuna was understood as god of many astonishments and miracles. At time of Bana this type of story was popular about him. Friendship relation between Nagarjuna and king of Satavahana was probably a historical fact. It is said that Nagarjauna had written a long letter to counsel summary of spiritual instruction of Buddhist religion to his friend king of Satavahana. That letter's translation, named Suhallekh in Tibetan language, is well-protected till now. Single string of pearl beads 'Ekavali' was much liked in all ornaments in Gupta-Period. So many times Kalidasa has mentioned that. Description of Ekavali is generally also given in Harṣacarita and

Kādambarī. Single string of pearl beads Ekavali with sapphire bead in middle is found in idols and paintings of Gupta-Period. It could easily be understood thinking about Ekavali in that era that it was special auspicious ornament. There are astonishing stories composed in jewelers and harems about special ornaments. It is mentioned in Maha Ummaga Jataka about giving mangal maniratna to king Kush by Indra. Kalidasa had said these as '*jaitrābharaṇa*'."[54]

String of beads made from pearl and quartz were worn by rich people but string of beads made from Rudra-eyed was worn generally by ascetics.

Describing about Harsha, Bana has written that his necklace named Shesh was hung falling from shoulder and his breast was wrapped in a fold of rays from the pearls in his necklace. "Sheshhar was ornament of special men of that time. It would be called as balebada of pearls which was narrow in upper part and bulky from lower part and wrapped on body it seems like the serpent from front. Bana has described in detail, in Kādambarī also, about Sheshahar. Kādambarī had sent it especially for Chanderapeed. Many samples of Sheshahar is found in idols of Gupta-Period.

Waist ornament-

Ornament of waist was Kardhani or Mekhala. Kardhani was essential part of garment because this was used to tighten Adhovastra tightly. Kardhani was made of gold. It contained many strings in which pronun was attached. Men and women wore this in similar way.

Bana has written, in Kādambarī, that king Tarapeed, distressed with grief of childlessness thinks, "When my son would trouble his mother, running behind sound of pronun attached in gold kardhani (*kanakamēkhalādhaṣṭikā*) and following sound of anklet with bells behind domestic swans and running one section to another section?"[56] Beautiful strings of kardhani were also in waist of daughter of Chandala.

Along with precious metals kardhani of rush was also in use. It is described in Kādambarī that Harsha, son of Yajyavalkya, had worn kardhani of rush.

Arm ornament-

Bajubanda or Bhujabanda was ornament of upper arm. Describing king Shudraka, in Kādambarī, Bana has written that two Bajubandas made of indraneelamani was tightened on his upper arms. Both were seemed like two snakes come there for greed of sandal ointment. It was arising doubt to see that as if two chains had come for tightening very lightning royal majesty '*aticapalarājyalakṣmībandhanigaḍa kaṭakaśankāmupa janayatēndramanīkēyūrayugmēna malayajara sagandhalubdhēna bhujangadvayēnēva vēṣṭitabāhuyugalama*' (Poorvabhagah, page-17). Again,describing the scene ,after dismission of court, Bana has written that cloth of many people were torn by insertion of pointed part of fishes shaped in Bajubandas and moving due to haste-'*atirabha sañcalana cālitāngada patrabhangamakarakōṭipāṭitāśukapaṭānāma* '(Kādambarī , Poorvabhagah, page-27).

It is clear from these descriptions that indraneelamani was fitted in Bajubanda. Bajubanda was ring shaped and shape of fish was shaped on end of that. Bajubanda was seen like snake because it was wrapped around arm and shaped mouth of fish on end.

Bajubanda of Shudraka was called 'Keyura' and 'Angada' in Kādambarī. It seems that Bajubanda was called 'Keyura' or 'Angada' in Harsha-Period. But according to A.Biswas Keyura and Angada were different types of Bajubanda. Describing three types of Bajubanda he has written "Upper-arm ornaments or armlets can be classified under three varieties. Keyura was wrought with beaded patterns edged in one or more rims. Some bore crisscross or net patterns and some consisted of several square panels inset with pearls or gems. They were placed on the upper arm by inserting the hand through them. Some may have clasps to be fitted with screws. Angada was an entwining type of armlet made in the form of a coil. Bana has picturesquely described them as "entwining the arm like a couple of snakes, fond of the smell of sandal applied to the body." In a third variety the keuras are replaced by a pile of bangles (*kankanas*) which may range upto twelve."[57]

Kankana or Kangana and Kara were ornaments those were worn on fore arm. Kangana was called Valaya in Sanskrit. Bana has written about king Shudraka, in Kādambarī , that sometimes he organized concert and his precious stone fitted kankana moved because he himself played double drum-'*sa kadācidanavarata dōlāyamānaratnavalayō*'(Poorvabhagah, page-13).

Again, describing women of king Tarapeed's royal palace Bana has written that those beautiful women were looked very lovely from continous sound of precious stone fitted kankanas, moving in tembling hands-'*karatalacalanmanivalayakalakalaramaṇīyama*' (Poorvabhagah, page-124).

In seventh century it was tradition to wear Kada in wrist. Kada was made of gold and pewter. "A Kada made of gold (*hāṭakakaṭaka*) was in wrist of Malati and emerald was fitted on both end of Capricorn shaped mouth: *marakatamakaravēdikāsanātha.* Capricorn shaped mouth (Grahamukhi or Makaramukhi) and Naharamukhi kadas are current in Indian ornaments till now."[58] Describing dress of Shabar youth, in Harṣacarita, Bana has written that he had worn a kada made of pewter, decorated with white godanta beads, which was placed on his roe-arm, the back of which was covered with a bundle of the rootlets of Nagadamana fastened together by the bristles of boars-'*gōdantamaṇicitrama trāpuṣama valayama vibhrāṇama*'(Ashtam Uchchhawas, page-414). "There was extensive tradition to wear ornament made of pewter or gilat in low castes. Shankara has given meaning of godanta as a type of snake. Shri Kane has given meaning as beads made of godantiharatala, which seems correct."[59]

It is also known from description of Bana that ring was worn in fingers. Men and women wore rings. Ring was made of conch shell and emerald. It is described in Harṣacarita that Savitri had worn ring made of conch shell (kambunirmit urmika) and Lord Brahma had worn ring made of emerald.

Leg ornament-

Bāṇa Bhaṭṭa has mentioned Noopur or anklet that was worn in feet. There is description, in Harṣacarita and Kādambarī, of

Noopuras fitted with precious stones and attached with pronun. Clashing sound came out from Noopur when women went away wearing it.

Along with these ornaments there was tradition of ornament, made of flowers, in seventh century. Several places, in Harṣacarita and Kādambarī, there is mention of ornaments made of flowers. Crown was made of flowers of jasmine and malati. Daughter of Chandala had worn garland made of black leafs of sandal. There is mention, in Kādambarī, of garland made of flower and leafs of champa. Flowers were also used to decorate the hair tied up behind. It is clear from these descriptions that flower and leafs were used as ornament in Harsha-Period. About importance of flowers, in Indian toilet, A.Biswas had written "Flowers were an important accessory in the Indian toilet. It was a common practice to wear garlands of fragrant flower and use sprays for tucking into the coiffures. The women knew the use of appropriate flowers for decorating the different parts of the body. Their choice changed from season to season. At one place, for instance, there is mention of women making use of different kinds of flowers: Kunda wreathed round the head; Kurabaka stuck in the top-knot; Kadamba placed at the parting of the hair; sirisa decorating the ears; garland of bakula adorning the neck and breast; pollen of lodhra emitting a yellow glow from face; bangles of flowers enhancing the beauty of the hands; and a lotus held in the hand. It was the time when life looked like a season of flowers."[60]

Accomplishing-

People had given special attention on beauty of their body in Harsha-Period. Different toilet items were used to bleach body. Describing servants, who were bearing toilet-items of wives of samantas who came in royal palace at time of Harsha's birth, Bana has written "After them(wives of samantas) followed servants bearing garlands in wide baskets, with bath powder sprinkled upon the flowers; dishes laden with bits of camphor, clear as crystal granules; jeweled caskets of saffron scents; ivory boxes, studded with rows of sandal-hued Areca nuts and tufted with slim khadira fibres dripping mango oil; vermilion and powder boxes red and pink, with murmuring bees sipping Parijata perfumes; betel trees with bundles of nuts hanging from the young slips."[61]

It is known from descriptions of Bana that sandal ointment, sandal dust, powder (*paṭavāsa cūrṇa*) and ubatan (paste) was used to bleach beauty of body. Along with, water mixed with musk, powder of the stigma of the crocus, liquid of camphor and wring out liquid of soft leafs of sandal etc was used to fragrant body. Bana has written that Kādambarī had made his body white by smeared white sandal '*acchācchēna candanarasēna dhavalīkṛtatanulatāma*' (Kādambarī, page-420). Again Bana has written that when Mahashveta was coming down from roof of palace then Taralika was also coming behind her bearing different type of flowers, bête, body ointment, patavas churna (powder). It is described in Harṣacarita that Harsha's body turned pale from ubatan of gorochana-'*gōrōcanāpiñjaritavapuṣi*' (Chaturth Uchchhawas, page-228). People used mirror to look their face.

It is known from descriptions of Harṣacarita and Kādambarī that women coiled (*avatansa*) and threaded lock their hair (*alakinee*) to decorate hair. Along with hair spared untied which hanged upto buttocks (*nitambacumbiśikhaṇḍa*). Coil of women's hair was decorated with flowers. Amla oil was applied in hair. There is mention of sahakara oil in descriptions of Bana. Probably this was fragmented oil that was applied in hair. Vermilion was applied by married women to the hair parting. Along with wives of samantas their servants were also come with them in royal palace bearing vermilion-boxes (*sindūrapātrāṇī*) at time of Harsha's birth.

The hair of men was cut. Bhandi had made his hair cut (*kāritaśōkaśmaśruvapanakarmaṇā*) grown from mourning and bathed in room of Mahapratihara. Some people allow the hair to grow upto navel. It is described in Harṣacarita that by side of Dadhicha a man accompanied with short nails, beard and hair-'*nīcanakhaśmaśrukēśama*'(Pratham Uchchhawas, page-43).

To decorate forehead sectarian mark was made. A set of three horizontal lines were also made on forehead. Liquid of soil, gorochana and mainsail (*mana: śilāpanka*) was used to made sectarian mark. A set of three horizontal lines was made from ashes.

It was tradition to apply lampblack in eyes. Eyes of book reader Sudristi were looking beautiful because lampblack was applied in her eyes. A line of lampblack was enlarged while applying lampblack. It is called 'ekashalakanjana' in Harṣacarita.

Saffron was applied to beautify the cheeks. It is mentioned, in Kādambarī, that leaf-platter was painted with saffron on the cheeks of queen Vilasavatee.

Any artificial cosmetic was not used to colour the lips. Men and women both were desirous of betel leaf. Betel leaf was eaten by people specially to colour the lips.

Ointment and dust of sandal was used to beautify breast. Along with the work of painting was done on breast with black agar. Describing luxurious life of king Tarapeed, in Kādambarī , Bana has written that their (women of palace) cloths were marked by leaf-platter with black agar painted on raised breast –'*ullasitakuca kṛṣṇāgurupankapatralatāngīta pracchadapaṭama*'(page-124). In this manner king Tarapeed had asked distressed queen Vilasavatee "Today why you has not painted your raised breasts with black agar like deer spoted moon?-' *kimiti ca hariṇa iva hariṇalāñchanē na likhita: kṛṣṇāguru patrabhanga payōdharabhārē*' (Kādambarī , page-131). It is clear from these descriptions that leaf-platter was painted with black agar on the breasts. These paintings can be compared with present tattoos that are in vogue. Tatoos of present time are painted on different parts of body but paintings of Harsha-Period were only painted on the breasts.

Dense red Alta or Mahavar was used for beautify feet. Leaf-platter was painted on feet with mahavar. Saffron was applied on the sole of the feet. In Harṣacarita and Kādambarī women's feet are described as coloured with alta. Describing Malati, in Harṣacarita, Bana has written that her feet, glowing with clotted lac and stained with saffron on the upper surface –'*piṇḍālaktēna pllavitasya kunkumapiñjaritapuṣṭhasya caraṇayugalasya*' (page-56).

It is known from these toilet items that people of seventh century were desirous. These toilet items are also used today in our country with some corrections.

Health and Hygiene:-

It is thrown light on different diseases and process of treatment of seventh century from descriptions of Harṣacarita and Kādambarī.

It is known from descriptions of Bana that people of that time were suffering from diseases in which following are illustrious- burning fever, kutapakala fever, insomnia, ringworm, cough releted diseases, leprosy and eye disease. Prabhakara-Vardhana, father of Harsha, was suffered with burning fever. Main symptoms of burning fever were intense thirst, head-ache, sinking eye, hot breath and twist in body etc. Kutapakala named fever was just a type of fever. Insomnia was a disease which was cause of sleeplessness. In Kādambarī, there is mention of an eye-disease, apart from night-blindness, which is cause to seem two objects of one object.

In Harsha-Period, medical treatment was done with the help of Ayurveda. There were two methods to prepare medicine in Ayurveda- first, boiled decoctions collected from different herbs. Second, without boiled decoctions, collected from different herbs, was used as medicine. Those boiled decoction were used as medicine after cooling. Old aged south Indian priest used without boiled liquid of herbs (*asaṁyakṛta rasāyana*). When Harsha returned at palace, after hearing illness of his father, then he detected an odour of boiling oil, butter and decoctions emitting a steam scented with various herb droughts. It is mentioned in Kādambarī that when body of Pundarika was burning in Kamajvara (disease of love) then Pundarika had collected soft leafs, present nearby, of sandal etc trees and ring out liquid of them, that was naturally fragmented and cold, and smeared it on head and entire body upto foot. He had collected camphor, extracted from cracked skin of nearby trees, and smashed from his hand and applied it to dry his sweat. Covering his chest from bark garment, soaked in liquid of sandal, he had fanned him with leaf of banana by dripping fine drops of water.

In Kādambarī there is mention of bruising stone of bahera and making it powder, melted liquid of gugul and liquid of shilajeet extracted from mountains. Probably these were used as medicine to cure diseases.

There is description of Himagriha in Kādambarī. In that himagriha cloths, made from mrinalatantu, were fragranted with liquid of comphore wring out from new foliage of comphore. Somewhere karnapoor made from flower-bud of jasmine were wet in liquid of lavali fruit. Somewhere, cool medicine liquid full in vessels of stone, were fanned from leaf of lotus. In this manner, servants were busy in preparing medicins of shitopachara (cooling treatment). In himagriha camphor liquid was flowing like river. Kādambarī was embracing puppet of ice to cool her body that was burning from fever of love. Again and again she was touching puppet of camphor on her cheeks. She was touching, again and again, puppet of sandal mud from her feet. From this description of Bana it is known that a medical treatment of fever was shitopachara in seventh century. Cool environment was created around patient to cure through this system. Sandal and camphor were rubbed on body. Cloths wetted in liquid of sandal and camphor was worn. Patients embraced puppet of ice.

People of seventh century took physical exercise and pranayama for health. Several times, in Harṣacarita and Kādambarī, it is mentioned about doing physical exercise by princes. It seemed to Mahashveta, by seeing dead body of Pundarika, as if he was doing pranayama by remorse and longing a peculiar pranayama (*apūrvaprāṇāyāmamivābhyasyantama*). This sentence of Bana indicates that people had done pranayama. It is known, from description of Bana, that people had special attention about cleanness of body. There was tradition to bath three times (morning, noon and evening) in a day. Hiuen-Tsang has also written that Indian people are very particular in their personal cleanliness, and allow no remissness in this particular.

Ayurvedic doctors were appointed to cure royal family members. In Harṣacarita there is mention of Sushena and Rasayana named Ayurvedic doctors. Rasayana named Ayurvedic doctor was expert scholar of Ashtanga Ayurveda and scholar of Ayurveda, written by Punarvasu. He was expert to cure diseases correctly by recognizing diseases with his acute wisdom. Bāṇa Bhaṭṭa has not given any information about system to cure general people. Probably, general people cured themselves by local knowledge and with help of roots and herbs used medicinally.

Food and Beverage:-

It is thrown light on food and beverage, vogue in seventh century, from descriptions of Bāṇa Bhaṭṭa. That time Indian food was filled with variety. There was tradition of vegetarian and non-vegetarian food. After food, people ate betel leaf, smoke dhoormavartika (sigar) and used mukhavas (materials for mouth fragrant). Mukhavas was dust to fragrant mouth which was made from sahakara (mangos), karpoora (camphor), kakkola-fruits, lavanga (cloves) and parijataka (coral trees).

Wood, coal made from wood and dry dung-cakes (*khuravalayairvilikhitājiravitardikāni*) were used for fuel. Utensils that were used to cook food, to put and to serve, were flat iron plate (tava), griddle (tai), thin metal rods (salakhen), small pan (kadahi), utensils of copper, earthen water-pot, saraiya of galvarka and small plate of masara etc "Both word galvarka and masara are important. These words are also used in the Mahabharata, Divyavadana and Mrichchhakatika. Masara could be related to Sanskrit word ashmasara. Kings of east countries had brought utensils of ashmasara to present Yudhishthir. Much probable that masara was name of Yashava (English zed). This was imported from Varma. Before that Bana has added adjective peet. Light yellow coloured yashaba was called peet masara. Scond was hakika stone which was used to made utensils for eating and drinking. For that, probably, galvarka word was used."[62]

Wheat, rice, gram, green gram (munga), urad, rajamasha, paunda, pooli, nivar (rice of tinni) etc were main grain of Harsha-Period. Sugar-cane was cultivated for production of raw sugar. There is mention, in Harṣacarita, of two types of sugar- red coloured raw sugar (*pāṭala śarkarā*) and white sugar (*karka śarkarā*). Sattu (dimin) was produced from gram. People were desirous of milk and curds.

Fruit was also an essential part of food. Saints were generally living on fruit. There is mention of mango, blackberry, banana, pomegranate, maulasiri, fruit of palm tree, fruit of draksha, date, dadima, aadu, plum (*cheta*), fruit of myrobalan (*amvla*), lemon and bahera etc in

Harṣacarita and Kādambarī. Fruit of myrobalan, fruit of draksha, lemon and bahera were also used to prepare medicine.

It is known from descriptions of Harṣacarita and Kādambarī that people were desirous of delicious food. Purodas and aamiksha named food were cooked at time of Somayagya. It was prepared by mixing curd in hot milk and presented to vaishvadeva. Probably other food items of milk and curds would also be prepared. Bearers of kitchen appurtenances of kings were bearing potherbs, bamboo shoots and flowers at time of Harsha's army march. It is clear from this description that potherbs, bamboo shoots and flowers were used to make vegetable dish. People ate vegetable dishes made from brinjal, edible tuber, sehijan, pumpkin, cucurbit etc Khirani and mainaphal were preserbed after drying and which were used as dried fruit.

There was vast tradition of non-vegetarian food in seventh century. Kings and feudatories were desirous of non-vegetarian food. Main food of wild region people was non-vegetarian. At time of Harsha's army march some bearers of kitchen appurtenances were bearing goats attached to thongs of pig-skin, a tangle of hanging sparrows and forequarters of venison. Some were bearing collection of young rabbits. It is clear from this description that, meat of goat, deer, birds and rabbits was eaten by people.

Somarasa was main beverage. Somarasa was prepared from plant of Soma. Bana has written, in Dwitiya Uchchhawas of Harṣacarita, that the terraces in front of the doors green with little beds of soma plants all fresh from recent watering –'*sēkasukumāra sōmakēdārikāharitāy amānapraghanāni*'(page-78). When Harsha had said Bana in first meet, as petit-maitre then Bana had opposed and said that I am a Brahman born in the family of the Soma-drinking Vatsyayanas-'*brāhmaṇōsmi jāta: sōmapāyīnāma vaṁśē vātsyāyanānāma*' (Harṣacaritam, Dwitiya Uchchhawas, page-135). It is clear from this description that soma-drinking had became as a symbol of social status. There is mention of rum-booths like shower-baths in royal palace at time of Harsha's birth festival. People also drank wine distilled from mahua flower. Probably, somarasa was beverage of rich and wine distilled from mahua flower was beverage of simple or poor people. It is known from description of Bana that both men and women had drink of wine.

In Harsha-Period main source of drinking water was well. Water was pulled out from well with help of rope and earthen water-pot. Milk was also an important beverage.

Means of entertainment:-

Literary activities, festival, song and music, dancing and singing and different types of game and show etc were means of entertainment. Festivals, which organized on different occasions, were means of entertainment for people. Dance of beautiful women, laughing and joking activities were organised at time of Harsha's birth festival. Royal women were also dancing freely. In this manner, in Kādambarī, there is mention of organizing festival of holi every year in context of south Indian priest. People had brought an old aged slave woman on damaged cot and imitated doing wedding to irritate priest. People enjoy, nowadays also, by laughing and joking on occasion of holi festival.

Song and music was main means of entertainment. Bana has written about king Shudraka that sometimes he played double drumming himself by organizing music programme. Different types of instruments as flute, cymbal, ghungharu, vina, bheri, drum and instruments played by mouth etc were played at time of singing in royal palace. In royal palace doubts about music tones were also solved. King, queen and members of royal family were expert to play different types of musical instruments.

Sometimes dance programme was organized in the royal court. Prostitutes presented dance. Some varavilasinies had also expert in dance and sometimes they presented dance programme in royal court for entertainment of king.

Literary activities as presentation of poem, joking stories, aakhyayika and telling history, solving puzzle, careful study of poem, reciting poem, drawing, elegant speech etc were means of entertainment. Time to time, symposium was organised related to these amusements in royal court. "Symposium of poem, symposium of ancient

Indian learning, symposium of aakhyama, symposium of drawing, symposium of vina, symposium of water and symposium of post etc type different symposiums were grace of royal courts. This healthy tradition was continued from Gupta-Period to medieval and after that."[63]

It is known from descriptions of Bana that different games were organized for entertainment of people. Elephant war and horse racing was organized to entertain people. Kings enjoyed by hunting animals in forests. Some games were indoor games as chess, chaupar and game of ball and dimin etc which were played by sitting in rooms.

In Harṣacarita and Kādambarī there is mention of magicians or jugglers who were expert in deception of the sight and did possible of impossible things. It is clear that those magicians and jugglers also entertained people by their presentation.

A glimpse of livelihood:-

Bana has presented true picture of village livelihood, city livelihood and forest dwelling livelihood consequently through description of forest village of Vindhya forest, Ujjayini city and activities of Shabar army.

Harsha-Vardhana had seen, during march towards Vindhya forest in search of Rajyashri, a forest settlement full of homes of foresters. Bana has presented that forest settlement livelihood so attractive and detailed that colourful picture of village livelihood with its full diversity is looked in front of eye as if we are seeing it by travelling.

There is description of Ujjayini city in Kādambarī. Bana has presented that picture of Ujjayini city, in his ornamental language, in which we find clear glimpse of city fame, prosperity of citizens, architecture of city, roads and markets, continuously presented arts, practice of literature and music etc

Bana has also described about livelihood of foresters along with village livelihood and city livelihood. There is given description, in Kādambarī, of hunting forest animals by Shabar (bheel) army in Vindhya forest. A glimpse of livelihood of forest living castes was found from activities of Shabar army chief and his companions. It is known about body structure and dress of shabars by description of Shabar army chief.

It is known from description of village livelihood, city livelihood and livelihood of foresters, which is given in Harsha Charit and Kādambarī, that society of seventh century was divided at two classes. One class of society was associated with rich who lived in towns. This class had got every type of convenience. Kings, feudatories and businessman were included in this class. Second class was associated with general and poor people. People of this class had problem to obtain even essential commodities. Farmers, workers, servants of royal court, saints and forest living castes were included in this class.

It is concluded from these facts that a gap between rich and poor was also present that time like present. Where rich lived luxurious life other side poor lived their life anyhow. But there were not cases of starvation in India of seventh century, like India of twenty first century. Asensitive historian like Bāṇa Bhaṭṭa must had certainly mentioned that type of incident if it happened. Probably, people of that period had not face problem of starvation because of abundance of natural resources and proper system of distribution.

Indian society of Harsha-Period can be understood entirely from description which is given about Indian society in Harṣacarita and Kādambarī. Society in the seventh century was based on Varna system. Along with some castes and sub-castes were present in contemporary society as – tamoli, rajaka, nishad, shabar (bheel), baheliya, Gandhi, chandal etc Women had respectful place in society but men had supremacy. Bana has also mentioned about living condition of people. It is thrown light on dress of people, ornament and toilet items, health, food and beverage and means of entertainment from description of Bana. Actual and complete picture of society has come in front of us from descriptions of village livelihood, town livelihood and livelihood of foresters. In that picture it appears that society was divided in two classes, where one class had luxurious life in that very place second class had to live his life anyhow.

References:-

1. Buddhist Records of The Western World- Samuel Beal- Low Price Publication Delhi-Page-82.
2. Do- Page-69.
3. Harṣacaritam- Chawkhamba Vidyabhawan Varanasi- Page- 20.
4. Kādambarī - Poorvabhagah- Chawkhamba Vidyabhawan Varanasi- Page- 11-12.
5. Kādambarī : Ek Sanskritik Adhyayana- Dr. Vasudevasarana Agrawal- Chawkhamba Vidyabhawan Varanasi- Page-65-66.
6. Harṣacaritam- Chawkhamba Vidyabhawan Varanasi- Page- 400.
7. Kādambarī - Poorvabhagah- Chawkhamba Vidyabhawan Varanasi- Page-192.
8. Rajvansh: Maukhari aur Pushyabhuti- Prof. Bhagawati Prasad Panthari- Bihar Hindi Granth Akadamy Patna- Page-313-15.
9. The Harṣacarita of Bana- Trans. By E.B.Cowell & F.W.Thomas- Motilal Banarsidass Pvt. Ltd. Delhi- Page-115.
10. Do- Page-122.
11. Kādambarī - Poorvabhagah- Chawkhamba Vidyabhawan Varanasi- Page-362.
12. The Harṣacarita of Bana- Trans. By E.B.Cowell & F.W.Thomas- Motilal Banarsidass Pvt. Ltd. Delhi- Page-258.
13. Kādambarī : Ek Sanskritik Adhyayana- Dr. Vasudevasarana Agrawal- Chawkhamba Vidyabhawan Varanasi- Page-181.
14. The Harṣacarita of Bana- Trans. By E.B.Cowell & F.W.Thomas- Motilal Banarsidass Pvt. Ltd. Delhi- Page-153- 154.
15. Kādambarī - Poorvabhagah- Chawkhamba Vidyabhawan Varanasi- Page-398.
16. Harṣacarita: Ek Sanskritik Adhyayan- Dr. Vasudevasarana Agrawal- Bihar Rastrabhasha Parishad Patna- Page-98-99.
17. Kādambarī - Poorvabhagah- Chawkhamba Vidyabhawan

Varanasi- Page-355-56.

18. The Position of Women in Hindu Civilization- A.S.Altekar- Motilal Banarsidass Pvt. Ltd. Delhi- Page-125.
19. Kādambarī - Poorvabhagah- Chawkhamba Vidyabhawan Varanasi- Page-334.
20. Do- Page-335.
21. Rajvansh: Maukhari aur Pushyabhuti- Prof. Bhagawati Prasad Panthari- Bihar Hindi Granth Akadamy Patna- Page-325.
22. The Position of Women in Hindu Civilization- A.S.Altekar- Motilal Banarsidass Pvt. Ltd. Delhi- Page-172.
23. Kādambarī : Ek Sanskritik Adhyayana- Dr. Vasudevasarana Agrawal- Chawkhamba Vidyabhawan Varanasi- Page-213-14.
24. Harṣacarita: Ek Sanskritik Adhyayan- Dr. Vasudevasarana Agrawal- Bihar Rastrabhasha Parishad Patna- Page-254.
25. Kādambarī - Poorvabhagah- Chawkhamba Vidyabhawan Varanasi- Page-371.
26. The Harṣacarita of Bana- Trans. By E.B.Cowell & F.W.Thomas- Motilal Banarsidass Pvt. Ltd. Delhi- Page-59.
27. Rajvansh: Maukhari aur Pushyabhuti- Prof. Bhagawati Prasad Panthari- Bihar Hindi Granth Akadamy Patna- Page-320.
28. Harṣacarita: Ek Sanskritik Adhyayan- Dr. Vasudevasarana Agrawal- Bihar Rastrabhasha Parishad Patna- Page-151.
29. Do- Page-151.
30. Do- Page-151-52.
31. Do- Page-152-53.
32. Do- Page-97.
33. Do- Page-76.
34. Do- Page-199.
35. Do- Page-153.
36. Do- Page-153-54.

37. Do- Page-154-55.
38. Do- Page-155-56.
39. Do- Page-156.
40. The Harṣacarita of Bana- Trans. By E.B.Cowell & F.W.Thomas- Motilal Banarsidass Pvt. Ltd. Delhi- Page-86.
41. Kādambarī : Ek Sanskritik Adhyayana- Dr. Vasudevasarana Agrawal- Chawkhamba Vidyabhawan Varanasi- Page-53.
42. Harṣacarita: Ek Sanskritik Adhyayan- Dr. Vasudevasarana Agrawal- Bihar Rastrabhasha Parishad Patna- Page-56.
43. Do- Page-15.
44. Do- Page-15.
45. Kādambarī : Ek Sanskritik Adhyayana- Dr. Vasudevasarana Agrawal- Chawkhamba Vidyabhawan Varanasi- Page-56.
46. Harṣacarita: Ek Sanskritik Adhyayan- Dr. Vasudevasarana Agrawal- Bihar Rastrabhasha Parishad Patna- Page-82.
47. Do- Page-76.
48. Kādambarī - Poorvabhagah- Chawkhamba Vidyabhawan Varanasi- Page-210.
49. Do- Page-192.
50. Harṣacarita: Ek Sanskritik Adhyayan- Dr. Vasudevasarana Agrawal- Bihar Rastrabhasha Parishad Patna- Page-24.
51. Do- Page-157-58.
52. Kādambarī - Poorvabhagah- Chawkhamba Vidyabhawan Varanasi- Page-383.
53. Harṣacarita: Ek Sanskritik Adhyayan- Dr. Vasudevasarana Agrawal- Bihar Rastrabhasha Parishad Patna- Page-21.
54. Do- Page-202.
55. Do- Page-46.
56. Kādambarī - Poorvabhagah- Chawkhamba Vidyabhawan Varanasi- Page-135.
57. Indian Costumes- A.Biswas- Publication Division- Page-

105.
58. Harṣacarita: Ek Sanskritik Adhyayan- Dr. Vasudevasarana Agrawal- Bihar Rastrabhasha Parishad Patna- Page-24.
59. Do- Page-190.
60. Indian Costumes- A.Biswas- Publication Division- Page-99.
61. The Harṣacarita of Bana- Trans. By E.B.Cowell & F.W.Thomas- Motilal Banarsidass Pvt. Ltd. Delhi- Page-111-12.
62. Harṣacarita: Ek Sanskritik Adhyayan- Dr. Vasudevasarana Agrawal- Bihar Rastrabhasha Parishad Patna- Page-96.
63. Kādambarī : Ek Sanskritik Adhyayana- Dr. Vasudevasarana Agrawal- Chawkhamba Vidyabhawan Varanasi- Page-25- 26.

■ ■ ■

Chapter-4

Bāṇa Bhaṭṭa and Culture in India during Seventh Century

Indian culture has continuity from beginning to present. Many descents and ascents came in long history of Indian culture. Indian culture has preserved its distinction by enduring attack of different cultures and assimilating them. Indian culture started from Hadappan civilization but its foundation was actually laid at time of Rigvedic and post-rigvedic era. Vedas and Upanishadas are filled with incitements factors of this culture. These incitement factors have disciplined behavior of Indian people from ancient time to present. There are light thrown on different aspects of contemporary Indian culture by books written in different time-slots of Indian history.

There is deliberation of different aspects of Indian culture in Harṣacarita and Kādambarī. These descriptions are expressed uninterrupted about wealthy tradition of Indian culture. Behaviour, tradition, manners and customs of vedic era were also in vogue in Harṣa -period. These are also in vogue now a day.

Samskara:-

There is provision of different Samskaras in Indian culture. "The word Samskara means refinement. It is a religious ceremony of refinement in various stages of life that polished and made a disciplined man of a child unaffected by good or bad."[1] Behind determining Samsakaras this belief was working that person's life spent peacefully endowed with Samskaras. Satisfied, happy and prosperous country is constructed from persons endowed with Samskaras.

It is thrown light on different Samskaras, current in seventh century, from descriptions of Harṣacarita and Kādambarī. At proper place he has mentioned different important Samskaras of birth to death as Garbhadhan, Jatakarma or Namakarana, Karnabhedan, Chudakarma, Upanayan, Samavartana, Vivah, Vanaprastha and Shraddha. Today these Samskaras, those were current in seventh century, are also important part of Indian culture.

First Samskara is Garbhadharana in which women became pregnant by grace of god. In Indian culture, birth of a child is connected with grace or wish of god. It is believed in Indian religious books that god takes birth particularly as form of the individual soul. "Saints have cleared it that one supreme god has born as individual soul by establishing himself in the womb. This tradition is continued after that time when god established first time in the womb. One grandson and son of grandson and that god is radiant in whole world in form of individual soul-

utaiṣā̃ pitōta va putra ēṣāmutaiṣāma jyēṣṭha uta va kaniṣṭha:.

ēkō ha dēvō manasi praviṣṭa: prathamō jātā: sa u garbhē anta:..

- Atharva Veda 10/8/28

[That god (*jivatma*) established again (*sa u*) in the womb (*garbhe antah*), who was born first time (*prathamah jatah*) by entering in mind, as father, son, elder brother, younger brother of many]"[2]

This belief was also in vogue in Harṣa - Period that supreme god establishes himself in the womb in form of individual soul. It is mentioned in Harṣacarita that queen Yashomati saw a dream in three hours' period of night and suddenly awoke with a cry 'Help, my lord! help'. When king asked about dream then the queen replied- "I know now, my lord. I saw in a dream two shining youths issue from the sun's disk, filling the heavens as with radiance of morning, and turning the whole world as it were into lightning. They wore crowns, earrings, armlets, and cuirasses: swords were in their hands: they were bathed in blood cochineal red. The entire world bowed before them with upturned faces and hands joined reverently at their foreheads. Accompanied by one maid like a moon incarnate, who issued from the ray Susumna, they lighted upon the earth, and while I screamed, cut open my womb with a sword and essayed to enter. My heart quaked, and I awoke with a cry to my lord."[3] Then hearing these words the king said to her with delight hearts "Queen, you are dejected at the hour of joy. Your parents' prayers are answered. Our wishes are fulfilled. Our family goddesses have accepted you. In his graciousness the holy god of the radiant crown will grant you joy and that soon, by the gift of three noble children."[4]

In this manner it is mentioned in Kādambarī that king Tarapeed saw a dream that the full moon, like lotus-stalk in elephants mouth, entered in mouth of Vilasavati who was slept on roof of royal palace. Shukanasa, minister of king Tarapeed, expressed his view about this dream that generally dreams came true that were seen in three hours' period of night. So, queen would soon give birth of a child like Mandhata.

In Harṣa -Period childless parents were also distressed like present. They were seen as bad in society. It was considered, that time also, that they were getting that punishment due to their work in former birth. King Tarapeed convinced his queen Vilasavati, who was distressed with childlessness and said "Queen! What can do about this God-controlled object? It is meaningless to cry excessively. We are not suitable for grace of gods. Actually our heart is not suitable to take joy of ambrosia taste like embrace of son. In former birth we had not done work like bright auspicious act. Living creatures get fruits of that acts, in present birth, which were done in former birth. The ordinance of fate, even many efforts, can not be changed. Though man have to do everything those are possible. Queen! From now on you have at most adoration to teachers. Do double pray to gods. Display special affection in reception of saints. The saints are big god. If you will pray them with big efforts then they will grant boon of desire."[5] Mentioning work of queen Vilasavati, according to suggestion of her husband, Bana has written "From now on she started to display respect in adorn of god, pray Brahmans and honour teachers. She did which and where she heard about religious rite, everything for birth of child. She tolerated every type of big troubles by doing this. She slept, on bed of musalas made from kusha, in temple of Durga,where darkness was spread by smoke of continuous burning gugul, by wearing white cloth and without food with pure body. She bathed sitting under good omen cows, endowed with mark of hands made from kumkum etc by old aged Gopies, with gold made pitchers full of auspicious water, attached with different type of flowers and fruits, covered with leaf of the banyan tree and attached with all jewels. She got up in morning. She bestowed gift to Brahmans by putting sesame seed and all jewels in vessel made of gold.

She took auspicious bathe by going at crossroads in night of the fourteenth day of dark half of the month and by sitting in middle of circle made by country doctors and offering different type of sacrifice to give pleasure to guardian deity of all points of the compass. She went to those surrounding temples where offered different items to gods after accomplishment of their work and people had faith in those gods who had fulfilled their desire. She took bath in ponds of famous Nagakulas. She worshipped adoration and circumambulation to the peepal etc trees. After bathing in early morning she offered food, made from curds and unbroken boiled rice, to crows by both hands attached with trembling kankanas fitted with precious stones. She worshipped goddess Amba by offering flower, dhoop, sandle, pooa, meat, kheer and swollen parched rice. She asked questions to medicants with faith by offering vessel filled with food items. She had much faith in prediction of astrologers. She had respect to persons who understood omens. She believed in secret of sacred text that was traditional from old aged people and was in vogue from even. Vilasavati who was eager to see mouth of son caused to recite the Vedas by Brahmans who came to see her. She listened those ancient stories which had recited always. She had fastened tabeej of sacred verse which were written on bhojapatra with gorochana."[6] It is astonishing but true that today Indian people also thought similar like seventh century. Today Indian women also do different religious rites, keep fast and do other activities to obtain a son.

It is tradition of Indian culture that special attention was given on health and care of women in the state of pregnancy. In seventh century all comfortable circumstances were provided to pregnant women in family so that healthy child would bear. It was also taken special emphasis on health and care of pregnant women in modern medical science. Mentioning special care of queen Yashomati, in the state of pregnancy, Bana has written- "Her friends, never for an instant leaving her side, brightened the house, as in anticipation of the approaching birth festival, with eyes wide-open in joy, as though strewing on every side a ceaseless protective charm in the shape of a rain of blooming lotus petals, white red and blue. Great physicians holding various herbs sat in their proper places, supporting her as the mountains support the earth."[7]

A special room was provided for women in the state of pregnancy that was called Sootikagriha. In sootikagriha special arrangements were made to provide security to mother and child and to protect them from different violent outbreak. In Kādambarī it is described detailed in context of description of queen Vilasavati's sootikagriha. Today this tradition is also in vogue in Indian villages with some changes but intention is same.

According to description of Bana Jagaran of sixth night and Uthavan programme was performed on ninth day of child's birth. On this occasion kings were bestowed cows and gold to Brahmans on auspicious moment. On tenth day Namakarana Samskara was performed in which name was given to newborn child. Discussing about her Namakarana Samskara Mahashveta said to Chandrapeedaa "My father had, because of childless, welcomed my birth more than son's birth. Then on tenth day, according to ritual, my name was given Mahashveta. That name was according to my beauty."[8] Distinguishing features of the child were kept in mind while giving name. Son of Tarapeed was given name Chandrapeeda because a dream that the moon was entered in mouth of his mother was related to his birth.

Certainly, Karnabhedana Samskara was also in vogue in seventh century. There is description, in Harṣacarita and Kādambarī, about wearing kundala and other ornaments in ear by men and women. Though Karnabhedana Samskara is not mentioned in descriptions of Bana but it is indicated from ear ornaments that Karnabhedana Samskara was in vogue. Ear of men and women were pierced.

Describing about Chudakarma Samskaras, in Kādambarī, Bana has written that in future Chudakarma etc Samskara's were completed of Chandrapeeda and gradually childhood was spent- '*kramēṇa kṛtacūḍākaranādi kriyākalāpasya śaiśavamatīcakrāma candrapīdasya*' (Kādambarī, page-158). The first shaving of a child's head was performed in Chudakarma Samskara and lock of unshaved hair was spare according to family tradition.

After Chudakarma Samskara two important Samskara were performed - Upanayana and Samavartana. The samskara in which child was sent to Gurukul (school) for education was called Upanayana Samskara. Auspicious moment was decided for this samskara. It is mentioned in Kādambarī that king Tarapeed handed over Chandrapeeda to teachers, along with Vaishampayan in an auspicious day and moment, for obtaining all type of knowledge. The Samskara in which students came back home with permission of teacher after obtaining all type of knowledge was called Samavartana. In Kādambarī Bana has written "king Tarapeed sent army chief Balahaka along with many horsemen and foot soldiers to bring Chandrapeeda, in auspicious moment, when he knew that Chandrapeeda had become youth and practiced all arts and obtained all knowledge."[9] It is known from descriptionn of Kādambarī that Upanayana Samskara was performed at age of six years and after ten year education Samavartan Samskara was performed at age of sixteen years. Army chief Balahaka told Chandrapeeda "After leaving home it is your tenth year in school. You had come here when you were six years old. Now you are entered in sixteen year including these years. So you have to meet mothers after departure from here and enjoy luxurious life of youth according to your mind and take the enjoyment of throne after worshiping feet of teachers."[10]

There is provision of Grihasthashrama (the second or domestic stage of life) in Indian culture. This ashrama (stage of life) is important to all ashramas because it grants four Purusharthas (goal of man) i.e. Dharma, Artha, Kama and Moksha. In Rigveda it was advised people to remain in Grihasthashrama-

ihaivasta mā vi yauṣṭama viśvamāyuvaryaśnutama .
krīṛantau putairnaptṛbhimēdimānau sva gṛhē ..

Rigveda 10/85/42

In other words, remain in Grihasthashrama and get full age without opposing anyone. Stay at your home and be joyful by playing with son, grandson and make home an ideal.

People entered in Grihasthashrama after completion of Vivah Samskara (Marriage). Generally this samskara was completed after education and starting of adolescence. It can be considered from description of Bana that wedding of boys was completed after age of sixteen years. It seems from description of Rajyashri's wedding, that is given in Harṣacarita, that wedding of girls was completed in starting of adolescence i.e. in age of fourteen-fifteen years.

It is known from description of Harṣacarita that wedding proposal was sent from boy's side to girl side in seventh century. It is mentioned in Harṣacarita that Grahvarma, the Maukhari king, had sent proposal of wedding with Rajyashri to Prabhakara-Vardhana.

It was indicated, from descriptions of Harṣacarita and Kādambarī, different types of weddings as Brahma Vivah, Rakshasa Vivah and Gandharva Vivah were in vogue. Wedding of Rajyashri and Grahvarma, described in Harṣacarita, was Brahma Vivah because in this wedding father of Rajyashri had selected Grahvarma to bestow her daughter. Describing characteristics of Shabars Bana has mentioned that wives of others, who were brought forcefully, are their wives- 'kalatrani bandigriheetah parayoshitah' (Kādambarī, page-67). Doing wedding forcefully without wish of women was called Rakshasa Vivah. Thus there was tradition of Rakshasa Vivah in Shabaras. Wedding of Chandrapeeda & Kādambarī and Pundarika & Mahashveta, mentioned in Kādambarī was Gandharva Vivah because they had liked each-other and wedded willingly.

There is light thrown on wedding system by wedding of Rajyashri and Grahvarma which is described in Harṣacarita. Wedding proposal was taken to consideration with family members and their consent was taken. King Prabhakara-Vardhana had discussed on wedding proposal of Grahavarman with his queen and sons then in the presence of the whole royal household, he poured the betrothal water. It is known from description of Harṣacarita that Grahavarman entered in Kautika Griha (Kohabara), on time of auspicious moment for wedding after arrival of marriage procession, where he saw Rajyashri. Then he came out of kohabara took Rajyashri by the hands and marched round the fire with Rajyashri. "Here Bana had mentioned first kohabara and latter work of march round the fire, that is tradition of Punjab, which is also in vogue in Kurukshetra. It is changed in area of Delhi-Meratha. Work of march round the fire is performed first and worship by women in front of gods mark, made by the palm on the wall, has performed latter."[11] Grahavarman bowed with Rajyashri to their parents after completion of wedding. Then he entered in Vas Griha (sleeping room) where its portals were figured the spirits of Preeti (love) and Rati (joy). One side figured the god of love holding bow and arrow. There is mention of Kamadeva with Preeti and Rati in Mandasor-script of Bandhuvarma: shloka13; Matsyapurana 162/54-55; *prīti: syā: dakṣiṇē tasya ... ratiśca vāmapārśvē tu.* Grahavarman spent ten days in his father's house and then he managed to secure his dismissal with provisions named in dowry and his bride to his native country. It is clear from this description that dowry was in vogue in seventh century.

"Women were married, as Hiuen-Tsang had mentioned, once. So describing devotion of Gajasadhanadhikrit feudal king Skandagupta to his lord, in Harṣacarita, Bana has written that he had Prasad (favour) of his prabhu (dev Harṣa) like a noble wife and fast fixed by love to one lord-*ēkabhartṛbhaktiniścalāma kulānganāmīva prabhūprasāda bhūmimārūṛha:* (Shashtha Uchchhawas, page-350)."[12]

In Harṣa -Period there were different types of religious practices, persuasions and worships to escape from death, grief and recover from illness. Describing activities of people, at time of king Prabhakara-Vardhana's illness, for his health Bana has written "Here loving kinsmen were keeping a fast to appease Ahibradhna, lying before his image. There were young nobles burning themselves with lamps to propitiate the Mothers. In one place a Dravidian was ready to solicit the Vampire with the offering of a skull. In another an Andhra man was holding up his arms like a rampart to conciliate Candi. Elsewhere distressed young servants were pacifying Mahakala by holding melting gum on their beads. In another place a group of relatives was intended on an oblation of their own flesh, which they severed with keen knives. Elsewhere again young courtiers were openly resorting to the sale of human flesh."[13] It is clear from this description that this type of belief was in vogue in all religious sects of that time. They believe that gods would please with these works and grief and contention would die out.

It is light thrown, from description of Harṣacarita, on rituals done after death. After death people carried dead body to the crematorium on bank of river, funeral rites were performed by putting fire into the mouth of dead, sraddha ceremony was done and Pinda offered (cake or ball of meal) to paternal ancestors. Bana has written that Harṣa had self taking upon proffered shoulders the bier of king Prabhakara-Vardhana. The feudatories and townsmen headed by the family priest had bore the bier to the river Sarasvati where funeral rites performed upon a pyre befitting an emperor. Describing offering water to his father by Harṣa and having bath for funeral work Bana had written "In the empty audience chamber the clamorous cry of 'Victory' was still. Thus the prince passed on to the Sarasvati's bank, and having bathed in the river, offered water to his father. After the funeral bath, he stayed not to wring his hair, but having put on a pair of white silk robes, proceeded home full of sighs, umbrella-less, with none to clear his path, and, though a horse was led up, on foot."[14] Describing Daskarma Samskara of Prabhakara-Vardhana and bestow gift to Brahmanas Bana had written "The Brahman who consumes the departed spirit's first oblation had now partaken of his meal. The horror of the days of impurity had passed. The various appurtenances of the royal bier, beds, chairs, chowries, umbrellas, vessels, carriages, swords and the like, now become an eyesore, were in course of distribution to Brahmans. The bones, in shape like sorrow's spearheads, had been carried with the people's hearts to sacred fords. A monument in brick had been set up on the sepulchral pile. The royal elephant, victor in mighty battles, had been abandoned to the woods."[15] Pinda was offered for peace of dead soul. It is mentioned in Ashtam Uchchhawas of Harṣacarita that Harṣa devotedly waited upon Rajyashri in her sorrow and made her and her attendants partake of the food prepared for the panda offerings in honour of her husband. It is mentioned in Pratham Uchchhawas that all white were Mandakini's banks with the pindas to the manes let fall by Brahma when purified by bathing.

Shraddh has special importance in different important activities those were performed after death. Shraddh is a medium to display respect to the departed soul. Tradition of shraddh has been in vogue till now from ancient time. Throwing light on importance of shraddh in Indian culture Shri Mohanalala Mahato Viyogi has written "It had been important characteristic in Arya life that they had been rebellious to narrowness, inferiority and smallness. Everywhere they had fought against these evils. The life of Arya had made efforts to make mind broader. It is very reason that in Arya family not only his mother, father, wife, son, brother etc had important place but paternal ancestors, also going after them in heaven, had tightened in tie of shraddha. God, saints all were worshipped by family of Arya. As far as tree, animal, birds these all were affectionately worshipped by family of Arya.

A householder of Athara (4/34/7) has bestowed four earthen water-pot filled with milk and four earthen water-pot filled with water to his parental ancestors with this belief that they would be nurtured with milk and water where ever they present.-

catura: kumbhamaścaturdhā dadāmi

śrīrēṇa pūrṇā: udakēna daghnā .

ētāstvā dhārā upayantu sarvā: svargē lōkē madhumata

vintamānā upatvā tiṣṭhantu puṣkariṇī samantā: ..

It has said in second mantra (Yajurveda 2/34) –

ūrja bahantīramṛtama kṛtama payaḥ kīlālama pariśratama ..2..

svadhā stha tarpayata mē̃ pitdṛna ..

[It is flowing water, milk, juicy grain and juice of ripe and fallen sweet fruit. Paternal ancestors, stayed in haven, you would satisfied.]

It is an extraordinary virtue to express respect and make connection with persons who are dead or stayed in heaven. This is other fact that dead person are in condition to accept or not to accept this type of respects but a happy Arya family did not forget them. Along with hospitality, work related to god, alms etc he remembered dead family members or paternal ancestors with full respect. This work was considered auspicious act. It was auspicious duty, supported with religion, for any Arya householder that he did not restrict himself to live by earning and maintenance of family members, he also carried on religious tasks as yagya, offering to god, pitriyagya etc. Some tasks were daily and some were performed on special occasions."[16]

Astrology and Palmistry:-

It is known from descriptions of Harṣacarita and Kādambarī that in Harṣa -Period auspicious moment was counted before begining of any auspicious work. Astrologers determined auspicious moment on base of situation of heavenly bodies. Astrologers were able to predict future on base of their knowledge. Describing an astrologer named Taraka, who had reached in royal palace at time of Harṣa 's birth, Bana has written "At that very time instant approached the astrologer Taraka, a man very highly esteemed by the king. Hundreds and hundreds of times he had shown supernatural insight by announcing facts beyond the ken of man, a calculator, deeply read in all the treatises on astronomy, extolled and liked among all astrologers, endowed with knowledge of the three times, and a Maga."[17] Astrologer Taraka had predicted that this child (Harṣa) would become Chakravarti king. People of India had belief continuously on astrology in every era. In India people have also belief in astrology even in twenty first century. Every day good and ill consequences of the zodiac are published in newspapers. People cause to make their horoscope with help of computer. Astrologers solve different problems, sitting in studios of different television channels, with the help of laptops.

In seventh century prophecy was made on base of sign and lines that were present in palm and the soul of the foot. It is mentioned in Harṣa Chartia that auspicious marks such as the lotus, the shell, the fish and the makara were present in the soul of Harṣa 's foot which told of his sovereignty over the four ocean- '*jalajaśaṁkhamīnamakarasanāthatalayā kathitacaturambhōdhibhōgacinhāviva caranau dadhānama*' (Harṣacaritam, Dwitiya Uchchhawas, page-123). It is described, in Kadambri, about auspicious marks those were present in palm and the sole of the foot of Chandrapeeda. His both hands were marked with sign of the shell and the wheel like god Vishnu and auspicious lines. Both foots were decorated with mark of flag, chariot, horse and umbrella and the lotus mark. It was concluded on base of these marks that Chandrapeed had sign of Chakravarti kings. People believe, even today, on prophecies on the basis of lines of palm.

Hospitality and Humbleness:-

Guests were considered as god in Indian culture. Here hospitality has a long tradition. It is thrown light on hospitality that was in vogue in seventh century from descriptions of Bana. It is known from description of Harṣacarita and Kādambarī those feet of guests were wiped with cloth after washing. After that they took breakfast after seating. People took food after feeding the guest. About hospitality of Kapinjala Mahashveta told "Instantly I had greeted respectfully by standing up and self spread out mast for him (Kapinjala). When he sat then I had washed, he would not consent, his foot and wiped with my shawl and sat on free ground space with him."[18] In this manner describing greet respectfully by Kādambarī to Mahashveta and Chandrapeeda Bana has written "Kādambarī had washed foot of Mahashveta with own hands and sat on bed after wiped that by her shawl. Her trusting and fast friend Madalekha, beautiful like Kādambarī, had washed, feet of Chandrapidm though he had not consent."[19] Sometimes later when Kādambarī was to give betel leaf to Mahashveta then Mahashveta had said "friend Kādambarī! It is our duty to give respect first to new coming guest. So you give betel leaf first to him."[20] This tradition of hospitality had been special characteristics of Indian culture which is also continued today.

There is given special emphasis on humbleness in Indian culture. Cultured and humble people were praised in religious books. People had criticized harshly who have bitterness, enemity and jealousy. Indians are naturally humble. Describing the behaviour of people of Ujjayini, in Kādambarī, Bana has written that they are humble even though they are mighty (*virenapivinayavata*).

"Show courtesy to respected people, teacher, acharya etc is said as 'jewell' of influential or great people in Harṣacarita and said jewellery as only stone in comparison to courtesy- '*alankārō hi paramārthata: prabhavatāma praśrayātiśaya: , ratnādikastū śīlabhāra:*'(Ashtam Uchchhawas, page-427).

It is mentioned in Harṣacarita that when a student of Shaiva saint Bhairavacharya reached to meet king Pushyabhuti then king greeted him with respectful words and after seated him he talked to him-'*kṣitipatirapyugatamucitēna cainamādarēnānvagrahīta āsīnama ca prapraccha*'- (Tritiya Uchchhawas, page-173).

And saint addressed king as 'Mahabhaga' respectfully.

Kings addressed saints as 'Bhagavan' or 'Bhagvan' with courtesy. When acharya Bhairavacharya met king then he addressed king with 'Svasti' word in low sound- '*gangāpravāhahrādagambhīrayā girā svastiśabdamakarōta*'

And king greeted respectfully at a distance (on seeing) by bowing his head – '*dūrāvanata: praṇāmabhinavama cakāra*;

When acharya requested king Pushyabhuti to seat on his own tiger-skin then he answered with courtesy that a teacher's seat should be like himself respected, not desecrated and then he seated himself on a rug (asana) brought by his attendants-'*mānanīyama ca guruvannōllanghanamarahatī gurōrāsanama*'; And when Bhairavacharya reached in royal palace to meet king Pushyabhuti then showing modesty – king bestowed himself with inner-palace, attendants and treasury-'*tasmai ca rājā sānta:puraṁ saparijanama sakōṣamātmānama nivēditavāna'* (Do, page-179-81).

Deva Harṣa also addressed acharya Divakaramitra 'Bhagavan' and 'Bhadanta' when he met him in the forest of Vindhyatavi and not accepted to seat on acharya's seat with courtesy and sat down on ground in front of him and told with courtesy – 'the labour of offering me a seat seems only to make me a stranger- '*parakaraṇamivā sanādi dānōpacāra cēṣṭitama . kṣitāvēvōpāviśata*' (Ashtam Uchchhawas, page-426-27).

Kings were addressed with 'tat', 'dhiman' and 'mahabhaga' by acharyas, saints and medicants etc. (Tritiya Uchchhawas, page- 180 and Ashtam Uchchhawas, page-430-31).

According to description of Harṣacarita young-old, man-woman different words were used for addresses were as follow- Bhadra (for respected people), Ayushman (by teacher for his student and by old for young), Mahanubhav (for man related to high class), Mahanubhava and Bhadre (for women related to high class), Ayushmati, Kalyanini, Punyamati, Arye (for old aged women). (Ashtam Uchchhawas,page-436-37)."[21]

"It is written in Harṣacarita, by displaying different types of respectful greeting and expression of affection between young-old, when Bana reached to his village after meeting with

Harṣa – 'In due course Bana greeted some and was greeted by others, was kissed head by some (by elders), and kissed head of others (to younger), was embraced by some (by elders) and embraced others (to younger), was welcomed with a blessing by some, welcomed other by blessing and when elders were seated, he took a seat brought by his excited attendants-'*kramēṇa ca kā̃śrcidabhivādayamāna: kaiśrcidabhivādyamāna: kaiśrcicchirasi cumbyamāna, kā̃śrcinmūrdhi , kaiścidālingayamāna: kā̃śrcidālingana, anyērāśiṣānugṛhyamāṇa:, parananugṛhanana ... sambhrāntaparijanōpanītama cāsanamāsinēṣu guruṣu bhējē* '- (Tritiya Uchchhawas, page-143).

After father's death when Rajya-Vardhana returned after completing battle against Hunas then extending his long stout arms he clasped his younger brother Harṣa 's neck and touched his chest, neck, shoulder and cheek-'*sudūraprasāritēna ... dīrghēna dōradaṇḍadvaēna gṛhītvā kaṇṭhē ...vakṣasi punaḥ kaṇṭhē punaḥ skandhabhāgē punaḥ kapōlōdarē nidhāya*'- (Shashtha Uchchhawas, page-311-12)."[22]

There are described different styles to express respectfull greeting in Harṣacarita and Kādambarī. According to Bana, following were styles to express respectful greetings-

1. with the four parts of the body

2. by touching earth to head

3. by touching knee, hand and head on earth

4. by bowing head towards earth

5. by bowing in ground with expanded both hands

6. by putting knee and palms on earth

7. by holding foots

8. by touching hand on ground

9. by embracing courtyard with the five parts of the body

10. by rubbing head on upper part of foot.

Confirming the description of respectful greetings, those were in vogue and similar to these types of respectful greetings, Hiuen-Tsang had written “There are nine methods of showing outward respect- (1) by selecting words of a soothing character in making requests; (2) by bowing the head to show respect; (3) by raising the hands and bowing; (4) by joining the hands and bowing low; (5) by bending the knee; (6) by a prostration; (7) by a prostration on hands and knees; (8) by touching the ground with the five circles; (9) by stretching the five parts of the body on the ground.

Of these nine methods the most respectful is to make one prostration on the ground and then to kneel and loud the virtues of the one addressed. When at a distance it is usual to bow low; when near, then it is customary to kiss the feet and rub the ankles (of the person addressed).”[23]

Yamapatta:-

There is laid special stress on purification of character in Harṣa -Period. There is criticized sinful act and people were motivated to do good behavior. It was also believed in Harṣa -Period like present that when man dead, who had been involved in sinful act, the agents of Dharmaraja (god of justice), took away his soul in hell. That man had to suffer that type of the pangs of hell as he had done work on earth. Big sizes of Yamapatta were displayed on crowded places, to restrain people from sinful act. Paintings related to results of sinful act were displayed with drawing of Yamaraja in thoseYamapattas. It is mentioned in Harṣacarita that when Harṣa reached the market of skandhavar, by hearing news of father’s illness, then he saw Yamapattika, the shower of Yamapatta. Bana has written “No sooner had he entered than in the bazaar street amid a great crowed of inquisitive children he observed an Inferno-showman, in whose left hand was a painted canvas stretched out on a support of upright rods and showing the lord of the dead mounted on his dreadful buffalo. Wielding a reed-wand in his other hand, he was expounding the features of the next world, and could be heard to chant the following verse:-

Mothers and fathers in thousands, in hundreds children and
wives
Age after age have passed away: whose are they, and
whose art thou?"[24]

It is clear from this description that Yamapattas were medium to publicity for messages. It is also known from this description that there were appointed special employees to spell out these messages which were called 'Yamapattika'.

Yamapatta were like modern advertisement hoardings. The only difference was that advertisement hoarding is used for publicity of product whenever Yamapatta was used for publicity of morality. About motive of Yamapatta C.Sivaramamurti had written "The psychology of depicting such scenes for people with a religious bent of mind is to avail of the opportunity, when the mind is receptive, to present ideas that could have a permanent impression and so determine their future conduct."[25]

Even today a miniature of Yamapatta in form of calendar, that gave message like Yamapatt, are found in Indian markets.

Opinion of bad Omen:-

It is known from description of Harṣacarita and Kādambarī that in seventh century people were regarded twitching of the eyelid and activities of animal-birds as bad omen. Twitching of the left eye had been regarded as bad omen. When Harṣa was hunting in the skirts of the Himalayas then one night he saw a dream and his left eye incessantly throbbed (*dakṣiṇētaramakṣi paspandē*). Instantly after that he received news of his father's illness. Mahashveta told in Kādambarī "My right eye, informer of bad omen, incessantly throb (*durnimitanivēdakamaspandata dakṣiṇamalōcanama*). From this I doubt in my mind that now god has created a new misfortune."[26] It is mentioned in Harṣacarita that while Harṣa was commanding his march for a world-wide conquest then he installed his right arm, which by a reminding throb at the moment brought itself as it were to notice, in the office of subduing the eighteen continents. It is clear from this description that throbbing right was regarded as auspicious and it indicated to obtain something.

Deer, passing from right to left, uttering dreadful cry by crow, coming lampblack naked saint straight against, howling jackals by open mouth in direction of sky and uttering dreadful cry by vulture etc were considered as symbol of bad omen. When Harṣa was about to depart, by hearing news of father's illness, then there taken place three ill omens. "Deer passed away from right to left, facing the sun's flaming circle, a crow on a burnt-out tree ultered its dreadful cry and straight against him came a naked Jain, bedecked with peacock's tail-feather, a fellow all lampblack as it seemed with the collected filth of many days besmirching his body. According to book of omen above mentioned all three matters were considered as bad omen. It is right for deer that it takes out by circumambulating lion, if it gives its left to lion then it indicates death of lion: *vināśamupasthitama rājasīhasya*. It is said in Kādambarī that if a deer passes away circumambulating a woman then it is bad for that women: *prasthitāmivāna dhiṣṭadakṣiṇa vatmṛgāgamanāma*. According to Vrihatsamhita (95/19) if crow utters facing sun by seeing towards east then happened royal fear. Meaning of nagnatak was naked Jain or Digambar. Amatya Rakshasa had said, in Mudrarakshasa (anka 4), bad omen to seeing kshapanaka."[27]

It is described in Harṣacarita that at time of Prabhakara-Vardhana's illness there happened many bad omens in royal palace. "Bana had said sixteen mighty signs, thus- earthquake, the ocean rolled with waves noisily plashing upon each other, seeing comet high in heavenly spaces, seeing then also beneath a sky, in the sun's circle shorn of its radiance and lurid as a bowl of heated iron, seating moon in the round rim of flaming halo, the quarters glowed red as though they had in anticipation entered fire, flowing showers of bloody dew on the earth, blocking the portals of the heavens with untimely masses of dark cloud, heat-riving bursts of thunder-storms, dimming brilliance of the sun by dust-showers, discordant howling by rows of jackals lifted high their muzzles, disheveling locks of the family goddesses, ranging feverishly about the Lion Throne by a swarm of bees, the croak of crows hovering above the women's quarter, , swooping upon a bit of a gem fitted in the Lion Throne like a piece of juicy meat by an old vulture. These types of bad omens or mighty signs were very popular at time of Bana. There is described in detail about these types of mighty signs and bad omens in Vrihatsamhita written by Varahamihir."[28]

Auspicious and Inauspicious Dream:-

There is mention of different types of auspicious and inauspicious dreams in Harṣacarita and Kādambarī. There was conception, in Harṣa -Period, that dreams seen in last hours' period of night or daybreak would become true. This type of thinking is also current today. In seventh century dreams were divided in two categories- auspicious and inauspicious. When Rajya-Vardhana had gone for battle against the king of Malwa then Harṣa had seen in a dream that a heaven kissing pillar of iron broken in pieces. Harṣa's heart was throbbing by result of this dram because this type of dream was considered as inauspicious. In Kādambarī there is mention of the dream of king Tarapeed in which he had seen that the full moon had entered in mouth of Vilasavati. Sukanasa, minister, cheered by hearing about that dream and told king that soon he would see mouth of son. It is known from this description that this type of dream was considered as auspicious.

Tantra-Mantra Shriparvata:-

Astonishing place has special importance in Indian culture. Some places became famous for fulfilling heart's desire of people. People had travelled that places to solve their different problems. It is known from description of Bana that Shriparvata was famous for astonishing result. Praying for victory of Harṣa Bana had written – "victorious is Harṣa who guards the world by a wall of fire of glorious majesty-Shriparvata for fulfilling the desires of all his friends."[29] Dr. Vasudevasharana Agrawal's opinion, about Shriparvata, is – "Fame of Shriparvata, situated in Andhrapradesh, was spread everywhere at time of Bana. That was considered as centre of charm and miracles. People were visited to shriparvata for fulfilling their heart's desire: *sakalapraṇayīmanōrathasiddhiśrīparvata:*. It was people's thinking that shriparvata was protected by a wall of fire burnt around that. Shankar had quoted that Shiva had created a ring of vehement fire to protect from difficulty created by Ganesha at time of Tripurdahana and that very fire protects shriparvata. Bana had written this hearsay. Shriparvata is mentioned in Teerthayatra Parva of the Mahabharata and written that Mahadeva with devi and Brahma with gods stayed on Shriparvata. Shriparvata is recognized as Shrishaila which is situated on south bank of Krishna River and far away eighty two mile from Kurnool in direction of Ishanakona. Here Mallikarjuna named Shivalinga, one of twelve jyotirlingas, is situated. According to Shrishailasthalamahatmya Chandravati, daughter of King Chandragupta had sent a garland for Mallikarjuna Shiva of Shrishaila. Shri Altekara had recognized Chandravati as daughter of the Gupta king Chandragupta and as Prabhavati gupta queen of the Vakataka king. It is known that there was arrangement of a garland made by her to worship daily on Shrishaila. Certainly Shriparvata was famous for astonishing fulfillment at time of Bana and south Indian old priests of that place were cause to worshipped as written in Kādambarī: *śrīparvatāścaryavārttāsahastrābhijñēna jaraddravida dharmikēna.*"[30]

Other Opinions:-

Some other opinions, those were current, are also mentioned in Harṣacarita and Kādambarī. Some opinions of them are also in vogue today. Cow dung was considered as auspicious and ground was smeared with that. It is mentioned in Kādambarī that ground of Jabali's adobe was smeared with cow dung (*haritagōmayōṣalēpanaviviktatalasya*).

People were tied auspicious thread coloured in liquid of gorochana on occasion of wedding etc. People were gave away alms on different occasions. Harṣa was gave away his accumulated wealth for charity on every five year.

People have persuasions to obtain desired things. It is mentioned in Kādambarī that king Tarapeeda was grateful after seeing his son's mouth because he had got this good fortune after thousand persuasions.

Children wore locket in neck made of nail of tigers, to protect from evil spirit of ghosts and spirits and evil eye. It is mentioned in Harṣacarita that Harṣa's neck was ornamented with a row of great tiger's claws linked with gold (*hāṭakabaddhavikaṭavyāghra nakhapanktimanḍitagrīvakē*).Musta-rd was also put on Harṣa 's head to protect him.

People of seventh century had belief in existence of ghosts, spirits and fiend. They believed that ghosts, spirits and fiend live on trees of cremation ground and ugly persons born as fiend. People also thought that ghost and fiend possessed people or people were possessed by an evil spirit.

It can be concluded that it is helpful to understand different aspects of Indian culture from descriptions of Bāṇa Bhaṭṭa . Different samskaras, which are described in Indian religious books, were in vogue in seventh century. Thinking and behaviour of people was affected by these samskaras that were determined for birth to death. Shradh and Pindadana were performed after death to satisfy soul of paternal ancestors. Some samskaras, that were current that time, are also in vogue today. People had belief on astrology and palmistry. By reading tradition of alms, style to greet respectfully, different bad omens, auspicious and inauspicious dreams and traditions it seems that Indian culture had a long tradition which is continued today.

References:-

1. Some Aspects of Indian Culture- C. Sivaramamurti- Publication Division- New Delhi- Page-143.
2. Arya Jivan Darshan- Shri Mohan Lal Mahato 'Viyogi'- Bihar Hindi Granth Akadamy Patna- Page-100.
3. The Harṣacarita of Bana- Trans. By E.B.Cowell & F.W.Thomas- Motilal Banarsidass Pvt. Ltd. Delhi- Page-105.
4. Do- Page-105.
5. Kādambarī- Poorvabhagah- Chawkhamba Vidyabhawan Varanasi- Page-133-34.
6. Do- Page-137-39.
7. The Harṣacarita of Bana- Trans. By E.B.Cowell & F.W.Thomas- Motilal Banarsidass Pvt. Ltd. Delhi- Page-109.
8. Kādambarī- Poorvabhagah- Chawkhamba Vidyabhawan Varanasi- Page-287.
9. Do- Page-163.
10. Do- Page-164.

11. Harṣacarita: Ek Sanskritik Adhyayan- Dr. Vasudevasarana Agrawal- Bihar Rastrabhasha Parishad Patna- Page-84.
12. Rajvansh: Maukhari aur Pushyabhuti- Prof. Bhagawati Prasad Panthari- Bihar Hindi Granth Akadamy Patna- Page-333.
13. The Harṣacarita of Bana- Trans. By E.B.Cowell & F.W.Thomas- Motilal Banarsidass Pvt. Ltd. Delhi- Page-135-36.
14. Do- Page-160.
15. Do- Page-164.
16. Arya Jivan Darshan- Shri Mohan Lal Mahato 'Viyogi'- Bihar Hindi Granth Akadamy Patna- Page-93-94.
17. The Harṣacarita of Bana- Trans. By E.B.Cowell & F.W.Thomas- Motilal Banarsidass Pvt. Ltd. Delhi- Page-109-10.
18. Kādambarī- Poorvabhagah- Chawkhamba Vidyabhawan Varanasi- Page-313.
19. Do- Page-392-93.
20. Do- Page-394.
21. Rajvansh: Maukhari aur Pushyabhuti- Prof. Bhagawati Prasad Panthari- Bihar Hindi Granth Akadamy Patna- Page-335-37.
22. Do- Page-339.
23. Buddhist Records of The Western World- Samuel Beal- Low Price Publication Delhi-Page-85.
24. The Harṣacarita of Bana- Trans. By E.B.Cowell & F.W.Thomas- Motilal Banarsidass Pvt. Ltd. Delhi- Page-136.

25. Some Aspects of Indian Culture- C. Sivaramamurti- Publication Division- New Delhi- Page-47.
26. Kādambarī- Poorvabhagah- Chawkhamba Vidyabhawan Varanasi- Page-333.
27. Harṣacarita: Ek Sanskritik Adhyayan- Dr. Vasudevasarana Agrawal- Bihar Rastrabhasha Parishad Patna- Page-89-90.
28. Do- Page-97.
29. Harṣacaritam- Chawkhamba Vidyabhawan Varanasi- Page-11.

30. Harṣacarita: Ek Sanskritik Adhyayan- Dr. Vasudevasarana Agrawal- Bihar Rastrabhasha Parishad Patna- Page-08-09.

■■■

Chapter-5

Bāṇa Bhaṭṭa and Religion in India during Seventh Century

We get a detail description of religion in India during seventh century from Harṣacarita and Kādambarī. There were mainly three religions – Hindu (Brahman religion), Bauddh and Jain in India. Different communities were also existed in these religions. It is thrown light, from description of Bāṇa Bhaṭṭa , on worship system, tradition of continuously doing Yagya, tendency of general people about religion along with religious faith of the kings of Puṣyabhūti clan. Describing Ujjayini, in Kādambarī, Bana has written that there were temples established on crossroads. Different gods were worshipped by establishing in temple.

The kings of Puṣyabhūti clan had faith in the Hindu religion (Brahman religion). Mentioning religious faith of king Puṣyabhūti, in Harṣacarita, Bana has written "Wherefore from boyhood upwards he, untaught by any man, entertained a great, almost inborn, devotion towards Shiva the adorable, readily won by faith, upholder of the universe, creator of creatures, annihilator of existence. From all other gods he turned away. Not even in drams did he take food without worshipping him whose emblem is the bull. Devoted to the Lord of Beings, the increate, ageless, guru of the immortals, the foe of the Demons' City, the lord of countless Hosts, spouse of the Daughter of the Mountains, him before whose feet all world bow, he thought the three spheres void of all other deities. The dispositions of his subjects also were conformable to their monarch's mind. Thus: - house by house the holy lord of the Cleaving Axe was worshipped: the winds blowing in those pure districts were fragrant with much resin melted in the sacrificial pits, they dropped a rain of dew from the milk used for bathing, and they whirled along petals of Bel twig chaplets. It was with gifts and presents customary in Civa's worship that the king was honoured by citizens, dependants, councilors, and neighbouring sovereigns, whom his arm's might had conquered and made tributary. Thus: - they gratified his heart with huge Civa bulls white as Kailasa's peaks, and ringed about their horn-tips with gold-leaf creepers; with golden ewers, with oblation vessels, censers, flowered cloth, lamps on jeweled stands, Brahmanical threads, and *mukhakocas* inlaid with bits of precious gems. His queens also complied with his desire, voluntarily undertaking the threshing of the scattered rice, deepening the glow of their hands by staining the temples with unguents, occupying all their attendants in stringing flowers."[1]

It is clear from this description that king Puṣyabhūti, founder of Puṣyabhūti clan, was not only devotee of Shiva but nurturing the Shaiva persuasion. King Puṣyabhūti had laid foundation of Puṣyabhūti dynasty after defeating Shrikanth Naga with help of Mahashaiva Bhairavachary of south India.

In Puṣyabhūti clan a king was born in course of time a king of kings, named Prabhākaravardhana , famed far and wide under a second name Pratapashila. Real founder of Puṣyabhūti dynasty was Prabhakar-Vardhana. Prabhākaravardhana had proceeded traditional religion of Puṣyabhūti clan. Describing attachement to Hindu religion of Prabhākaravardhana Bana had written "Beneath his rule the golden age seemed to bud forth in close packed lines of sacrificial posts, the evil time to flee in the smoke of sacrifices meandering over the sky, heaven to descend in stuccoed shrines, Dharma to blossom in white pennons waving over temple minarets, the villages to bring forth a progeny of beautiful arbours erected on their outskirts for meetings, alms' houses, inns, and women's marquees, Mount Meru to crumble in a wealth of utensils all of gold, a very cornucopia to bear fruit in bowls of riches lavished upon Brahmans."[2]

Prabhākaravardhana entirely devoted to Sun. In Harhsa Charita it is mentioned "The king was by natural proclivity a devotee of the sun. Day by day at sunrise he bathed, arrayed himself in white silk, wrapt his head in a white cloth, and kneeling eastwards upon the ground in a circle smeared with saffron paste, presented for an offering a bunch of red lotuses set in a pure vessel of ruby and tinged, like his own heart, with the sun's hue. Solemnly at dawn, at midday, and at eve he muttered a prayer for offspring, humbly with earnest heart repeating a hymn having the sun as its centre.[3]

It is indicated from description of Harṣacarita that Rājyavardhana was inclination towards Buddhist. It is described in Harṣacarita that greatly distressed Harṣa was closely attended by mythologist (experts in allaying sorrow). "Harṣa's grief was lessening under their influence and his thoughts recurring to Rājyavardhana who had gone outwards. Here Bana has compared life of Rājyavardhana to life of Buddha and imagine it that Rājyavardhana may also not seek a hermitage as a royal sage like Buddha. In copper inscription of Bansakheda Rājyavardhana Prathama, his son Aditya-Vardhana and his son Prabhākaravardhana are said entirely devoted to Sun and Rājyavardhana , is said Paramasaugata and Harṣa is said Paramamaheshvara. This mention of copper inscription about Rājyavardhana has surprisingly supported by Harṣacarita. Scholars have not attention on this because of hiding double meaning of this expression. It will be clear from meaning of following sentences –

1. *api nāma tātasya maraṇama mahāpralayasadṛśamidamupaśrutyāryō̃ bāṣpajalsnātō na gṛhaṇīyāda valkalē.*

In other words, when Arya Rājyavardhana learnt about this death, a type of the world's dissolution, may not after a bath of tears assume two robes of bark like Arya (Buddha) had worn two robes of bark after hearing four scenes of deep grief related to death (from his charioteer).

2. *nāśrayēda va rājarṣirāśramapadama.*

May not Rājyavardhana seek a hermitage as a royal sage like Rajarshi Buddha had entered in abode of Alara Kalama.

3. *na viśēda vā puruṣasīhō giriguhāma.*

May not man-lion as he is, enter a mountain cave like shakya-lion (Gautam) had entered in Indrashaila cave

4. *astrasalilanirbharabharitanayananalinayugalō vā paśyēdanāthā̃ prithīvīma.*

May not his lotus eyes brim with a flood of tears, may he yet look upon the lordless earth like Buddha had distressed by seeing appeared earth orphaned from mardHarṣa na at time of bodily posture of ground touch.

5. *prathamavyasanaviṣamavihvala: smarēdātmanāma vā puruṣōttama:.*

May not tormented by the poisonous pangs of a first loss, may the best of men yet remember himself like Purushottama Buddha had meditation of 'Ata' (soul) at time of mardHarṣa na.

6. *anityatayā janitavairāgyō vā na nirākuryādupasarpantī rājalakṣmīma.*

May not ever indifference due to the transitoriness of things lead him to slight the advances of sovereign glory like Buddha had not accepted royal treasury presented by Bimbisara after asceticism.

7. *dāruṇadukhadahanaprajvalitadēhō vā pratipadyētābhiṣēkama.*

May not all aflame with the fire of direful pain, may be have recourse to the coronation bath like Buddha had bathed by creating stream of water when flame was appeared from body in abode of Mahakashyapa.

8. *ihāgatō vā rājabhīrabhidhīyamānō̃ na parācīnatāmācarēta.*

Once arrived here may he not, when pressed by the kings, display a contrary mind like Buddha had displayed a contrary mind, also requested by Suddhodana, after returning in Kapilavastu."[4]

King Harṣa -Vardhana was follower of Hindu religion and devotee of Shiva. Describing preparation before march of Harṣa to conquer the world, Bana has written "On a day with care calculated and approved by a troop of astronomers numbering hundreds, was fixed an hour of marching suitable for the subjugation of all the four quarters. The king had bathed in golden and silver vessels, like autumn clouds which were skilled in pouring water; had with deep devotion offered worship to the adorable Nilalohita; fed the up-flaming fire, whose masses of blaze formed a rightward whirl; bestowed upon Brahmans sesamum vessels of precious stones, silver, and gold in thousands, myriads also of cows having hoofs and horn tips adorned with creepers of gold-work; sat upon a throne with a coverlet of tiger skin; duly anointed first his bow and then his body down to the feet with sandal bright as his own fame; put on two seemly robes of bark silk marked with pairs of flamingos; formed about his head a chaplet of white flowers to be, like the moon's digit, a sign of the supreme."[5]

After that Harṣa entered in new built temple close to the Sarasvati River and bestowed hundred villages to Brahmans. Bana had written "The starting place was fixed at a large temple built of reeds not far from the city and close to the Sarasvati. It displayed a lofty pillared gateway, an altar supporting a golden cup adorned with sprays, affixed chaplets of wild flowers, wreaths of white banners, strolling white-robed people, and muttering Brahmans. During the king's stay there the village notary appeared with his whole retinue of clerks, and saying, 'Let his majesty, whose edicts are never void, oven now bestow upon us his commands for the day,' so presented a new-made golden seal with a bull for its emblem."[6] After that Harṣa bestowed upon the Brahmans a hundred villages delimited by a thousand ploughs.

"In Harṣacarita king Harṣa had said as servant of Brahmans – '*karmakara iti viprai:*', 'founder of dharma (*āvartanamiva dharmasya*)' and patron of Varna and ashrama system like Manu (*mānāviva kartari varṇāśramavyavasthānā*).

Shiva's conveyor 'bull' is marked on head of Sonepat-coin of Harṣa and Paramamaheshvara, Maheshvaraeva sarva (bhaumah) Paramabhattaraka Maharajadhiraja shri Harṣa is written on coins found from Nalanda.

Figure of a horseman and script of 'Harṣa deva' is marked on front and figure of a lady seated on throne is marked on back of that coin of Harṣa which is found."[7]

"It is also written in Harṣacarita that Deva Harṣa had assured the prince of the king of Pragyajyotisha, who had vowed in childhood that he had not to bow his head apart from Shiva, about establishment of friendship and told 'the prince's design too is excellent. Stoutarmed himself, with me, a devotee of the bow, for his friend, to whom save Shiva need he pay homage- *svayaṁ bāhuśālī māyi ca samālambitaśarāsanē*
suhṛdi harādṛtē kamanyayama namasyati' (Saptam Uchchhawas, page-392-94).

Undoubtedly king Harṣa was follower of Brahmana religion and entirely devoted and attached to Maheshvar Shiva like first ancestor Puṣyabhūti."[8]

It is known from description of Harṣacarita that Harṣa had decided to accept Buddhist after completion of revenge of his brother's death and expedition to conquest of the world. Harṣa had met with acharya Divākaramitra in the forest of Vindhya during searching Rajyashri. Divākaramitra, childhood friend of Rajyashri's husband Grahavarman, had become medicant after accepting Pravrajya. Harṣa was impressed by Divākaramitra. When Harṣa had saved Rajyashri from dying with help of Divākaramitra then introducing him Harṣa told Rajyashri that my child, salute this holy man. He was your husband's second heart and is our guru- '*vatsē ! vandasvātrabhāvantama bhadantama. ēṣa tē bharturhṛdayama dvitīyamasmākaṁ ca guru:*' (Harṣacarita, Ashtam Uchchhawas, page-446).

In this description Divākaramitra had said as second heart of Grahavarman. Probably Grahavarman had accepted Buddhism. It is also indicated from this description that Harṣa had also inclination towards Buddhism.

Harṣa had not accepted Buddhism till completion of his vow of conquest of the world. Along with, he had not given permission to accept Buddhism till that time. It is mentioned in Harṣacarita that Rjyashri had requested Harṣa to give permission to assume the red robe. Rajyashri's betel-bearer Patralata expressed her wish to Harṣa "Sir, the queen bids me say that she never remembers to have uttered before a loud remark in your highness' presence, far less a command; but this outrageous tyranny of sorrows makes her speak, and this sad plight, brought about by evil fate makes her forget her due respect. A husband or a son is a woman's true support; but to those who are deprived of both, it is immodesty even to continue to love, as mere fuel for the fire of misery. Your highness' coming stopped my resolution to die, even on the point of accomplishment; let me therefore in my misfortunes be allowed to assume the red robe."[9] Then Harṣa told to Divākaramitra "From this day forth, while I discharge my vow, and console my subjects in their sorrow for my father's death, I desire that she should remain at my side and be comforted with your righteous discourses, and your passionless instruction which produces salutary knowledge, and your advice which calms the disposition, and your Buddhist doctrines which drive away worldly passions. At the end, when I have accomplished my design, she and I will assume the red garments together."[10]

It is clear, from these descriptions, that at beginning Harṣa was follower of Hindu religion but later he attracted towards Buddhism. He decided to accept Buddhism after completion of his vow. It is known, from descriptions of Si-Yu-Ki, that Harṣa and his sister Rajyashri were followers of Buddhism at arrival of Hiuen-Tsang.

It is thrown light on different religions and sects, from writing of Bāṇa Bhaṭṭa ; those were in vogue in seventh century. Mentioning condition of the king's favourite servants, friends and sachivas, after death of Prabhākaravardhana , Bana has written "On the same day the king's favourite servants, friends, and ministers, whose hearts were held tight by the bonds of his many virtues, went forth, and in spite of the remonstrances of tearful friends, abandoned their loved wives and children. Some consigned themselves to precipices: some stationed themselves at holy fords in the neighbourhood. Some in agony of heart spread couches of grass, and quieted their great sorrow by abstinence from food: some, beside themselves with passionate grief, plunged like moths into the flame. Some, in whose hearts burnt a fire of fierce pain, took vows of silence and sought refuge on the mount of snows: some to cool their heat lay on couches of twigs along the Vindhya slopes, where wild elephants bedewed their bodies with a shower bath from their trunks. Some, indisposed for a courtier's life, abandoned the gratifications within their reach, and lived on a limited diet in vacant forest openings: some by feeding on air became emaciated hermits, rich only in virtue. Some assumed red robes and studied the system of Kapila in the mountains: some, tearing off their crest jewels, bound the ascetic's knot upon their heads, and made Civa their refuge: others by enveloping themselves in trailing pale-red rags displayed the bright afterglow of their love. Others again reached old age in sylvan hermitages, where the deer licked their forms with the ends of their tongues: other finally took vows, and roamed as shaven monks, bearing water in pots and in the hollows of their eyes, both equally red in colour and rubbed by their hands."[11] Bana has thrown light on different religious sects of that time through this description.

Regarding this Dr. Vasudevasarana Agrawala has written "It is imagination but taking advantage of this context Bana has given precious material at one place to throw light on religious history of India. Somadeva, in Yashastilakachampoo (9th century), has given good introduction of different sects and their principles. Shri Handiki has given detailed consideration, from historical point of view on these in his book. It is indicated also in dramas of Naishadhacharita of ShriHarṣa and Prabodhachandrodaya etc about name of these sects and persuasions. But mention of Bana is more valuable because of early half of seventh century. Bana's material has thrown light on historical development of different philosophies and religious sects of early time of Shankaracharya."[12]

Mentioning the holy man's presence in abode of acharya Divākaramitra, gathered from various provinces, Bana had written "Then in the middle of the trees, while he was yet at a distance, the holy man's presence was suddenly announced by the king's seeing various Buddhists from various provinces seated in different situations,- perched on pillars, or seated on the rocks or dwelling in bowers of creepers or lying in thickets on in the shadow of the branches or squatting on the roots of trees,- devotees dead to all passion, Jainas in white robes, white mendicants, followers of Krisna, religious students, ascetics who pulled out their hair, followers of Kapila, Jainas, Lokayatikas, followers of Kanada, followers of the Upanishads, believers in God as a Creator, assayers of metals, students of the legal institutes, students of the Puranas, adepts in sacrifices requiring seven ministering priests, adepts in grammar, followers of the Pancaratra and others besides, all diligently following their own tenets, pondering, urging objections, raising doubts, resolving them, giving etymologies, disputing, studying, and explaining, and all gathered here as his disciples."[13]

"In this list Bana had given sample of philosophical world of his time. It is important for religious history of India. Many important changings would took place in religious field after seventh century also and consequently name of Shiva, Kapalika and Kalamukha etc special sects would added which figure has drawn in 'Yashastilaka' Champu (Yashastilaka written by Shrikrishanakant Handiki, page-346-60).

Many facts of this list are likely to give attention. Jain word was generally used that time for Bhuddhist. Bana has himself used word Jaini sajjanata for group of Buddhist sainthood. Generally 'Jinanath' adjective was used that time for Buddha. Jain word was reserved for Jains after non-existence of Buddhist. Persuasion of Shaiva and Pashupat is not mentioned in this list that was predominance that time. Actually Maskari medicant were particularly Pashupata of that time. Bana had said Pashupata Bhairavacharya and his disciple as Maskari. Two separate classifications of Bhagavatas is appeared from names of Bhagavata and Pancharatrika. Different forms of Bhagavata religion was developed in Kushana and Gupta era. Followers of Vaikhanasa persuasion were worshiped Vishnu and his four assistants-Achyuta, Satya, Purusa and Aniruddha. Satvata people worshipped Narayana a form of Vishnu. Their characterists were imagination of Nrisingh and Varah idol form of Mahavishnu. Many idols of Nrisingh and Varah of Vishnu are found in Mathura-art of Gupta-Period which seems inspired form of principle of Satvas. Principle of Mulpancharatra was ancient from these both. Followers of that tantra were called Pancharatra or Pancharatrika. They believed in formation of four – Vasudeva, Sankarshana, Pradyumna and Aniruddha. Those were called Ekantin who worship only Vasudeva: According to Narada Pancharatra there were two types of Ekantin- pure, who worship Vasudeva only believing as god (*vāsudēvaikayājina*), and second mixed, who believed in other gods-form of Vishnu (i.e. Shiva, Indra, Brahma, Parvati, Sarasvati, Brahmani, Indrani etc) besides Vishnu. Gradually different sects were assimilated in one sect. At time of Bana only remained these two broad categories- Pancharatrika and Bhagavata. In future those all were called as this one name as Bhagavata and their mutual micro difference was vanished. But till now huge literature of hundreds of books of Vaikhanasa Satatva and penal codes and tantras of Pancharatras are preserved. Study of those sects from historical point of view can throw new light on religious history of Kushana and Gupta era.

Three names of Jain saints are illustrated as Arhata, Shvetapata and Kesalunchan. But now there is no knowledge of mutual types of avantara sects except broad types of Digambara and Shvetambara.

The philosopher of these four types – Shankhya, Vaisheshika, Naiyayika and Vedanta were also taking shelter of different types of changing stance about perpetual and impermanence of man and nature by stepping into an arena of wrestling ground and manifested new innovations which is an interesting subhect of philosophical history of Vikrami first century. Minanshaka and Vaiyakarana were attempting to work together by joining shoulders. Meditation over supreme spirit of Kumarila and Bhartrihari is proof of it. People of Karandhami or dhadhuvadi considered Nagarjuna as their guru and giving form of their belief of different types of attainments and astonishing effects of medicines as philosophy. Later this belief became famous from name of Rasendra philosophy in which it was believed that a body could be made immortal by suitable use of medicines.

These philosophers had competition particularly with Buddhist; along with they had not less competition among themselves. There was manifesting new innovations in area of philosophy and everyone had to take care of his home. New edge of practice was put on old practice and they had tested by new changing stances to cut other's persuasions."[14]

There is description of Bhairavacharya in Harṣacarita. Bhairavacharya was related to southern Mahashaiva sect. His disciples were spread in whole world in number of thousands: *śiṣyērivānēka sahastrasaṁkhyairvyāptamartyalōkaṁ*. King Puṣyabhūti had defeated Shrikantha Nag with help of Betal Sadhana of Bhairavacharya. Describing Bhairavacarya Bana had written "Soon amid a great throng of recluses he beheld Bhairavacharya, who thus early had bathed, presented the eightfold offering of flowers, and attended to the sacrificial fire. Seated on a tiger-skin, which was stretched on ground smeared with green cow-dung, and whose outline was marked by a boundary ridge of ashes, he was wrapt in a black woolen cloak, as though, apprehending an entrance into an Asura cavern, he were rehearsing a dwelling in the darkness of hell. Like realgar paste purchased by the sale of human flesh, his flashing splendor, lurid as lightning, cast a glow upon his disciples. With his hair, knotted at the top and showing the round shells of his rosary hanging from one braided part, he seemed to be imprisoning the saints, who, presuming upon a smattering of knowledge, roamed overhead. His time of life, marked by a few white hairs, had just passed five-and fifty years. The hair-line on his skull was giving way to baldness, the orifices of his ears were covered with hair, and his forehead broad; while a slanting forehead-mark, made with ashes, produced the effect of a white line of skull bone burst by the heat of burnt gum repeatedly held over half his head. A natural frown, contracting the interval between his brows, seemed by the meeting of these to give him one long unbroken line of brow tawny in colour. His very long eyes, somewhat yellow as with *gutta serena* in the pupils, sparkling bright in the centre, and from their red corners sending out a film of rays, appeared to trace round him a many-coloured circle like a rainbow, and to shower about the parts of space an oblation to Civa variegated with rows of white, yellow, and red symbolical marks. The tip of his nose was curved like the end of Garuda's beak, his cheeks narrowed by the wide gash of his mouth, and the outgoing light of his teeth, somewhat indented, whitened the stretch of heaven as with the light of the moon, the crest of that Civa who was ever treasured in his heart. As if overweighted by the whole Caivite canon resting on the tip of his tongue, his lip hung a little downwards. A pair of crystal earrings, dangling from his pendulous ears, suggested that Venus and Jupiter were pursuing him in the confidence of acquiring a knowledge surpassing gods and Asuras. Upon one forearm, having an iron bracelet and bound with the line of a charm-thread of various herbs, he wore a bit of shell like one of Pusan's teeth broken by the holy Civa and out of devotion converted into an ornament. His right hand shook a rosary, like a Persian wheel containing the buckets for raising water from the well of all delightful emotions. His beard, dangling upon his breast and somewhat tawny at the end, was like a broom sweeping away all the dust of passions therein contained. Covered with a circle of very thick black hair, his bosom seemed scorched by the illumination won through meditation. The ring of a rather loose-hanging wrinkle ran round his middle: the flesh upon his buttocks swelled out in bulk: his girdling loin-cloth was of pure white linen: while circling round him in a tight *paryanka* band was an ascetic's wrap in hue white as ambrosia foam, as if Vasuki, manifested by the power of many unfailing charms, were performing the circuit of honour about him. His feet, whose soles were tender like red lotuses, appeared by the clear woven rays which fell from their nails to be crushing hell to pieces in the delight of carrying away its great treasures. They were constantly attended by a pair of pure white water-washed slippers, like a pair of *hamsas* become intimate with him during his pilgrimage to the holy fords of the Ganges. Constant at his side was a bamboo staff with a barb of iron inserted in the end, which might be compared to a goad for driving away the god whose function it was to remove obstacles to the full attainment of knowledge."[15]

"In this context following indications are important from cultural (particularly religious) point of view-

1. Asura-vivara Pravesha, which is mentioned by Bana at several places. Acharyas were called Vatika who performed Asur-Vivara-Sadhana. Here Bana has written that coming down in the underworld or deep hole was performed for entering in Asura-Vivara: patalandhakaravasam. This was any terrible tantrika experiment. Betal Sadhana was its main part. This type of terrible work was associated with Shaivadharma anyhow.

2. Selling of Mahamansa- This tradition was terrible and fearsome from the beginning. Praising ghost-fiend etc was performed by going in cremation ground and working as a hawker taking flesh of dead body. Many places these are mentioned in Kathasaritsagara (5/2/81). Princes were also said as selling Mahamansa, at time of Prabhākaravardhana 's illness, for well of him. According to Bana Sakta people were bought mainsail named precious material from that money

which had obtained by selling Mahamansa: *mahāmā̃savikrayakrītēna manaḥ śilāpankēna.*

3. Burning gugula on head: *śirōrdhadhṛtadagdhaguggulasantāpasphuṭiṭakapālāsthi.* The Practiser of Shaiva had burnt candle of gugula for worship of Shiva and from which bone was come into sight after burning of skin and flesh.

4. Worship of Mahamandala- Practicing by making around mandala from different coloures. Worship of Matrikas and kubera was performed by making mandala.

5. Shaivasamhita- At time of Bana Shaivasamhitas was composed that is clearly mentioned here.

6. Sphatikakundala- Sect of slit-eared saints, who wore kundala of Billore by slitting long tip of the ear, was associated with Kapalikas in seventh century."[16]

There is mentioned, in Harṣacarita and Kādambarī, different gods of Hindu religion i.e. Shiva, Brahma, Vishnu, Katyayani, Bhagavan Narayana, Nar-Narayana, Mahabhairava, Surya, Trayambaka Shankara, Laxmi, Madhu kaitabha, Parvati, Devmata Aditi, Durga, Bhagavati Chandika, Chaturmukha Shankara Bhagavana, and Nrisingh and Varah form of god. Shiva was important god in all these gods. Kings of Puṣyabhūti clan were Shaiva and they promoted worship of Shiva. Describing worship of Shiva in Sthanishvar Bana has written that house by house the holy lord of the Cleaving Axe (god Shiva) was worshipped -'*gṛhē gṛhē bhagavānapūjyata khaṇḍaparaśu:*'. Devotees of Shiva were burn gugula. They used milk for bathing Shiva and whirled along petals of belt wing chaplets. To praise god Shiva they gratified Shiva bulls ringed about their horn-tips with gold-leaf creepers, golden vessels for bath, golden ewers, censers, flowered cloths, lamps on jeweled stands, Brahmanical threads and mukhakoshas inlaid with bits of precious gems. "Chaturbhuja Shivalinga, Panchamukha Shivalinga and Ekamukha Shivalinga have been found, in Mathura art, of Kushana-period. There was general tradition to make Ekamukha Shivalinga in Gupta-Period. It is known that this was characteristics of Pashupata Shaivadharma. Actually Mukhavigraha was made in rock Shivalinga. It is known that tradition to gratify Mukhakosha or cover of gold on Shivalinga was continued in that tradition. These were called Mukhakosha because there was made shape of mouth on these covers."[17]

In Kādambarī there is mention of two forms of Shiva- Trayambaka Shankara and Chaturbhuja Shankara which were in vogue in seventh century. Mahashveta said to Chandrapeed, during telling his story, that she worshipped Trayambaka Shankara daily – '*pratidinamararcayantī dēvaṁ trayambakama*' (Kādambarī, page-354). When Chandrapeed reached to Mahashveta in sequence of his expedition to conquer the world then he saw the idol of Chaturmukha Shankara Bhagavana whose feet was worshipped by all people and was father of whole world- '*aśēṣatribhuvanavanditavaraṇama, carācaragurūna ,caturmukhama*' (Kādambarī, page-268). In Harṣacarita there is mention of making idols of clay (*pustakarmanā̃ pārthivavigṛhā*). Probably it was possible that idol of gods were made of clay. In absence of idols people were made Shivalinga of sand on bank of rivers and worshipped them after bath. In Harṣacarita there is mention of sand made Shivalinga made by ascetics of great powers and saintliness (*siddhaviracitabālukālinga:*).

Worship of Sun and pray at sunset was very much current in Harṣa -Period. There were repeated Aghamarshana Mantra at time of making an offering and sprinkled red sandle. Describing about making an offering to god Sun, in Kādambarī, by Hareeta Bana has written "Repeated pure Aghamarshana Mantra with pure heart after bathing and taking pranayama (breath exercise) and stand up by making an offering to suryanarayana with taking water in leaf-cup of puraina and currently breaked off lotus flowers."[18] Describing worship of Sun by king Shudraka, also in Kādambarī, Bana has written that he went to temple after making an offering of water pured with repeating mantra and respectful greeting –'*mantrapūtēnatō yāñjalinādivasakaramabhiprāṇamya dēvagṛhamagatama*' (Kādambarī, page-33). Saints of Maharshi Jabali's abode also worshipped Sun after bath. Bana had written "Visibly it seems that Sun was applied that sandal on his body which red sandal had sprinkled after bath by those saints at time of making offering –'*snānōtyiṭēna munijanēnārghyavighimupapādayā ya: kṣititvē dattastamambaratalagata: sākṣādivaraktacandanāṅgarāgama ravirudavāhata*' (Kādambarī, page-99-100). There is also mention, in Harṣacarita, of making offering to sun by kings of Puṣyabhūti clan.

Concept of Kula-devata was also in vogue in seventh century along with these gods. In Kādambarī there is mention that when Chandrapeed came back in royal palace after completion of his education then minister Shukanasha told, by expressing pleasure, that Kuladevata was pleased that day- '*adyaprasannā: kuladēvatā* (Kādambarī, page-203).

In seventh century there was tradition to worship god by establishing them in temples. In Kādambarī there is written, by describing Ujjayini, that temples were constructed on crossroads of the city. Golden pitchers were put on tapering towers of those temples and above that white flags were flapped.

In Kādambarī there is description of temple of Durga, temple of Chandika devi, and temple of four armed Shankara Bhagavana. Mentioning worship performed by queen Vilasavati in temple of Durga, Bana has written that she slept, on bed of musalas made from kusha, in temple of Durga, where darkness was spread by smoke of continuous burning gugul, by wearing white cloth and without food with pure body – '*anavaratadahayamānaguggulabahuladhūmāndhakāritēṣu caṇḍikāgṛhēṣu musalaśayanēṣu suṣvāpa*' (Kādambarī, page-137). Chandrapeeda had seen a desolate siddha temple of Shiva which was constructed in Chandraprabha, skirt of Kailasha Mountain. In that temple idol of four armed Shiva was established. That idole was seated in a mandapa which was constructed on four pillars of sphatikamani (*catu: stambhasphaṭikamaṇḍapikā talapratiṣṭhitama*). That idol was made of pure muktashila: *amalamuktāśilāghaṭitalingama.*

In Kādambarī actual drawing of Chandika devi temple. There was a buffalo bull made of iron placed on platform of black rock in front of Chandika devi. Red hand mark of red sandal was marked on different places of his body. The courtyard of temple was turned as slipping spot from blood of offering. There were two doors in garbhagriha of temple and there were fitted double door-leaves in both doors. There were spread out cloths on that platform when idol of Bhagavati coloured in red colour of mahavara like all dead animals in feet of Durga. There were present many weapons as hatchet-spear etc for slaying animals in that temple. Neck of devi was decorated with garland of vilvapatra attached with different fruit-leaves and coloured in red sandal. That garland looks like shaven heads of children. Joyful chandika was became ecstatic from harsh sound of beating large drum at time of killing animals for offering and worshipped by blooded flower of Kadamba. It seemed that she was expressing her cruelty from this facial expression. It seemed that Bhagavati chandika had dressed like abhisarika for going to Bhagavana Mahakala dressed in beautiful-golden cloths and decorated forehead with tilaka of vermilion made by Bhilanies, with contact light of pomegranate flowers that flowers made karnapura was worn in her ears, with red cheeks, with red lips coloured with betel leaf and looks like blood, with face of red eyes, crooked eyebrow by shrinking and with red cloth coloured in flower of kusumbha. Fire of lighted lamps, lighted in inner part of mandapa with wafted smoke of burning black gugula, looks like by becoming red as she was scolding forest buffalo for fault of swinging stick of trishula at time of scratching back side of shoulder by red fingers coloured in blood of Mahishasura.

There is light thrown on Yajna, method of worship and religious faith of Harṣa -Period from description of Harṣacarita and Kādambarī. People performed sacrificial ladle and uttered sacred verses in Yajna. People had belief, behind these Yajna, that they would be pure by performing this act and would obtain the pleasure of the heaven. About his ancestor Arthapati, Bana has written "Mahatma Arthapati had conqured heaven without any endeavour of blazed fire decorated with alms according to vedic rites and uncountable Yajna like elephants with heavy trunk similar to stable pillars for tightening animals-

vidhānasampāditadānaśōbhitai: sphurammahāvīrasa
nāthamūrtibhi:.
makhairasaṁkhyairājayatsu rālayama sukhēna
yō yūpakarairgajairiva ..15.."[19]

In Harṣacarita there is discussion of continuous Yajna performed in Shrikantha Janapada. Evil thinking and narrowness of Varnas of Shrikanth Janapada had demolished from smoke of Yajna. Bana has written "There (Shrikantha Janapada) false doctrines faded away there, as if washed out by a rain of tears due to the smoke of the Triple Fire. Sinful ways vanished, as if consumed by the burning of the bricks for altars. Demerit was scotched, as if cleft by the axes which fashioned sacrificial posts. Caste confusion ceased, as if cleansed by a rain from the smoke clouds of oblation fires."[20]

In Kādambarī Bana has written, by praising king Tarapeeda, that he had become pure after performing many Yajnas: *anēkasaptatantupūtamūrti:* (Kādambarī, page-114).

Yajnas were performed at home of Brahmans on family level. Bana has mentioned SomaYajna, in dwitiya Uchchhawas of Harṣacarita, which was performed at home of Brahmanas in his village. Increasing popularity of Yajna in seventh century is indicated by this mention of Bana. About this Dr. Vasudevasarana Agrawala has written "This time again it is known the increasing popularity of Yajna karmakanda. That background is reflected by this description of Bana which revival movement of Mimansashastra was done by Kumarilabhatt- in those houses young students attracted by somaYajna were assembled whom foreheads was white with sectarial marks made of ashes, in front of them green beds of soma plant were planted, the rice and panicum for the sacrificial cake laid out to dry on the skins of the black antelope, the oblations of wild rice strewed by the young maidens, the fuel, leaves and bundles of green kusha grass brought by disciples, there were heaps of cow-dung and fuel, cows were seated in courtyard for dropping the milk for the daily offering, the sacred limits purified by heaps of udumbara branches brought to make pegs to mark out the altars for the three sacrificial fires, the panda of Vishva deva were placed on place to place, the sprays of the trees in the courts grey with the smoke of the oblation, the young spotted goats were playing those were brought for Pashubandha Yajna."[21]

Clarified butter, milk and purodas (sacrificial material) were offered in fire pit of Yajna. Recital of the Vedic mantras was performed. In Kādambarī there is mention of black incense sticks (*kṛṣṇāgurudhūpalēkhatī*).

In Harṣa -Period people had faith, like present, in power of mantras. It is known from description of Kādambarī that

Aghamarshana mantra, which was current that time, had power to pure by removing all sins. Chandrapeeda told Mahashveta that merely having sight of you is abundant like Aghamarshana mantra to make pure by removing all sins- '*tvadīyamālōkanamapi sarvapāpraśamana maghamarṣaṇamiva pavitrīkaranāyālama*' (Kādambarī, page-280). In present time people had cause to recite Mahamrityunjay mantra to release from influence of heavenly bodies.

It is known from descriptions of Bana that saints or ascetics had told one's beads by taking string of beads of rudraksha or quartz in their hand. By mentioning the abode of Jabali, Bana has written that counting was performed only on string of rudraksha beads at time of recital of god name not some one's body was counted- '*gaṇanā rudrākṣavalayēṣu na śarīrēṣu*' (Kādambarī, page-86). There is description, also in Kādambarī, about Jabali "He was uttering Mantra with tring of rudraksha beads, like necklace of Sarasvati made of white rock crystal and stringed white large pearls, by keeping in his trembling fingers." [22]

People became saint or ascetic to obtain relief from worldly grieves. It is known from descriptions of Kādambarī that women also renounced the world like men. It is described in Kadamabri the Mahashveta was surrounded with women of different sects in which Shaiva, Buddhist, Shvetambara Jain and ascetic women were included. There is also mention, in Kādambarī, of ascetics who carried out ascetic practice by standing in water.

In seventh century religious superstitions were also in vogue. Bana has thrown light on superstitions and hypocrisy through description of the south Indian priest of Chandika temple. In Kādambarī describing the priest of south Indian Bana has written "An old dravida priest lived in that temple (Chandika devi). It seems from his bulky veins which were spread on his whole body that large lizard, the common house-lizard and chameleon were stucked on his body by thinking his body as trunk of a tree. Big marks of ulcers on his whole body were seen as large beads, all auspicious signs were scraped one by one from his body due to which holes were appeared. A hanging lock of hair beside ear, substitute for kundala of ear, was seemed as a short string of rudraksha beads. Black tumor was appeared on his forehead due to falling it again and again at Bhagavati's feet. His one eye was burst by applying siddhanjana of any cunning person. So he was smoothing needle of wood to apply trikala anjana in his second eye. His teeth had come out from his mouth. He was applying juice of bitter pumpkin daily on them for retaliation. His hand was dry by any inadvertently hurt of bricks. So habit of massage was acquitted. His disease of timirandha was increased by applying katukavarti again and again regularly in his eyes. He had collected teeth of pig to break stones. He had stored lampblack, which was applied in eyes, in cavity of fruit of Ingudi. He had stitched a nerve of his prakoshtha by needle so that fingers of his hand were shortened by squeezing. Silk socks of his feet were torn. So his toe of foot was cracked and everywhere appeared scar. He had attacked by fever untimely due to use of uncooked herb juice. He also gives trouble to Bhagavati Chandika, in this old age, by requesting to give him kingdome of south country. He had heard from mouth of any badly educated medicant that one had became king who had a mole on particular place. So he was hopeful to become rich by these words. He had shell that was coloured with black ink which was prepared from coal cooked in green leaf juice. He had written Durgastotra on a slate. He had collected small booklets of kuhaka (illusory magical art), tantra (use of medicine) and mantra (mantra of shabara tantra etc) by writing on talapatra with ink of lampblack and mahavara. He had written persuasion of mahakala heard from ancient followers of Pashupata sect. He suffered from disease of money from this thinking that scheme by which the buried money could obtain. He was stricken to the wind of alchemy by continuous thinking of these words by which copper could be converted in gold. The fiend of thinking to reach in the underworld of demons was chasing him. Confusion was created in his mind by desire of sexual intercourse with girls of Yakshas. He had collected many mantras those were capable to disappear anybody before the eyes. He had knowledge of thousand astonishing stories related to Shriparvata. His ears were flated by regular slap of men those were angered with vehicles of fiends those came running by regular throwing consecrated seeds of mustard. He behaved proudly as follower of Shaiva. Any traveler did not go near him by seeing that he was not playing properly the vina made by the bottle-gourd. He used to rage, at day time also, like mosquito and sing anything by swinging his head. He was dancing by singing devoted song of Bhagirathi (the Ganga) that was written in language of his country. He maintained asceticism like horses in absence of a wife. Because of this he had spread dust of vaseekarana on those foreigner and old women ascetics who used to stay whenever in this temple. He was angered, because of angered temperament, when his astapushpika tabeej, which was made by collecting eight flowers, was lost here and there. He was also ridiculed Chandika by grimacing in several ways."[23]

It is clear from descriptions of Bana that dravida worshipper was reached on bank of mental bankruptcy because of his great belief on superstition. People made fun of him. Every year on occasion of the holi people, who take part in the holi festival, had carried on old lady on a cot and acted a part of his wedding with her. He had not got anything even after staying sleeping in different temples that were famous for desired attainment. He had been also cherished unfavorable condition of illness like family. He also showed his foolishness, full with many addictions, like there born his many children. Many times people of that state were called without any reason and dragged away him by putting his leg. But he also accepted this disrespect thinking as current behavior.

Through this description Bana has made satirical remarks on religious superstition and dissimulation. He has demarcated that man became mentally bankrupt by superstitions. The body of old dravida worshipper was became decrepit because of following superstition. Actually superstition and dissimulation are similar like woodlouse for any person and society which weaken person, society and ultimately country from internally. It is duty of any historian to raise consciousness in people about defect of this type of improper custom. Through this description Bana has completed duty of an alert historian by his satirical remarks on religious superstitions of seventh century.

It is clear from description of Harṣacarita that there was not any type of hatred among religious sects in India during Harṣa -Period. People of different sects made deliberation, refutation and elaboration by sitting at one place but there was not present any type of religious bitterness. So there was present religious tolerance in seventh century in which people of all religions and sects were living peaceful life with their thinking and beliefs.

"To live in harmony with followers of different religions and philosophies in abode of Buddhist acharya Divākaramitra and mutual tolerance among different religions is an indication of liberation and affection.

From ancient time Ashramas had important place in spreading, coordination, increasing unity and contribution in history of Indian religion, culture and knowledge. It is possible that other abode of Brahmana and Buddhist were also present that time in country like abode of acharya Divākaramitra those were worked for substantial growth equality of all religions and involved to establish coordination. We can say, by keeping this structure of ashramas in view, that those had great contribution in Indian knowledge and culture and hand to establish nearness and unity in different religions."[24]

Rulers of Puṣyabhūti clan had also promoted religious tolerance. They were followers of Shaiva persuasion but they had not compelled follower of any other religion and sects to accept this persuation. "King Puṣyabhūti the first king of Puṣyabhūti clan and Prabhākaravardhana were Paramashaiva and devotee of Aditya but they had good-thinking and respect for Buddha and Buddhist forever as king Harṣa had respect, good-thinking and faith in his heart for god-godess of Brahmans as former time even after acceptance of Buddhist.

Describing Sthanvishvara, the capital of Parama-Maheshvara adiraja Puṣyabhūti, Bana has told that place as abode-place of Brahmanas and Buddhists. So Brahmana saints think that place as tapobhoomi (*yastāpōvanamiti munibhi:)*; good people (religious) think that place as sadhu-samagama (*samāgama iti sadbhi:*) and medicants think that place as 'abode of Shakyamuni'(*śākyāśrama iti śāmibhi:)* (Tritiya Uchchhawas, page-165-66).

It is clear that king Puṣyabhūti was the first man who treated with respect to all types of religions and saints in his state.

At time of illness of king Prabhakar-Vardhana when Brahmanas were performing fire for peace, muttering prayers of rudra ekadashi in samhitamantras in temple of Shiva and Shaivas were busy in worship of Shiva then Buddhist acharyas were also busy in recitation of 'mahamayuri' (a field of knowledge) *krimāṇaṣaḍāhutihōmama..... prayataviprаprastuta saṁhitājapaṁ japyamānarudraikādaśīśaśabdāyamānaśivagṛhama ... paṭhayamānamahāmāyūrīpravartyamāna* ... (Pancham Uchchhawas, page-265).

It was result of this generosity and respect of kings of Puṣyabhūti clan to all religions that good thinking and affection was continued in people and all sections of that time as it is clear from descriptions of Hiuen-Tsang and Harṣacarita."[25]

It can be concluded that there is given glimpse of religious scenario of seventh century in books of Bāṇa Bhaṭṭa . It is clear from descriptions of Harṣacarita that kings of Puṣyabhūti clan were mainly follower of Shaiva persuation. But Rājyavardhana had proclivity for Buddhist. Harṣa had also decided to accept Budddhism in last part of his life. It is clear from description of Hiuen-Tsang that Harṣa and Rajyashri had accepted Buddhism at time of his travel in India. It is also known, from description of Harṣacarita and Kādambarī, about different religions and sects those were in vogue that time. Polytheism was current in Hindu religion. It seems from description of Bana that whole religious scenario was divided in different persuasions and sects. But there was not any type of bitterness on religious level. "Mutual good-thinking and respect for each other was present in all religions and we found follower saints of different religious and philosophies lived together and involved in religious discussion in abode of vindhyatavi (abode of Divākaramitra) on the same idealism as the great Ashoka had expressed desire that people of all religion would live together and become 'bahushruta' by involving in discussion of each-others religions likely to hear."[26]

References:-

1. The Harṣacarita of Bana- Trans. By E.B.Cowell & F.W.Thomas- Motilal Banarsidass Pvt. Ltd. Delhi- Page-84-85.
2. Do- Page-102-03.
3. Do- Page-104.
4. Harṣacarita: Ek Sanskritik Adhyayan- Dr. Vasudevasarana Agrawal- Bihar Rastrabhasha Parishad Patna- Page-115-16.
5. The Harṣacarita of Bana- Trans. By E.B.Cowell & F.W.Thomas- Motilal Banarsidass Pvt. Ltd. Delhi- Page-197.
6. Do- Page-198.
7. Rajvansh: Maukhari aur Puṣyabhūti- Prof. Bhagawati Prasad Panthari- Bihar Hindi Granth Akadamy Patna- Page-209-10.
8. Do- Page-210.
9. The Harṣacarita of Bana- Trans. By E.B.Cowell & F.W.Thomas- Motilal Banarsidass Pvt. Ltd. Delhi- Page-254.
10. Do- Page-258.
11. Do- Page-161-62.
12. Harṣacarita: Ek Sanskritik Adhyayan- Dr. Vasudevasarana Agrawal- Bihar Rastrabhasha Parishad Patna- Page-106.
13. The Harṣacarita of Bana- Trans. By E.B.Cowell & F.W.Thomas- Motilal Banarsidass Pvt. Ltd. Delhi- Page-235-36.
14. Harṣacarita: Ek Sanskritik Adhyayan- Dr. Vasudevasarana Agrawal- Bihar Rastrabhasha Parishad Patna- Page-195-96.
15. The Harṣacarita of Bana- Trans. By E.B.Cowell & F.W.Thomas- Motilal Banarsidass Pvt. Ltd. Delhi- Page-263-65.
16. Harṣacarita: Ek Sanskritik Adhyayan- Dr. Vasudevasarana Agrawal- Bihar Rastrabhasha Parishad Patna- Page-58-59.
17. Do- Page-56.
18. Kādambarī- Poorvabhagah- Chawkhamba Vidyabhawan Varanasi- Page-79.
19. Do- Page-04.
20. Harṣacaritam- Chawkhamba Vidyabhawan Varanasi- Page-81.

21. Harṣacarita: Ek Sanskritik Adhyayan- Dr. Vasudevasarana Agrawal- Bihar Rastrabhasha Parishad Patna- Page-31.
22. Kādambarī- Poorvabhagah- Chawkhamba Vidyabhawan Varanasi- Page-90.
23. Do- Page-458-61.
24. Rajvansh: Maukhari aur Puṣyabhūti- Prof. Bhagawati Prasad Panthari- Bihar Hindi Granth Akadamy Patna- Page-239-40.
25. Do- Page-237-38.
26. Do- Page-239.

■ ■ ■

Chapter-6

Bāṇa Bhaṭṭa and Educational Aspect in India during Seventh Century

In seventh century there was a well-organized system of education in India. People were skilled in all skills and arts after completion of education. Women were also educated and expert in different skills along with men. It is thrown light on educational scenario from descriptions of Harṣacarita and Kādambarī. Homes of Brahmanas, abode of ascetics and institutions supported by state were place of teaching. There was a defined curriculum for education. It is also thrown light on technique of teaching from description of Bāṇa.

Aim of education in Harṣa-Period was- to acquire skill in all streams of education and arts. It was expected from an educated person that he would be expert of all shastras, he has potential to enquire into secrets of religious books, he would be dexterous in poetic conversation and a skilled orator. It was given education of music, drawing, the art of sculpture, drama etc arts to students. So to acquire expertise in these arts was also an aim of education. It is mentioned in Harṣacarita about Dadhicha that he was trained in all the sciences and the circle of the arts in house of maternal grandfather- '*aśikṣatāyaṁ tatraiva sarpā vidyā: sakalāśca kalā:*' (Harṣacarita, Pratham Uchchhawas, page-47). Sarasvati had granted boon to his son at the very hour of his birth that by my favour all the Vedas with the mystic portions, all authoritative books, and all arts would be fully and spontaneously manifested in him: '*samyakasarahasyā: sarvēvēdā: sarvāṇī ca śāstrāṇī sakalāśca kalā mataprabhāvāta svayamāvirbhāviṣyantī iti varamadāta*'(Do. Page-67). Describing charateristcs of Vatsa, brother of Sarasvata, Bāṇa has written that he was at rest from all the doubts of different schools. He had opened all knotty points in the sense of books. He was poet, eloquent and without envy-

‘*śamitasamastaśākhāntarasaṁśītaya: udghāṭitasamagra granthārcagranthaya:, kavaya:, vāgmina:, vimatsarā:* (Do, page-70).

It is described about Rajyashri that she gradually grew up in daily increasing familiarity with friends expert in song, dance etc. and with all accomplishments- ‘*rājyaśrīrapi nṛttagītādiṣu vidagdhāsu sakhīṣu sakalāsu kalāsu ca pratidivasamupacīyamānaparicayā śanai: śanairavarddhatē*’ (Harṣacarita, Chaturth Uchchhawas, page-239).

It is known from descriptions of Bāṇa that an aim of education was also to get employment. There was given training to students to construct community hall, hostel, well, temple, bridge and instruments through vocational education. Students were successful in getting jobs by knowledge of scientific applications and skill of crafts. Describing Ujjayini city in Kādambarī Bāṇa has written that people of that place had constructed community halls, hostels wells, temples, bridges and instruments according to instructions of smriti shastras. They were expert of scientific applications and crafts. Under vocational education there was given education related to work of carpenter, work of evory and metallurgy.

It is known about educational centres of seventh century from Harṣacarita and Kādambarī. That time there were three types of education centres- home of Brahmanas, abode of ascetics and educational institution supported by state.

It is described in Tritiya Uchchhawas of Harṣacarita that people of village were warmly welcomed Bāṇa when he reached in his village after gratified beyond measure by king. He was delighted by own hospitality and with a joyous heart he made his inquiries from people- “Have you been happy all this time? Does the sacrifice proceed without hindrance, gratifying the Brahman groups by its faultless performance? Do the fires devour oblations with ritual duly and without flaw performed? Do the boys pursue their studies at the proper time? Is there the same unbroken daily application to the Veda? The old earnestness in the practice of the art of sacrifice? Are there the same classes in grammar exposition, showing respect by days not idly spent in a series of emulous discussions? Is there the old logic society, regardless of all other occupations? The same excessive delight in the Mimamsa, dulling all pleasure in other authoritative books? Are there the same poetic addresses, raining down an ambrosia of ever-new phrases?"[1]

It is clear from this description that home of Brahmans were main study centres. In Harṣacarita and Kādambarī it is mentioned to this extent that even parrot and maina, those were lived at home of Brahmanas, were recited sacred text of Vedas. Describing about continuous study in homes of his relative Brahmanas Bāṇa has written that all peaceful through the cessation of the labours of the Brahman techers, while busy repetitions were now commenced by the parrots and mainas- '*śukasārikārabdhādhyayanadīyamānōpādhyāyaviśrāntisukhāni*' (Harṣacarita, Dwitiya Uchchhawas, page-79).

Second centre of education were- abode. Abode of Divakaramitra is mentioned in Harṣacarita. In that abode scholars of different sects, those came there from various provinces were explaining their sacred texts diligently by hearing, studying repetition, raising doubt, resolving them giving etymologies, debate and practice. That abode was an ideal educational institution for Buddhist study. "Extremely humble disciples were gravely busy performing the ritual of the chaitya (*caityakarmakurvāṇa:*). Great followers and skilled scholars in the Shakya Shastras were explaining the Abhidharma kosh written by Vasubandhu. Lectures were given on ten laws those were instructed for medicants. There were muttering jataka-stories of Bodhisattva and people were gaining insight from them. It was characteristics of Gupta-Period Buddhism and literature to telling and hearing many stories of jataka mala written by Aryashura and Divyavadana etc books with new style. Nature of people, who lived in abode, had become peaceful by following law of Saugata Bhagavan Buddha."[2]

Abode of maharshi Jabali is described in Kādambarī. That abode was study centre related to Hindu religion. Describing educational environment of that centre Bāṇa has written "There were continued instructions related to shradh. There was continued lecture on yajya vidya. There was continued criticism on religious books. There was continued thinking on meaning of all shastras. There was continued construction of hermitage. Courtyard was smeared. There was continued cleaning of homes of sages. There was continued meditation of god. There was continued study of mantras. There was continued sequence of yoga practice. There was continued offering to vana-devies."[3]

In descriptions of Bāṇa it is also mentioned that type of educational institution which were supported by state. According to story of Kādambarī, king Tarapeeda had caused to construct a school outside town to educate his son Chandrapeeda. Bāṇa has written "king Tarapeeda had caused to construct a school, long and wide up to half kosha and similar like a temple, on bank of Shipra river to prevent his son from bad company. An enclosed space was provided under that and a wall was constructed and white washed. That school was looked like garland of snow-peaks. A broad and circled ditch was dug out around that. Vast and firm gate was fitted in that school. Only one gate was constructed to enter into that. A big horse-shelter was constructed in that school. Exercise-room was constructed in that enclosed space. Teachers of all subjects were appointed in that school. In that school king had kept Chandrapeeda like cub had kept in cage. Chandrpeeda was forbid from going out of school. Only sons of acharyas were stayed as relative and all objects were kept out those could attract mind of children. So he had made that type of arrangement that mind of child was not involved in any other object. After that king tarapeeda had handed over Chandrapeeda along with Vaishampayana to acharyas on an auspicious moment and day to obtain education."[4] It is known from this description that schools were established by states.

Describing incidents of his life Bāṇa has written that he had spent his time in gurukulas. Certainly these gurukulas were study centre of other type. Position of these gurukulas was different from study centre of Brahmana's home and study centre of abode. It is possible that those gurukulas were established or supported by state which is mentioned by Bāṇa.

Curriculum of seventh century was full of varieties. Syllabus was constructed to expertise students in all shastras and art. Describing education of Prince Chandrapeeda Bāṇa had written

"Prince Chandrapeeda had learned all field of knowledge in short time from acharyas. All shastras and arts were entered in pure-hearted Chandrapeeda similar to pure mirror of mani. Chandrapeeda had obtained expertise in many arts as grammar, mimansa, nyaya, dharmashastra, polity and wrestling and different type of weapons as bow, chakra, shield, sword, shakti, spear, battle-axe, club and mastered these type of so many arts as charioteer, in elephant-driving, in horse-riding, in different types of instruments as vina, venu, mridanga, kansyapatra, majeera, dadur etc, in art of dance structured by Bharata, in music invented by acharya Narada, in education of elephant, in the skill to know age of horse, in the skill to know distinguishing feature of men, in drawing, in drawing figure on cloth and walls, in writing books, in gandharvashastra, in understanding sound of birds, in Astrology, in investigation of precious stones, in work of carpenter, in work of ivory, in architect, in ayurveda, in use of machinery, in poison-remover work, in digging a tunnel, in swimming, in crossing, in jumping, in climbing on height, in science of sexual intercourse, in knowledge of illusion, in fables, in dramas, in stories, in poetries, in the Mahabharata, in Puranas, in history, in the Ramayana, in knowledge of all scripts, in knowledge of all countries, in knowledge of signs, in all crafts and in Chhandashastras."[5]

It is known from this description that curriculum was divided mainly in four parts-

1. Education of religion and philosophy,
2. Education of literature and art,
3. Education of polity and law and
4. Vocational education.

Education of Veda, Purana, the Ramayana, the Mahabharata, education of yajya, method to perform shraddha, dharmashastra and smriti, mimansashastra, shlokas and shlokas related to asceticism were included in education of religion and philosophy. Criticism, debate and refutation and elaboration etc were also exercised on dharma-shastra.

About position of education, which was given at home of Brahmans in his village, Bāṇa had asked to his kinsmen that there is the same unbroken daily application to the Veda? : *pratidinama vicchinnō va vēdābhyāsa:?*, The old earnestness in the practice of the art of sacrifice? : *kaccītsa ēva cirantanō yajñavidyākarmaṇyabhiyōga:?*, The same excessive delight in the Mimamsa, dulling all pleasure in other authoritative books?: *sa ēva vā mandīkṛtētaraśāstrarasō mīmā̃sāyāmatirasa:?*, Are there the same poetic addresses, raining down an ambrosia of ever-new phrases?: *kaccīta ēvābhinavasubhāṣitasudhāvarṣiṇa: kāvyālāpā?*

Praising his four cousins Ganapati, Adhipati, Tarapati and Shyamala Bāṇa has written that they had knowledge versed in the acts of all monarchs and sages of old. Their minds were inspired by the Maha-Bharata. They had thirsting for no elixir but that of listening to well-turned phrases.

In Kādambarī it is said about citizens of Ujjayini that they were able to read all scripts. They had passion for the Maha-Bharata, Purana and the Ramayana- '*sarvalipijñēna mahābhāratapurāṇarāmayanāṇurāgiṇā*' (Kādambarī, page-108). Citizens of Ujjayini had knowledge of smriti shastras. They had devotion to Vedas. They had passion for listening poetic addresses-' *śrutarāgiṇā subhāṣitavyasaninā*' (Kādambarī, page-108).

Different books, related to Buddhism, were taught in abode of Divakaramitra. It is known from Harṣacarita that Abhidharmakosha written by Vasubandhu, Jataka stories of Buddha, ten laws of Bhagavan Buddha and spiritual instruction were included in curriculum of that abode. Medicants were also following the instructions of these books after study.

Different books of literature, history, grammar and different aspects related to arts as music, dance, expertise to play different musical instruments, painting, training related to army etc were included in education of literature and art. Describing about education of prince Chandrapeeda, Bāṇa has written that he had obtained expertise in stories, dramas, fables and poetry. It is known from this description that form of literature as story, drama, fable and poetry etc were taught that time.

Famous literature books of Harṣa-Period were mentioned in Harṣacarita and Kādambarī. Important books of that period were – Vasavadatta written by Suvandhu, prose-poem written by Harishchandra, dramas written by Bhasa, books written by Kalidasa, Vrihatkatha written by Gunadhya, Sangraha written by Vyadi, Nitishastra written by Kamandaka, different poetry dramas, ancient and modern stories, Natyashastra written by Bharata and Kamashastra. It is clear from mention of these literature books that these were famous books of that time. Certainly these books were a part of curriculum. Different forms of literature were developed by teaching of these books. Many books were composed. This fact is proved by high quality books as Harṣacarita and Kādambarī written in Harṣa-Period. Indian literature was enriched from these types of books.

In Harṣa-Period different types of poems were written in different parts. In Harṣacarita Bāṇa had written "In the North plays on words are mainly admired, in the West it is only the sense; in the south it is poetical fancy; in Ganda pomp of syllables-

'*ślēṣaprāyamuḍīcyēśu pratīcyēśvarthamātrakama.*
utprēkṣā dakṣiṇātyēṣu gauṛē ṣvakṣaraḍambarama..7."[6]

It is also clear from descriptions of Bāṇa that number of poem writers was increased that time. There was shortage of good composers of poem. Some poets composed their poems by changing some varnas of other poets for their own benefit. They had not anxiety to dignity of literature. Bāṇa has addressed these poets as 'kukavi' and compare them with countless like dogs, following their own vile nature from house to house. They were treating as bad in world of literature. He has written "Most commonly the poetasters of the world have their perceptions ruled by desire, loquacious and willful like red-eyed kokilas. Countless such there are like dogs, following their own vile nature from house to house, - not many are there like Sharabhas, possessing creative power. A poet is not reckoned among the good and is detected as a 'thief' by his only changing the words of former writers and by his concealing the signs of different styles."[7]

It is known from mention of chitrashalas those were constructed in towns, where dramas were played in Harṣa-Period. These dramas were important medium of entertainment. It is mentioned about Chandrapeeda that he had also got expertise in drama.

History was also included in curriculum. Describing his cusions Bāṇa has written that they all were scholar of history- '*mahāpuruṣavṛtāntakutūhalina:*'. It is described in Kādambarī that parrot, which was brought in royal palace of Shudraka by daughter of Chandala, was skilled in telling story of Purana and history-' *purāṇētihāsakathālāpa nipuṇa:*'. Skandagupta, Gajasadhanadhikrit of Harṣa, had told stories of kings killed by conspiracy to arouse Harṣa. It is proved, from this type of stories related to political events, that history was written and read that time. Harṣacarita is also a history book.

There was given special emphasis on grammar in curriculum of education. In Kādambarī Bāṇa has written that Chandrapeeda had knowledge of all scripts, known language of all countries and skilled in Chhandashastra. In Kādambarī there is mention of topics of grammar at many places by symbolic manner. The parrot, presented in royal court of Shudraka, was able to speak ornamental words clearly and correctly by dividing varnas according to intra-syllabic vowel symbol and nasality- '*yadayama sankīrṇavarṇapravibhāgāmabhivyakta mātrānusvāra saṁskāryōgāma viśēṣasaṁyuktāma giramudīrayati*' (Kādambarī, page-26). It is mentioned about officers present in royal court to arrange system of alms such that royal palace was famous to know beggers of Prathama, madhyama and uttama category with the help of royal official those were famous to arrange system of alms as grammar is famous for bibhakti of prathama-madhyama-uttama puroosh, sup-ting etc, order of gachchha-ghas etc in place of gam ada etc placed in prakriti, karaka of shadvidha karta etc, akhyata like gachchhati pashyati, sampradan or fourth karaka, dhatu of bhu etc and pada of uchaih nichaih prabhriti avyaya- '*vyākaraṇamiva prathamamādhyamōttamapuruṣa vibhaktisthitānēkādēśakārakākhyāta sampradānakriyāvyayaprapañcasusthitama*' (Kādambarī, page-190-91). Bāṇa has written, by describing Mahashveta that she was separate from conflict of happiness and sorrow as words are separate without samasa (*asamasta padavṛtti mivādvadvāma*) and she had worn dress suitable to yatis (saints) as yati and gana of arya chhanda were put according to an intra-syllabic vowel-symbol (*āryāmivōpāttayatigaṇōñcita mātrāma*). It is clear from these descriptions that chhanda, division of varnas, matra-anusvar, samasa, correctness of language etc topics were included in contents of grammar.

Education of music, training to play different instruments, dance, song, drawing & painting were also included in curriculum. One aim of education was to get skill in these arts. In Kādambarī there is mention of getting education of different instrument to play, music and dance by Chandrapeeda. Bāṇa has written that he had learnt to play different types of instruments as veena, venu, mridanga, kansyapatra, majeera, dadur, he had read books of dance written by Bharata and books of music composed by acharya Narada. In Harṣacarita it is mentioned about Rjyashri that meanwhile Rajyashri gradually grew up in daily increasing familiarity with friends expert in song, dance and with all accomplishments. In a comparatively limited period she came to maturity.

Education of dancing was also given in Harṣa-Period. There is mention of dancing by female members of royal family at time of Harṣa's birth festival. It is also thrown light on methods of dancing of that time by description of Bāṇa. He has mentioned arbhati dance done by Natas in sequence of describing hot season. Nata, dancing in arbhati style, were performing Ras dance in round as rechaka or by making flirtatious movement of waist, hand and shoulder:
raiṇavāvartamaṇḍalīrēcakarāsarasarabhasārabdhanartanarambhārabhatīnaṭā: Five characteristics of dances are

mentioned by Bāṇa-
1. mandalinrita, 2. rechaka, 3. Rasrasa, 4.rabhasarabdhanarttana and 5. Chatulashikhanarthana.

1. mandalinrita- Shankara had said mandalinrita as hallinaka in which a male danced as a leader in middle of circled line of female dancers. This particular dance was said hallisaka in Sarasvatikanthabharana written by Bhoja. It is known that hallisaka word was derieved from 'ileeshiyan' (illeshiyan mistory dance) dance of Yunan near about first Christian year. Tradition of rasa dance of Krishna and hallisaka dance was co-related with each-other any time.

2. rechaka- According to Shankara it was three types-katirechaka, hastarechaka and greevarechaka i.e. it's characteristics was doing movement of waist, hand and shoulder during dance.

3. rasa- When eight, sixteen or thirty two persons were dancing in form of a circle then it called as rasa dance.

4. rabhasarabdha narttana- Speedy movement of hand-foot during dance which expressed unrestrained temperament and effort.

Thus, which style of dance was formed including these four was named as arbhati or dance which was performed by speedy movement of hand-waist shoulder with expression of unrestrained temperament and effort was called arbhati dance. Leaping and jumping, beating and wounding, rebuking, turmoil, sudden disturbance created by firing etc and scene of illusion or deception were displayed through dancing in group was called arbhati. Ornament of sense, disaster, different frightened places indicating death etc unrestrained and vehement disposition were also displayed by rhythmical movement of parts of body in dances which were performed at ileeshiyan place of Yunan. And at last when parts of body were reached extreme of temperament by hurling, which were called rechaka in own country, and devastation and misfortune was reached on extreme level then suddenly arose a divine light in those dances. Thus it is known that arbhti dance style was born by mixing of both hallisaka and rasa.

According to Natyashastra, there were four modes or style of dance as Bharati, Sattvatee, kaishiki and Arbhati. It is known that these names had geographical base. Bharati was associated with Bharata Janapada or kurukshetra, Satvatee was associated with Sattvatas (Yadavas) of Gujarata and Kathiyavada, Kaishiki was associated with Vidarbha desha or Barara which was called as Krathakaishika. It is known from this that arbhati was also associated with particular country. Till now arbhata is not determined certainly. But writers of Yunan had mentioned 'Arabitae' or 'Arbiti' named caste those were lived in southern part of Baluchistan in west side of Sindhu which were in west of Sonamiyani. Arabius River was flowed in country of those people. Both Ariryan and Strabo had said this province as last part of India. Sikandara's army of Yunan, at time of return, had made way through this province. I think that this was the ancient Arbhata country which dancing style, mixed with rasa of India and hallisaka of Yunan, was called Arbhati. Bāṇa has also written that Natas had started arbhati-style dance by throwing away their free hair here and there: *caṭulaśikhānarttanārambhārabhaṭīnaṭā*. Till now it is characteristics of Baluch and tribesman to dance with this type of free hair and shaking head & body by speedy movement of arts of body."[8]

Education of singing was also given with dancing. Songs were singing on different occasions. Books related to music were written to give education of music and song. Chandrapeeda had obtained expertise in music composed by acharya Narada. It is described, in Kādambarī, that Mahashveta was singing the praises of Shankara along with playing vina. Her song of praise was endowed with dhruva (dhrupada), distinguishing feature of song and different voice were articulated by modification of main musical mode. There is given many times in that song as a drunken woman was clapping the hands excessively. In that song there was present murchhana-shrati etc different parts of song as there was present two perception named shabdi and aarthi in mimansashastra.

In Harṣacarita, comparing melody song of Sudrishti with state of Harṣa, Bāṇa has written "This song is similar to state. Song is according to sound of flute and state is hereditary. Opposite voice of gandhar and ninad are not present in song and there is not any rebellious in state. Tal and laya of song are absolutely clear and actions of state or place for judgement are famous. Song is praiseworthy because of following pattern presented by Bharata muni writer of Sangitashatra and state is praiseworthy because of following law of ancient king named Bharata."[9] There are thrown light in characteristics of Harṣa-Period songs. It was thought that a good song was followed by instruments, there was not present gandhar and ninad voice, there were absolutely clear tala and laya and based on laws of sangitashastra.

Education of painting was also included in curriculum. Chandrapeeda had got expertise also in painting and art to paint on cloths and walls. It is mentioned, in Kādambarī, about rule of king Shudraka that mixing of colour was done for painting (*citrakarmasuvarṇasankarā:*) but there were not persons of mix caste in subjects. It is known from descriptions of Bāṇa that photos were hanged in royal palaces. Describing incident of becoming sati by queen Yashomati Bāṇa had written that she was holding photo, which was her husband's photo, firmly like her mind for death- '*sannihitaprāṇasamama varanāya cittamīva citraphalaka vicalama dhārayantīma*' (Harṣacarita, Pratham Uchchhawas, page-286). It is also proved by mention of painting of Yamapatta and cause to paint figures on body (structure like tattoo) that education of painting was given that time.

There is mentioned, in Harṣacarita and Kādambarī, about counting auspicious moment and predicting future events by astrologers. In Harṣacarita it is said about Taraka named astrologer that he had announced facts beyond the ken of men according to mathematical calculations. He had deeply read in all the treatises on astronomy. "Vrihatkathasamhita written by other acharyas included in these treatises. According to Vrihatsamhita three parts of astrology are-grahaganita, samhita and horashastra and it is written that daivachitaka had expertise in samhita. There is given list of samhitas in second chapter of Vrihatsamhita."[10] Chandrapeeda had also got expertise in astrology (*grahaganitē*) and examining precious stones (*ratnaparīkṣāsu*). It is clear from this description that astrology was essential part of curriculum. People had belief in prophecy of astrological calculation.

There was system of education of military training and training of other useful arts. Training to use different weapons, to drive chariot and training to ride on elephant and horse was given under military training. Chandrapeeda had got expertise to use different types of weapons as bow, chakra, shield, sword, shakti, spear, battle-axe and club. He had also got training of wrestling, driving away chariot and riding on elephant and horse. He had obtained education of dice, education to cure from poison, digging underground tunnel, swimming, crossing, jumping, to climb on height, education of illusion and sexual intercourse. Education related to ayurveda and health was also given. Special virtues were developed in students after education of these subjects and they help them in spending life successfully.

Education of polity and ethics was also included in curriculum. Bāṇa has written that Chandrapeed had obtained education of ethics (*pramāṇē*) and politics (*rājanītiśu*). In Kādambarī it is described about king Tarapeeda that his wisdom was never disturbed in neetishastra –' *nītiśāstrākhinnbuddhi*'. In this manner Shukanasa, minister of king Tarapeeda, was skilled to use neetishastra- '*nītiśāstraprayōgakuśala:*'. It is clear from this description that king and their ministers were expert in neetishastra. It is also known from descriptions of Bāṇa that there was given special emphasis on ethics in administrative management. Judges (*dharmādhikārī*) were appointed for this. Describing about judges, which were appointed in court of king Tarapeeda, Bāṇa has written "High post holder judges worn high quality dresses were present in court like idol of dharma and sat on lofty chairs, clerks of judges were writing there thousands of letters by displaying good work compared to city of dharmaraja and considered whole world as a village because they had remembered all city and village names."[11] Certainly people who had education of law would be appointed on these posts.

Vocational education was also a part of curriculum in Harṣa-Period. There is mention, in Kādambarī, that Chandrapeeda had obtained expertise in work of carpenter (*dārukarmani*), work of ivory (*dantavyāpārē*), architect (*vāstuvidyāsu*), ayurveda (*āyurvēdē*) and use of machinery (*yantraprayōgē*). Describing expertise in architect of citizens of Ujjayini Bāṇa has written that citizens of that city had constructed meeting hall, hostels, wells, temples, bridge and machinery according to smritishastras-

'*smṛtiśastrēnēvāsabhāvasathakūpaprapārāmasurasadana sētuyantrapravartakēna*' (Kādambarī, page-107). Again it is described about citizens of that city that they were expert in all machines and crafts- '*sakalavijñānaviśēṣavidāvadānyēna dakṣēṇa*' (Do., page-108). It is known from description of Harṣacarita and Kadambri that art of jewellery, art of sculpture, work of metal and art to make different types of machines (as dharayantras fitted in buildings, Persian wheel, art to make plough) were developed in Harṣa-Period. Certainly students were educated in these arts. Students who were educated in these arts would be able to get job easily. Along with they would also able to start their own business.

In seventh century period of education was ten years. Students were got admission in age of six year after completion of Upanayana samskara and eduction was ended in age of sixteen after completion of samavartana samskara. When Balahaka, army chief of king Tarapeeda, had went school to bring Chandrapeeda from school to royal palace after completion of education then he had told Chandrapeeda "It is tenth year to live your in school after discharging home. When you were six year old then you had came here. Combining these you had entered in age of sixteen. So you had to enjoy youthful luxurious life with free mind departing from here and seeing mothers and worshipping feet of teachers and taking pleasure of throne."[12]

There is also thrown light on education system of Harṣa-Period from descriptions of Bāṇa. There were booklets of different subjects which were read by putting them on book-stand. Education was given with help of these booklets. There is description, in Kādambarī, of reading booklets of different subjects in abode of Jabali – ' *vācyamāna vividha pustakama*'(Kādambarī, page-83). Booklet readers were called *pustaka vācaka*. In Harṣacarita there is description of reading book by Sudristi. Sudristi had removed tie of booklet and laid it upon desk made of reed staks (*pustakama purōnihitaśaraśalākāpatrakē nidhāya*) then took few leaves and read. It is known from this description that binding leaves of books by making hole into them was not current that time.

Generally bhojapatra and palm-leaf was used to write with red and black ink. Black ink was prepared by burning coal in liquid of green leaves and lampblack. Red ink was prcpared by mahavara and gorochana. Small booklets were written on palm-leaf by ink. Describing old dravida priest, in Kādambarī, Bāṇa had written "He had a shell painted black by black ink prepared by burning coal in liquid of green leaves. He had written durgastrota on a small board. He had collected small booklets of kuhaka (illusory magical art), tantra (use of medicine) and mantra (mantra of Shabara etc) by writing on palm-leaf with ink of lampblack and mahavara."[13]

It is known about teaching technique of that time from descriptions of Kādambarī. There was given consideration of different subjects of shastras through spiritual instruction, lecture and criticism. Describing teaching techniques of abode of Jabali, Bāṇa has written that spiritual instructions related to shraddh was continued there –' *uddiśyamāna śrāddhakalapama*'. There was continued lecture on yajya- '*vyākhyāyamānayajña viddama*'. There was continued criticism on dharmashastra-' *ālōcya dharmaśāstrama*'. There were continued reading booklets related to different subjects- '*vācyamāna vividhapustakama*'. There was continued discussion on meaning of all shastras-' *vicāryamāṇa sakalaśāstrārthama*'. There was continued meditation of god-' *ābadhyamānadhyānama*'. There was continued accomplishment of mantras-' *sādhyamāna mantrama*'. There was continued sequence of Yoga-' *abhyasyamānayōgama*'.

Students had uttered lessons in loud speech to remember contents. Describing educational environment of abode of Jabali, Bāṇa has written that abode was resounding by reciting lessons of students-'*adhyayanamukharabatujanama*' (Kadamabri, page-82). Parrots of that place were also making noise by reciting those words after hearing. Uncountable mainas were reciting Vedas-' *anavarataśravaṇagrahītavaṣaṭkāra vācālaśukakulama , anēka sārikōnda ghuṣyamāna subrahmaṇyama*' (Do, page-82). It is clear from this description that reading by loud speech and learn by rote system was current that time.

Impartial discussion on scripture was current in abode of saint Jabali. Bāṇa has written that only wing of cock was fallen in that abode, not any one take side of any person in discussion of scripture. This type of educational environment was also in abode of Divakaramitra. All holy men who came there from various provinces were diligently following their own tenets, pondering, urging objections, raising doubts, resolving them, giving etymologies, disputing, studying and explaining. Study and teaching of Brahmana's home was described in Harṣacarita. It is known from that description that there were continued daily practice of Vedas, lecture was organized on grammar, meeting was organized on ethics, there continued study of mimansashastra and modulation of poetry was continued.

Qualified and subject specialist persons were appointed as teacher. It is described in Kādambarī that teachers of all subjects were appointed by big efforts to teach Chandrapeeda. Teachers taught their students with fully concentration. Bāṇa has written that Chandrapeeda had got expertise in all subjects in very short period by acharyas who taught their student finding suitable and talented. By proving this description of Bāṇa, Hiuen-Tsang had written "The teachers (of different subjects) must themselves have closely studied the deep and secret principles they contain, and penetrated to their remotest meaning. They then explain their general sense, and guide their pupils in understanding the words which are difficult. They urge them on and skillfully conduct them."[14]

Relation between teacher and student was good in seventh century. Directly there is not written anything about relation between teacher and student in Harṣacarita and Kādambarī but certainly it is known about thinking of people to teachers from these books. When Harṣa met first time to Divakaramitra then he had not to sit on seat in front of Divakaramitra in spite of Divakarmitra's repeatedly request to sit and sat down on ground. Introducing Divakaramitra to Rajyashri Harṣa had said to Rajyashri that my child, salute this holy man. He was your husband's second heart and is our guru. Then Rajyashri had made her obeisance to him. It is described in Kādambarī that there were taken permission before taken away Chandrapeeda to home army chief Balahaka had said to Chandrapeeda that now your education had ended so you have to take joy of state with other work after worshipping feet of gurus. It is clear from these descriptions that teachers had respectful position in society that time and people respected them.

There is thrown light on languages, those were current that time, from descriptions of Harṣacarita and Kādambarī. There is mention of bhasha kavi Ishana in Harṣacarita. Ishana was best friend of Bāṇa. "Reference to bhasha-kavi is writer of songs who writes in local language. It is known that bhasha word was use for apabhransha that time. According to Dandi, apabhransha language had publicity in ahira etc castes to write poem. Great poet Pushpadanta had mentioned poet Ishana in preface of Apabhransha Mahapurana."[15]

Sanskrit language was considered as high level language. Sanskrit was language of higher educated people. Popular language books were written mainly in Sanskrit. Harṣacarita and Kādambarī are also written in Sanskrit language.

It is clear from descriptions of Bāṇa that books were also written in Prakrit language. Prakrit language was speaking language of rural people. Kulaputra Vyuvikara, one member of Bāṇa's friend circle, was written book in Prakrit language.

It is known from description of Kādambarī that Sanskrit speaking people did not use Prakrit language. Bāṇa has written in context of describing Mahashveta that she (Mahashveta) was divine girl not Prakrit as people did not use Prakrit language who were educated in Yajyas. It is known from this description that people educated in Yajya or had knowledge of Sanskrit language were abstain from speaking Prakrit language. It is clear from this context that society was divided on base of language. In present trend of discrimination on base of language is also found. In India English speaking people saw those people as lower standard who speak mother tongue Hindi and other regional languages.

Describing old aged dravida priest Bāṇa has written that he was dancing by singing a devoted praise of the

Bhagirathi Ganga written in language of his own country. It is clear from this description that language of south India was different from north India.

It can be concluded and said that educational aspect of seventh century is known from description of Harṣacarita and Kadambri. Bāṇa Bhaṭṭa has manifested every aspect related to educational world as- aim of education, centre of education, duration of education, curriculum, system of reading and teaching or teaching technique and current languages etc. Curriculum of that time was framed to ascertain all-round development of students. There were made efforts to develop all characteristics in students by physical, mental and religious improvement.

References:-

1. The Harṣacarita of Bāṇa- Trans. By E.B.Cowell & F.W.Thomas- Motilal Bāṇarsidass Pvt. Ltd. Delhi- Page-71.

2. Harṣacarita: Ek Sanskritik Adhyayan- Dr. Vasudevasarana Agrawal- Bihar Rastrabhasha Parishad Patna- Page-197-98.
3. Kādambarī- Poorvabhagah- Chawkhamba Vidyabhawan Varanasi- Page-83.
4. Do- Page-158-59.
5. Do- Page-159-60.
6. Harṣacaritam- Chawkhamba Vidyabhawan Varanasi- Page-05.
7. The Harṣacarita of Bāṇa- Trans. By E.B.Cowell & F.W.Thomas- Motilal Bāṇarsidass Pvt. Ltd. Delhi- Page-1-2.
8. Harṣacarita: Ek Sanskritik Adhyayan- Dr. Vasudevasarana Agrawal- Bihar Rastrabhasha Parishad Patna- Page-33-35.
9. Harṣacaritam- Chawkhamba Vidyabhawan Varanasi- Page-147.
10. Harṣacarita: Ek Sanskritik Adhyayan- Dr. Vasudevasarana Agrawal- Bihar Rastrabhasha Parishad

Patna- Page-65.
11. Kādambarī- Poorvabhagah- Chawkhamba Vidyabhawan Varanasi- Page-185.
12. Do- Page-164.
13. Do- Page-460.
14. Buddhist Records of The Western World- Samuel Beal- Low Price Publication Delhi-Page-79.
15. Harṣacarita: Ek Sanskritik Adhyayan- Dr. Vasudevasarana Agrawal- Bihar Rastrabhasha Parishad Patna- Page-28.

■ ■ ■

Chapter-7

Bāṇa Bhaṭṭa and Indian Economy during Seventh Century

Economy of any country depends on economical activities of that country. Development in agriculture, husbandry, industry and business is essential for economical progress. Economy of seventh century also depended on progress of these areas. It is known about status of Harṣa -Period agriculture, husbandry, industry and business from descriptions of Harṣacarita and Kādambarī .

Economy of Harṣa -Period depended on agriculture. Tax collected from agriculture was main source of state's income. It is known from description of Harṣacarita that agricultural land of state was distributed in three categories- 1. Land given to samantas, 2. Land directly controlled by state and 3. Tax free land given to Brahmanas.

Feudatory system was in vogue in Harṣa - Period. It is clear from descriptions of Harṣacarita that there were different categories of samantas as samant, mahasamant, aptasamant, pradhanasamant, shatru mahasamant and pratisamant. Land was given to these samantas by state. Samantas were responsible for administration and collection of tax of jagirs. Tax was not collected in their area by king. They had to pay tax determined by state along with they had to maintain an army. This army had to fight according to need of state. Which army was standing in front of royal gate, at time of expedition of Harṣa to conquer the world, was constructed with army's of samantas came from different areas. When the king had started supervision of army then they had accepted respectful greeting of kings according to their status and divided them in different groups.

Direct tax was collected from that land which was in direct control of state. Official and employees of state were responsible for collection of tax and to deposit it in treasury. Farmers who had observation on these lands were called as agraharika by Bāṇa . Agraharks had to present some food items in service of king at time of his expedition. Describing presentation of food items in service of Harṣa , at time of his expedition, by agraharikṣ Bāṇa has written "Fools of agraharikas (who had observation of agriculture), issuing from the villagers on the route and headed by aged elders with uplifted waterpots, pressed furious near in crowds with presents of curds, molasses, candied sugar and flowers in baskets, demanding the protection of the crops: flying before their terror of irate and savage chamberlains, they yet in spite of distance, tripping and falling, kept their eyes fixed upon the king, bringing to light imaginary wrongs of former governors, lauding hundreds of past officials, reporting ancient misdeeds of knaves."[1]

Land was granted as alms to Brahmans by kings. Bāṇa has written that before expedition of army Harṣa had bestowed upon the Brahmans a hundred villages delimited by a thousand ploughs. Land given to Brahmans was tax free. It is mentioned in Harṣacarita that at time of expedition of Harṣa 's army there shrieking quarrelsome Brahmans, mounted on the tops of trees, were being expelled by the rods of chamberlains standing on the ground. "Actually Bāṇa has indicated here that according to letters of alms, which was given to Brahmans who had got villages in agrahara, there was condition that any type of material would not collected as tax from that land at time of camping and crossing royal army from that land. According to ancient tradition village given in agrahara were free from all type of taxes. This time, at time of expedition of army, chamberlains were wanted to collect taxes also from these villages. Government servants and agrahari Brahmans were quarreling on that topic. Chamberlains wanted to frighten them from their power then shrieking quarrelsome Brahmans mounted on the tops of trees were being expelled by the rods of chamberlains standing on the ground."[2]

Area of land was measured by ploughs for taxation in Harṣa -Peiod. Harṣa had bestowed the villages, before expedition of army, had area of one hundred seer or plough. "This mention is important because this is probability to find same indication of that large numbers that meaning is not determined till now, which are given mountain scripts along with names of countries. There was determined detailed area of every village and ascertained government tax (bhaga) of the land which was allotted in Gupta-Period. There is determined a certain relation between area and bhaga of government. It is said in Shukaneeti that tax of village, which had area of one kosha, was one hundred karshapana of silver. This number could be meaningful after knowledge that how many plough land was in area of one kosha. It is known that number of land measured in plough was indicated along with each village name and number of revenue collected in karshapana along with country name was written in letters of administration."[3] Probably tax was collected from land of samantas and government land owner farmers determined by measurement of plough.

It is also thrown light on preparation of land for agriculture, production of crops, use of fertilizer, watering and system of protecting crops by description of Harṣacarita. Raw material for industries was produced from agriculture along with production of food-grain. People were also depending on agriculture for fruit, flower, vegetables, grass for animals etc.

Land was prepared by plough for agriculture. Small cultivative lands were prepared with help of spade on land which was hard. Describing Shrikantha Janapada, in Harṣacarita, Bāṇa has written that their lands were prepared and land lotuses were rooted up by plough. Again in Harṣacarita describing forest village of vindhya forest Bāṇa has written "The outskirts being for the most part forest, many parcels of rice-land, threshing ground, and tilth were being apportioned by small farmers, and that with no little vigour of language, since it was mainly spade culture and they were anxious for the support of their families. No great amount of coming and going tramped the earth owing to the difficulty of ploughing the sparsely scattered fields covered with kush grass, with their few clear spaces, their black soil stiff as black iron"[4]

People sowed different crops after preparation of lands. Food grain and cash crop were included in crops. Paddy and wheat were min food grains. There were different types of paddy. Describing forest village Bāṇa has written that woodland districts turned grey by the smoke from granaries of wild grain in which heaps of burning Sastika chaff sent up a blaze. It is described in

Kādambarī that shyamaka (variety of paddy) was dry up in courtyard of huts of saints in abode of Jabali. Impenetrable Shyamaka grew in field of forest village. Bāṇa has also mentioned Gavedhuka named paddy which was a variety of paddy according to commentator Shankara. It is known from description of Harṣacarita that there was also produced wheat. Bāṇa has written that mouth of pitchers were covered with cup made from straw of wheat and flowers of Patala were put on that to fragment water. Sugar-cane, cotton plant, linseed and Indian hemp were produced as cash-crop. Describing forest village Bāṇa has written "The surrounding country was black with numerous sugar-cane enclosures, showing wide carefully tended branches, buffalo skeletons fixed on stakes to scare with their sharp points the rabbits which devastated the rising huds, and high bamboo fences which the antelopes lightly leapt when startled by ox-drivers' sticks which the watchmen hurled at them"[5]. Again he has written that people of forest village were moving along with bundles of cotton plants, plentiful loads of flax and hemp bundles.

It is known from description of Harṣacarita that vegitables were produced along with other plants in garden situated near home. "Home-garden of the forest householders was enclosed with clumps or plant of Eranda, Vacha (a plant had fierce fragrant), Vangaka (brinjal), Surasa (plant of tulsi), Surana (edible tuber), Shigru; the drum-stick/ house radish, Granthiparna, Gavedhuka paddy. The castor plant and a network of kashthalukalata creepers (creeper of the bottle-gourd), reared upon tall planted uprights, provided a shade.

It seems general tradition, from Harṣacarita, of placing nishkutas or gardens near homes. Bāṇa has also mentioned nishkutas in Dwitiya Uchchhawas (page-137)."[6]

Farmers were anxious about protecting crops. Farmers lived near field by constructing high platforms to protect crops. Bāṇa has written that near the village scaffolds constructed above ground suggested incursions of wild beasts. Along with this buffalo skeletons were fixed in fields to protect crops and a scarecrow made of straw was erected. Even today farmers had protected crops by erecting scarecrow made of straw.

Bundle of crops were put at threshing-floor after harvesting. After that grain was separated. There is described threshing-floor of forest village in Harṣacarita where heaps of burning Sastika chaff sent up a blaze.

Seeds of crops were preserved in homes. Farmers produced crops by sowing these seeds in their fields. Bāṇa has written that stores of Nala rice, Water lily roots, candied sugar, white lotus seed, bamboos, threshed rice and collection of Tamala seeds were ready at hand. Today also Indian farmers prevent seeds of different crops in their homes. They produce crops by sowing these seeds next year in fields.

Compost was used to increase fertility of fields. This compost was prepared by rubbish. This fertilizer was carried by bull-cart and spread in fields to increase fertility. Bāṇa has written "Here and there the preparation of unsightly fields of barren soil was being effected by numerous lines of wagons, bearing heaps of manure from old dust heaps and yoked to strong young steers, while to the creaking of their loose and noisy wheels were added the angry cries of the dust-grey ploughboys who sitting on the poles urged them on."[7]

Main means of irrigation were well and ponds in Harṣa -Period. Irrigation was done with help of Persian-wheels those were fitted on wells. "Describing Shrikantha Janapada, in Harṣacarita, Bāṇa has described about paddy and sugar-cane crops extending beyond their field and the ground bristles with cumin beds watered by the pots of the Persian Wheel. Bāṇa has also said that Shrikantha Janapada was graced with ponds like Visnu's navel (Tritiya Uchchhawas, page-160 and 162). It is very meaningful to compare ponds with navel of Vishnu. As Brahma, the creator of the universe was born from navel of Vishnu in the same manner ponds of that place were producer of agriculture or sita, the base of living world. In simple word ponds of that place had abundant capacity to watering crops for development of agriculture."[8]

There was tradition of husbandry in seventh century. Husbandry was means of subsistence for Gopalakas. Cow, ox, buffalo, dog, mangoose, shalijata were main domestic animals of that time. People also kept birds such as cock, duck, peacock, falcon, guinea-fowl and bhujanga. Gopalakas had protected cows to do business of milk. Calves of cows were also protected which were became ox after growing. Ox were used to plough field along with they were yoked in cart to carry weight. Describing forest village Bāṇa has written that Cowpens were encircled with dry branches. Tiger-traps, constructed in fury at the slaughter of young calves. It is described in Kādambarī that Kapila cows were present in abode of Jabali and that abode was delighted the groups of young calves. Cake made from these animals dung was used as fuel. Compost was made from dung and which was used to make fertile fields. It can be estimated from mention of protecting cocks that they were protected for chicken and eggs. People kept other birds for their hobby. Describing forest, situated near forest village, Bāṇa has written "Fowlers roamed hither and thither, loaded with cages for falcons, partridges, kapinjalas, and likely, their boys loitered about with aviaries hanging from their shounders."[9] It is clear from this description that birds were sold in markets by trapping. This was the main source of income of these fowlers.

Industries had important role in economy of seventh century. Main industries, which were known from descriptions of Harṣacarita and Kādambarī , were as follows-

1. <u>Iron Industry</u>-

Iron was essential for making defence weapons as sword, shield, spear, arrow, armour, small dagger etc in Harṣa -Period. Iron was also used for making instruments of agriculture as spade, ploughshare, sickle, axe etc. Describing Nirghat, nephew of Shabar army chief, in context of Vindhya forest Bāṇa has written that he was like a moving mass of black collieries and he was like a melting block of iron from the Vindhya. It is clear from this description that iron-ore was extracted from mines of Vindhyachala. Items of different shapes were made by melting iron-ore in furnace. This work was done by blacksmiths or specialists of this work. Describing forest village Bāṇa has written "Coolness of drinking arbours seemed to dispel the summer heat. In other place again blacksmiths were almost intensifying the heat by burning heaps of wood for charcoal.

It is clear from these descriptions that iron industry was in developed condition in seventh century. Heavy amount of state treasury was spent on production of weapons. Certainly weapons were stored to fulfill requirement of vast army of Harṣa . It is mentioned in Kādambarī that huge collection of varma (shield), arrow and chakra was stored in palace of king Tarapeeda.

2. Textile Industry-

It is known from descriptions of Harṣacarita and Kādambarī that textile industry was in developed condition in seventh century. Textile industry was ahead in technique. People liked delicate white cloths. Cotton and woolen cloths were also in use. Different types of cloths as- kshoma, badar, dukoola, lalatantuja, netra and pinga were in use in Harṣa -Period. Colouring and printing technique of cloth was also developed. Assam and Pundradesha or Bengal was centers of textile industry that time.

3. Sugar Industry-

It is known from description of cultivation of sugar-cane and availability of sugar that sugar was produced in seventh century. Two types of sugar- red sugar (*pāṭala śarkarā*) and white sugar (*karka śarkarā*) is mentioned in Harṣacarita. Sugar-cane was cultivated to supply raw material for sugar industry. There is a described waving field of sugar-cane. Raw sugar was also made from juice of sugar-cane.

4. Wine Industry-

It is known from descriptions of Harṣacarita and Kādambarī that people drank wine in large scale in seventh century. Two types of wine were used- Somarasa and wine made from flower of mahua (the tree Bassia latifolia). The rich people drank somarasa made from plant of Soma. General people drank wine made from flower of mahua. This wine was prepared at home. Describing forest village of Vindhya forest Bāṇa has written that decoction and distilled intoxication of mahua fruit was present in every house. There is mentioned, in Harṣacarita, that panasala of wine was established in royal court at birth festival of Harṣa . It is clear from this description that wine was produced at industry level.

5. <u>Ivory Industry</u>-

Craftsmanship of ivory and industry related to this work was developed in seventh century. When Bāṇa went to meet Harṣa in court then he saw Harṣa sitting on the throne which feet were made of ivory). It is known from description of Bāṇa that small boxes were made of ivory to put jewellery. Jewellery and combs were also made of ivory. It is known from description of Kādambarī that people, who lived in forests, supplied ivory for ivory industry. It is mentioned in Kādambarī that Bheels, who were wandering in forest of Vindhya, were taken bundles of hair of yak and deer together with ivory. Probably these Bheels sold these ivories in markets of nearest city.

6. <u>Wood and Furniture Industry</u>-

It is known from descriptions of Harṣacarita and Kādambarī that wood and furniture industry was also developed. Bedstead, chair, cot, four-legged seat, door, window, seat of wood, pillars of building in which shape of idol were made etc were made of wood. There is also mention of cane furniture. In Kādambarī it is mentioned that Chandrapeeda had got expertise in work of carpenters.

7. <u>Jewellery Industry</u>-

Extensive use of ornaments made of gold, silver, ivory and diamond were used in Harṣa -Period. Men and women both had desire of ornaments. There is mention of boxes of king and queen full of ornaments. It is clear from popularity and supply of ornaments that jewellery industry was developed. Goldsmiths were expert in making ornaments. Describing preparation of Rajyashri's wedding Bāṇa has written that the outer terraces resounded with the din of gold-workers engaged in hammering gold.

8. <u>Industy related to production of toilet items</u>-

People of seventh century had desire of toilet items. Important toilet items were- oil of mango, vermilion, patavas churna (powder), alta (lac dye), ubatan (paste), sandal dust, musk mixed water, dust of crocus, liquid of camphor etc. These toilet items were produced at industrial level because demand of these items was extensive.

People had employment, at large scale, in above described industries. Businessmen made profit by selling items produced in industries and paid tax to state. Thus these industries had important role in development of economy of seventh century.

It is also thrown light on trade and business of seventh century from description of Harṣacarita and Kādambarī . Business of that time could be divided in two parts – 1. Internal business and 2. Foreign business.

Internal business was done through roads. Kings were made these roads for convenient of their military expedition. Along with temporary lodging-place and place of drinking water was constructed place to place where travelers were take rest. Prabhakar-Vardhana had leveled land and portion out the earth by making the broad paths for his armies. Travelling had become easy after construction of these roads. It is clear from description of Harṣacarita that goods were carried on ox-carts. Businessmen supplied their materials from one place to other place in country through these carts. Wealthy cities were main centre for marketing commercial goods in Harṣa -Period. Describing market streets of Ujjayini Bāṇa has written "Market streets of that city were expanded like sea which was drunk by saint Agastya. Golden sand is spread on that way. There are hoards of conch shell, mother-of-pearl, pearl, coral and emeralds on paths of street for selling." (Kādambarī , page-105). Again he has written about citizens of Ujjayini that they had knowledge of languages of all countries. That city was centre of commercial activities and businessmen of all countries came there to do their business so citizens knew languages of all countries. Ujjayini was a wealthy city due to centre of commercial activities. Citizens of that city had crores of rupees. There is constructed sky kissing temple on crossroads of that city. Thus it can be imagined about the developed internal business of India by prosperity of Ujjayini city.

India had also commercial relationship with foreign countries in Harṣa -Period. "It is known from Harṣacarita of Bāṇa that eighteen continents of south-sea were considered as greater part of India at time of Harṣa . So Paramabhattaraka Rajya-Vardhana had suggested his younger brother Harṣa to stay in capital, at time of going alone to attack on the king of Malwa, and assured him that a concourse of lions in the matter of a deer is too degrading, moreover for the province of your prowess you had already the earth with her amulet wreath of eighteen continents.

Here the earth means country of India (In Arthashastra Kautilya had said India as prithivee, '*dēśa: pṛthivī*'- Adhikarana 9, chapter-1) and eighteen continents of south-sea were amulet wreath of eighteen countries or part and to conquer them was became as a subject of royal duty and valour.

So Harṣa had proclaimed at time of going against expedition of the king of Gauda, the killer of his brother Rajya-Vardhana, to roaming till 'dvipantara' (dvipantara= island of Indonesia; Sashtha Uchchhawas ,page- 344) along with sending instruction to all Indian kings to prepare their hands to give tribute.

Island of south-sea had been considered as part of India from Guptas so India, as Prof. Agrawal had indicated, was named Kumari dvipa. Name of islands, written below, were included in eighteen islands according to literature of Gupta-era-

1. Kumari dvipa (=India, the Himalaya to Kanyakumari)
2. Singhal dvipa (Shri Lanka)
3. Naga dvipa (Nikobar)
4. Indra-dyumna (Andaman)
5. Kathaha dvipa (Kedaha-malaya dvipakalpa Malay Peninsula)
6. Malay dvipa
7. Suvarna dvipa (Sumatra)
8. Yava dvipa (Java)
9. Varushaka dvipa (Barosa= Boros island)

10. Varuna dvipa (Borniyo)
11. Parnayupayana dvipa (Philipines)
12. Charma dvipa (Kardaranga)
13. Karpura dvipa (Probably this was name of Bornio due to production of high quality comphore)
14. Kamala dvipa (Kambodia)
15. Bali dvipa.

Together these all islands were famous from name of 'Dvipantara'.

Bāṇa has said Harṣa 's lip, smeared deep with betel and vermilion, was like a seal assigning away the various island continents in fief to loyal affection (*mudrayā hi sasindūrayā vilabhyatē* - commentator, in ancient time object of alms were given by smeared with vermilion). This mention of Bāṇa is authentic proof that 'Dvipantara' were part of India and so Indian king was authorized to bestow his beloved. Bāṇa has mentioned that in childhood both brothers (Rajya and Harṣa) fame was illuminated in dvipantara because it was part of India- (*dvipāntarē prakāśatāma jagmatu:*; Chaturth Uchchhawas, page-234).

It is proved from descriptions of Bāṇa , Shri Harṣa himself, Hiuen-Tsang and Itching that commercial and cultural relationship was dense and firm with Singhal and Indonesia etc dvipantaras through way of south sea at time of Harṣa .

In Pratham Uchchhawas of Harṣacarita Bāṇa has written by praising great poet Vyasa that he made the Mahabharata holy by his speech as the Bharata is hollowed by the river Sarasvati.........which story is spread in three world-

nama: sarvavidē tasmai vyāsāya kavivēdhasē .
cakrē pūṇyama sarasvatyā yō varṣamiva bhāratama .. 3..

....

kathēva bhāratī yasya na vyāpnōtī jagatrayama .. 9..
It is clear from this fact that story of the Mahabharata was spread in the three world or dvipantara beyond India at time of Harṣa ."[10]

"Relationship between India and China was close from ancient time by road rather than sea which was maintained in seventh century also. In Harṣacarita Bāṇa has written that Pandava Savyasachee (Arjuna) had attacked on China to acquire wealth for Rajasooya Yajya- '*pāṇḍava: savyasācī cīnaviṣayamatikramya rājasūyasampadē*' (Saptam Uchchhawas, page-380).

It is likely to view the reference of the Mahabharata with this context – It is mentioned in Anugita Parva under Aashvameghika Parva that Pandavas had reached on a place where great liquid of Mahata was stored- (shloka 1-6, chapter-64). Acquired wealth from that place was sixteen crore, eight lakh and twenty four thousand suvarna (Do, shloka-20)."[11]

"In Harṣacarita there is mention of China-cholaka (Saptam Uchchhawas), Cheenanshuka (silk made in China- '*cīnāśuka sukumāra*' (Pratham, Pancham and Ashtam Uchchhawas, page-64, 291, 433) and Kardaranga leathers (shield made in Kardaranga island = *kārdaranga carmaṇā kārdarangadēśabhavānāma - deshbhavanam*- commentator).

It is clear that Cheen-cholaka (it was royal dress, which was worn on kanchuka (inner coat) like 'over-coat'); and Cheenanshuka were imported from China and Kardaranga- leather (or shields, Saptam Uchchhawas) was imported from any island of Indonesia across south-sea.

In Harṣacarita there is clear indication of import of horses from foreign countries. In Saptam Uchchhawas there is mention of Uttunga horses of Tangana country and horses of Kamboja country in context of Harṣa 's cavalry. Though speed of Tangana horses was fast but their back was steady so horse riders had travelled comfortably.

Bāṇa has seen horses of different countries in royal horse shelter and counted their names as – Vanayuji (from country of Vanayu), Kambojee (from country of Kamboja), Aarbhatti (from country of Aarbhatta), Bharadwajee (from country of Bharadwaja), Saindhava (*sindhu dēśajai:*) and Paraseekee (paraseek or Iranian) - (Dwitiya Uchchhawas).

It is clear that horses were imported for cavalry from countries those were famous for war horses. It could easily be estimated that businessmen of horses also reached to India for business of horses like other businessmen of other countries.

It is known from descriptions of Harṣacarita and Hiuen-Tsang that Indian businessmen were earned 'ratnas' from islands by selling their panyas (goods of sale). Bāṇa has mentioned person (businessman) who had earned 'ratnarashi' from all islands and praised for his virtues. Mentioning Indian trade and businessmen Hiuen-Tsang has also written that they had earned different types of precious 'ratnas' and 'manies' from islands of sea in exchange of their panyas. He has given names of metals mainly gold, silver and copper (bronze?) etc which were here in abundant measure.

It is clear from description of earning 'ratnas' and 'manies' from islands in exchange of their panyas by Indian businessmen, which is given by Bāṇa and Hiuen-Tsang, that Indian industries were properly developed and as a result different types of Indian goods were exported to foreign countries and islands."[12]

Different unions of craftsmen and businessmen were formed in Harṣa -Period. These groups were active every time for improvement of their craft and business. In Harṣacarita Bāṇa has described about companies of craftsmen and sthapaties (mansions who had knowledge of architect) from different parts of countries who were summoned at occasion of Rajyashri's wedding to decorate and paint royal palace and construct marriage altar for wedding and hospitable treatment of sutradharas, expert in construction of marriage altar, by presenting white flower, sandal and cloths.

Bāṇa has also mentioned Sindhushena, the head of goldsmiths."[13]

Rajya-Vardhana, distressed with father's death, had told his beloved brother Harṣa that daily my sorrows increase, like money of merchant. Presence of merchants, who lend money on interests, is proved by this description. Probably, general people and businessmen borrowed debt, according to their need, from these merchants.

Knowledge about coin is also known from description of Harṣacarita and Kādambarī . Gramakshapatalika had presented a gold coin, on which bull was marked, to Harṣa at time of expedition of army. A bull is marked, on a copper-coin found from Soneepata. There is also mention, in Harṣacarita, about round shaped silver coin. Describing prosperity of citizens of Ujjayini Bāṇa has written that they had large number of gold coins.

It can be concluded and said that economy of seventh century was based on development of agriculture, husbandry, industry, trade and business. Raw materials for industry were also obtained from agriculture along with food grain. Very-numerous population was depending on agriculture. Different industries were also developed. Some important industries of that time were- iron industry, textile industry, sugar industry, ivory industry, wood and furniture industry. These industries had important role to provide employment. Different groups of craftsmen and businessmen were always active for development of their craft and business. Internal business was developed. Commercial relationship with foreign countries was also established.

References:-

1. Harṣacaritam- Chawkhamba Vidyabhawan Varanasi- Page-377-78.
2. Harṣacarita: Ek Sanskritik Adhyayan- Dr. Vasudevasarana Agrawal- Bihar Rastrabhasha Parishad Patna- Page-166-67.
3. Do- Page-141-142.
4. Harṣacaritam- Chawkhamba Vidyabhawan Varanasi- Page-406.
5. The Harṣacarita of Bāṇa - Trans. By E.B.Cowell & F.W.Thomas- Motilal Bāṇa rsidass Pvt. Ltd. Delhi- Page-228.
6. Rajvansh: Maukhari aur Pushyabhuti- Prof. Bhagawati Prasad

Panthari- Bihar Hindi Granth Akadamy Patna- Page-293.
7. The Harṣacarita of Bāṇa - Trans. By E.B.Cowell & F.W.Thomas- Motilal Bāṇa rsidass Pvt. Ltd. Delhi- Page-228.
8. Rajvansh: Maukhari aur Pushyabhuti- Prof. Bhagawati Prasad Panthari- Bihar Hindi Granth Akadamy Patna- Page-298.
9. The Harṣacarita of Bāṇa - Trans. By E.B.Cowell & F.W.Thomas- Motilal Bāṇa rsidass Pvt. Ltd. Delhi- Page-227.
10. Rajvansh: Maukhari aur Pushyabhuti- Prof. Bhagawati Prasad Panthari- Bihar Hindi Granth Akadamy Patna- Page-301-03.
11. Do- Page-306.
12. Do- Page-308-11.
13. Do- Page-312-13.

■ ■ ■

Chapter-8

Conclusion

Bāṇa Bhaṭṭa is the pole star of Indian literature. His intellect, creativity and Progressive thinking are expressed in his both books Harṣacarita and Kādambarī . Kādambarī is a story book but Harṣacarita is a historical book. Different aspects of contemporary Indian political situation, society, culture, religion, education and economy is described detailed in these books. He has impartially illustrated India of seventh century. He has not exaggerated Harṣa though he lived in Harṣa 's court. He was against flattery. He has criticized, in Harṣacarita , those poets who wrote flattery poems by their wish for own benefit. Historian A.L.Basham has praised Bana for this courage. Historical facts presented by Bana are also proved by other contemporary travel accounts, inscriptions and archaeological materials. Some historical facts are known only by description of Bana. View of Bāṇa Bhaṭṭa was broad. He has illustrated incidents exactly. One side he has illustrated luxurious life of kings other side he has not hesitation to point out difficulty of general people during marching of army for war. In this manner he has mentioned tolerance and generosity of Indian culture but he has also criticized the religious rites and dissimulation. Hardly ever any aspect of Indian life is untouched by descriptions of Bana. So descriptions of Bana are essential to understand India of seventh century entirly.

Events of establishing Puṣyabhūti clan to expedition of Harṣa to conquer the world is described in Harṣacarita . A royal clan was established in Shrikantha Janapada by a king named Puṣyabhūti. Prabhakara-Vardhana, Rājyavardhana and Harṣa -Vardhana like kings were born in this royal clan in the course of time. From descriptions of Bana it is known that credit to give stability of Puṣyabhūti clan was gone to Prabhakara-Vardhana. He had constructed roads for army in all directions by leveling river-side ditches, forest, trees, grass, bushes and mountains etc and bestowed them to his attendants. Prabhakara-Vardhana had two sons named Rājyavardhana and Harṣa -Vardhana and one daughter named Rajyashri. Rajyashri was married to king Grahavarma, the Maukhari king of Kanauja and Showed his diplomatic foresight. Now rulers of Kanauj and Thaneshwar could able to obstruct jointly the attack of Hunas and Malavas after this relationship. Harṣa -Vardhana was distressed and became angry with events of killing of Grahavarma by the king of Malwa, event of Rajyashri's imprisonment, event of killing Rājyavardhana by shashanka, the king of Gauda and vowed to conquer the world. Meanwhile he heard news of absconding Rajyashri from prison then he marched towards Vindhya forest to search her. Harṣacarita is ended with Harṣa 's meeting with Rajyashri.

In sequence of describing these events Bāṇa Bhaṭṭa has given important information about expansion of Puṣyabhūti dynasty, condition of king, their merits and demerits and duties, administrative structure, security arrangement, judicial system, revenue system etc. This throws light on whole political scenario of seventh century. He has drawn mental status of employees working in royal palaces. Through his writing Bana has thrown light on trouble to get employment, restlessness due to load of work, doing wrong and unlawful acts by servants and feeling asceticism by not receiving payment after work etc facts which are important from historical point of view. Conclusion of a survey, which is recently conducted to know the mental condition of Indian employees, has very much similarity to descriptions of Bana. He has made an effort to assess success of administration on touchstone of employee's satisfaction. Certainly Bana was a sensitive historian with modern thinking.

It is known about society of seventh century from descriptions of Harṣacarita and Kādambarī . Society was mainly based on Varna system. There were many castes and sub-casts in society. Bana has mentioned Bheels, Baheliya, Nishada (Kevata), Gandhee, Tamoli, Kumhar, Svarnakara etc castes. There was tradition to distinguish between son and daughter. On the whole condition of women was satisfactory. Women were also educated like men. They were expert in dancing, music and playing different instruments. Widows had to face different type of problems so they prefered to become sati in wish to die before husband death and relief from distresses. There was no obligation to become sati and not current as tradition. Bāṇa Bhaṭṭa has criticized it and said it as a work of fools. Tradition of veil was not current. It is known from descriptions of Bana that women used veil as virtuous conduct on special occasions as Rajyashri had used veil on occasion of wedding. In Kādambarī Bana has imagined fifth era as era of women. Today fifty percent seats are reserved in local bodies. There is continued demand to reserve seats for women in parliament. When this type of demand is fulfilled then in future women would be seen on important posts in administration. Thus imagination of Bana is seemed to fulfill in future. It is also thrown light on living condition of seventh century people from descriptions of Bana. He is described in detail about clothes worn by men and women, different types of cloths, their colouring and printing techniques and jewelleries worn on different parts of body. It is also thrown light on health and health science, food and beverage and means of entertainment from descriptions of Bana. In Harṣacarita there is description of forest village of Vindhyatavi. In this manner in Kādambarī there is description of Ujjayini city and characteristics of Shabaras. Glimpse of village life, town life and life of forest living people of seventh century is obtained from these descriptions.

Samskaras have important place in Indian culture. There is defined different samskaras for birth to death. Bana has mentioned samskaras those were in vogue in seventh century are- Garbhadhan, Jatakarma, Choodakarma, Upanayana, Samavartana, Vivah and Shraddh. Each samskara had its importance. Conduct and behaviour of Indian people was affected by these samskaras. Astrology and Palmistry was in vogue in seventh century. People of India are humble and consider guests like god. It is known from descriptions of Bana that people of seventh century gave special respect to guests. He has mentioned different styles of respectful greetings. Description of Bana is proved by list of respectful greeting presented by Hiuen-Tsang. Yamapatta were in vogue in seventh century. Paintings were displayed, which showed result of bad doing, so people abstain from bad conduct. It is known from description of Bana that different types of thought were in vogue about bad omen and good and bad dreams. There is mention of Tantra-mantra Shriparvata in Harṣacarita and Kādambarī . This mountain was famous for astonishment. People traveled there for fulfillment of their desire. Ground was washed with cow-dung because people were considered cow-dung as auspicious. People had also faith in ghosts and spirits. Children had worn Tabeej to protect them from evil and bad-eye of ghosts and spirits.

Many religions and sects were present in seventh century. Hindu religion (Brahman religion), Buddhist and Jain religion were mainly in vogue. Different persuasions were current in Hindu religion. Kings of Puṣyabhūti clan were follower of Shaiva persuasion. Rājyavardhana , Harṣa -Vardhana and Rajyashri had accepted Buddhism in latter days. Different gods were worshipped in Hindu religion. In Kādambarī there is mention of sky-kissing temples constructed at cross roads of Ujjayini city. Tradition to sacrifice was in vogue in forest living castes. In Kādambarī there is actual description of sacrifice that was performed in temple of Chandika devi. It is also thrown light on worship system and religious belief of that time from descriptions of Bana. There was tradition to perform Yajya in Hindus. It was belief that worldly and heavenly pleasure can be obtained from performing Yajya. In Harṣacarita there is mention of Somayajya that was performed at homes of Brahmanas. People had belief in power of mantra. Bana has criticized religious dissimulation through context of old dravida priest. Actually any society and country become hollow by religious dissimulation. In Harṣacarita there is mention of twenty one religious sects that were present that time. There was religious tolerance beside so many sects were current. It is known from description of Bana that followers of all sects were gathered in abode of Divakaramitra and practiced lectures on their own principles by hearing, considering repetition, doubt, verification, etymology and discussion.

Important information about education system of seventh century is given in Harṣacarita and Kādambarī . Education of all shastras and arts were given that time. Education of war, music, dance, architecture, painting and other arts useful for life were given under education of arts. Aim of this education was all round development of students. In Harṣa -Period there was three centres for education – home of Brahmanas, education centre established and supported by state and abode of saints. Students were admitted in age of six year and their education was completed is age of sixteen years. So education period was ten years. A certain curriculum for education was determined. Students got expertised in all shastras and arts after completion of that curriculum. In Kādambarī there is described detail of curriculum in which Chandrapeeda had got expertise. Relation between teacher and student was good. Expert in subjects became teacher. Students were disciplined and they respected teachers. It is thrown light on teaching technique from description of Bana. Students remembered their lesson by speaking loudly. Contents were cleared through spiritual instructions, lectures and criticism to develop understanding about subjects in students. Sanskrit, Prakrit and Apbhransha language was current in seventh century. Sanskrit was the language of Brahmanas, who perform Yajyas and people of high category. General people used Apbhransha and Prakrit language. Bana has mentioned his friend Ishana who wrote poems in lokabhasha or Apbhransha. It is known from descriptions of Bana that Prakrit was the language of people who lived in villages. Books were also composed in Prakrit language. Vayuvikara, a member of Bana's friend- circle, wrote poems in Prakrit language. It is mentioned in Kādambarī that people, who were expert in Yajyas, were avoid using Prakrit language. It is clear from this description that there were differences in society on base of language.

Knowledge about seventh century economy is also received from descriptions of Bana. Economy of that time was based on agriculture. Feudatory system was in vogue. Land was given to samantas by state. They were administrator of their land and deposited taxes in treasury of state by collecting. They had to maintaine an army which would fight from side of state on demand. Some land was in direct control of state and revenue was collected directly for state. Tax-free land was bestowed to Brahmanas by state. Tax was determined by measuring land with plough. Agricultural land was prepared with help of plough. Hard land of mountain areas was prepared as agriculture field with help of spade. Compost was also used to maintain fertility of fields. Compost prepared by rubbish was used as fertilizer. Well and ponds were main means of watering. Fields were watered by Persian wheels fitted on wells. Cash-crops were also produced along with grain crops. Paddy, wheat, gram, barley etc were main grain crops. Sugar-cane, cotton plant, linseed and Indian hemp were main cash-crops. Farmers were preserved seeds of different crops by drying it and used that seeds in next season to sow crops. Vegetables were produced in gardens adjacent to homes. It is known from descriptions of Bana that different industries were developed that time. Iron industry, textile industry, sugar industry, wine industry, ivory industry, wood and furniture industry, jewellery industry and industry related to production of toilet items were main industries of that time. It is clear from description of Harṣacarita and Kādambarī that internal business was in good condition. Commercial contact was also established with foreign countries. Chinacholaka coat and Chinanshuka named silk clothes, made in China, were imported from China. Shields made of Kardaranga leather was imported from Kardaranga Island. In Harṣacarita there is also mention of horses imported from different countries. Existence of different groups of craftsmen and businessmen is clearly proved by descriptions of Bana. These groups were active to develop their business. In Harṣacarita there is mention of profiteering merchants. Probably these merchants lent money on interest.

Mention of dates is essential to understand historical chronology. But Bana has not mentioned any date in his history writing. He has given actual drawing of India of seventh cenchury through his extraordinary writing. He has exposed every important aspects related to life of people. His descriptions are also proved by contemporary historical sources. Clearly it can be said that India of seventh century could not be understood without descriptions of Bana. Thus Bana is not only writer but also a historian.

■■■

BIBLIOGRAPHY

Books:-

1. Bhatt, Bana, Harsa-Charitam,The Chowkhamba Vidyabhawan, Varanasi, Trans. By Pt. Jagannath Pathaka, 1998.
2. Bhatt, Bana, Kadambari, The Chowkhamba Vidyabhawan, Varanasi, Trans. By Pandey Ramtej Sastri, 2002.
3. Bhatt, Bana, Kadambari (Kathamukha), The Chowkhamba Vidyabhawan, Varanasi, Edited by Sameer Sharma, 2000.
4. The Harsa-Carita of Bana, Motilal Banarasidass Publication Pvt. Ltd., Delhi, Translated by E.B. Cowell & F.W.Thomas, 1993.
5. Agrawala, Dr. Vasudevasarana, Harsha-Charita: Ek Sanskritika Adhyayana, Bihar Rashtrabhasha Parishada, Patna-4, 1999.
6. Agrawala Vasudevasarana, Kadambari (A Cultural Study), The Chowkhamba Vidyabhawan, Varanasi-1, 1988.
7. Panthari, Prof. Bhagawati Prasad, Rajvansh: Maukhari aur Pushyabhuti, Bihar Hindi Granth Akadami, Patna-3, 2000.
8. Altekar, A.S., The Position of Women in Hindu Civilization, Motilal Banarsidass Publishers Private Limited, Delhi, 2005.
9. Sivaramamurti, C., Some Aspects of Indian Culture, Publications Division, Ministry of Information and Broadcasting, Government of India, 1994.
10. Biswas, A., Indian Costumes, Publication Division, Ministry of Information and Broadcasting, Government of India, 2003.
11. India, Government and Economic Life in Ancient and Medieval Periods, Publication Division, Ministry of Information and Broadcasting, Government of India, 2009.
12. India, Society Religion and Literature in Ancient and Medieval Periods, Publication Division, Ministry of Infor-

mation and Broadcasting, Government of India, 2008.
13. India, Art and Architecture in Ancient and Medieval Periods, Publication Division, Ministry of Information and Broadcasting, Government of India, 2008.
14. Ancient India, Publication Division, Ministry of Information and Broadcasting, Government of India, 2007.
15. The way of the Buddha, Publication Division, Published on the Occasion of the 2500th Anniversary of the Mahaparinirvana of Buddha.
16. Beal, Samuel, SI-YU-KI, Buddhist Records of The Western World, Low Price Publications, Delhi, 2008.
17. Watters, Thomas, On Yuan Chawang's Travels in India (A.D. 629-645), Low Price Publications, Delhi, 2004.
18. Mahajan, V.D., Medieval India, S. Chand and co. Ltd., Ramanagar, New Delhi, 1997.
19. Basham, A.L., Adbhut Bharat, Shivalal Agrawal and co., Agra, 1997.
20. 'Viyogi', Pandit Mohan Lal Mahato, Arya Jivan Darshan, Bihar Hindi Granth Akadami, Patna-3, 1971.
21. 'Dinkar', Ramdhari Singh, Samskriti Ke Char Adhyaya, Lokbharati Publication, 15-A, Mahatma Gandhi Marg, Allahabad-1, 2005.
22. Majumdar, R.C. & Pusalkar, A.D. (eds.), History and Culture of the Indian People, III, Bombay, 1953.
23. Majumdar, R.C. & Pusalkar, A.D. (eds.), The Classical Age, Bombay, 1953.
24. Majumdar, R.C. & Pusalkar, A.D. (eds.), The Age of Imperial Kanauj, Bombay, 1955.
25. Majumdar, R.C. (ed.), History of Bengal-I, Dacca, 1943.
26. Sinha, G.P., Post-Gupta Polity, Calcutta, 1970.
27. Sircar, D.C., Political and Administrative System of Ancient and Medieval India, Delhi, 1974.

28. Tripathi, R.S., History of Kanauj to the Moslem Conquest, Varanasi, 1937.
29. Tripathi, R.S., Early Position of Harsha, Allahabad, 1932.
30. Mookerji, R.K., Harsha (3rd ed.), Delhi, 1965.
31. Sinha, B.P., The Decline of the Kingdom of Magadha, Patna, 1954.
32. Devahuti, D., Harsha, A Political Study (2nd ed.), New Delhi, 1983.
33. Devahuti, D., Harsha Shiladitya (Hindi), Meerut, 1987.
34. Goyal, S.R., Harsha and Buddhism, Meerut, 1986.
35. Goyal, Shankar, History and Historiography of the Age of Harsha, Jodhpur, 1992.
36. Mishra, S.M., Yashovarman of Kanauj, New Delhi, 1977.
37. Niyogi, Pushpa, Contribution to the Economic History of Northern India, Calcutta, 1962.
38. Gopal, Lallanj, Economic Life of Northern India, Varanasi, 1965.
39. Choudhary, A.K., Early Medieval Village in North-Eastern India (A.D. 600-1200), Calcutta, 1971.
40. Choudhary, R.K., Economic History of Ancient India, Patna, 1982.
41. Sircar, D.C., Landlordism and Tenancy in Ancient and Medieval India as Revealed by Epigraphical Records, Lucknow, 1969.
42. Sircar, D.C., (ed.), Land System and Feudalism in Ancient India, Calcutta, 1966.
43. Sharma, R.S., Indian Feudalism (2nd ed.), New Delhi, 1980.
44. Jha, D.D., (ed.), Feudal-Social Formation in Ancient India, Delhi, 1987.
45. Thakur, V.K., Urbanisation in Ancient India, New Delhi, 1981.
46. Sharma, R.S., Social Changes in Early Medieval India (A.D. 500-1200) (3rd print), New Delhi, 1983.

47. Sircar, D.C., Studies in the Religious Life of Ancient and Medieval India, Delhi, 1971.
48. Jaiswal, S., Origin and Development of Vaishnavism (2nd ed.), New Delhi, 1981.
49. Nandi, R.N., Social Roots of Religion in Ancient India, Calcutta, 1986.
50. Bhattacharya, N.N., History of Shakta Religion, New Delhi, 1974.
51. Bhattacharya, N.N., History of the Tantric Religion, New Delhi, 1982.
52. Pathak, V.S., Smarta Religions Tradition (A.D. 600-1200), Meerut, 1987.
53. Brown, P., Indian Architecture, Bombay, 1959.
54. Rowland, B., The Art and Architecture of India, Harmondsworth, 1959.
55. Desai, Devangana, Erotic Sculpture of India, A Socio-Cultural Study, New Delhi, 1975.

Journals, Magazines and News Papers:-

1. The Indian Historical Review (Vol. I, No. I, March, 1974. pp 1-9).
2. The Indian Historical Review (Vol. III, No. I, July, 1976. pp 43-58).
3. The Indian Historical Review (Vol. I, No. I, March, 1974. pp 10-17).
4. Prajna-Bharati (Vol. XIII, Year-2007), K.P. Jayaswal Research Institute, Patna.
5. Anusilana (Vol. XIX, Year-5, 2009), Department of Philosophy & Religion, Faculty of Arts, Banaras Hindu University, Varanasi.
6. Kadambini, Hindustan Times Ltd., 18-20, Kasturba Gandhi Marg, New Delhi, 110001.

7. Kurukshetra, Gramin Kshetra aur Rojgar Mantralaya, Krishi Bhawan, New Delhi, 110001.
8. Jagriti, Soochana aur Lok Sampark Vibhag, Punjab Sarakar, 117-118, Sector 17 B, Chandigarh, 160017.
9. Navaneet, Bharatiya Vidya Bhavan, Kanhaiya Lal Manik Lal Munshi Marg, Mumbai- 400007.
10. Yojna, Publication Division, Ministry of Information and Broadcasting, Patiyala House, New Delhi-110001.
11. The Hindu, Messrs Kasturi & Sons Ltd., Anna Salai, Chennai.
12. The Times of India, Benett Colman & Co. Ltd., New Delhi.
13. Dainik Jagaran, Jagaran Prakashan Ltd. New Delhi.
14. Rashtriya Sahara, Sahara India Mass Communication, 28 Barakhamba, New Delhi.
15. Hindustan, H. T. Media Ltd., Kasturba Gandhi Marg, New Delhi.
16. Hindustan Times, H. T. Media Ltd. Kasturba Gandi Marg, New Delhi.

■■■

Apendix

PUSHYABHUTI EMPIRE UNDER HARSHA-VARDHANA

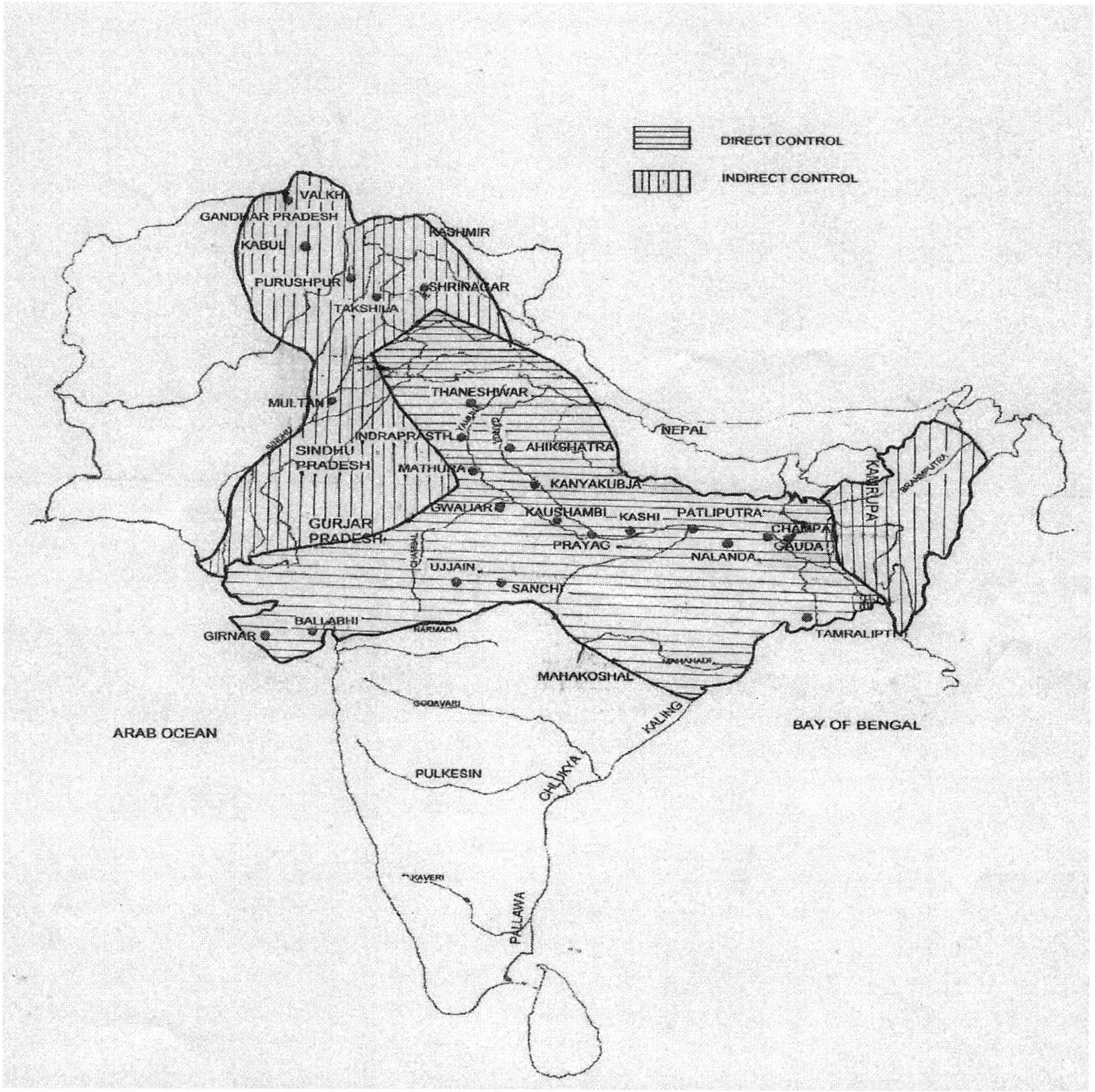

PUSHYABHUTI EMPIRE UNDER PRABHAKARA-VARDHANA

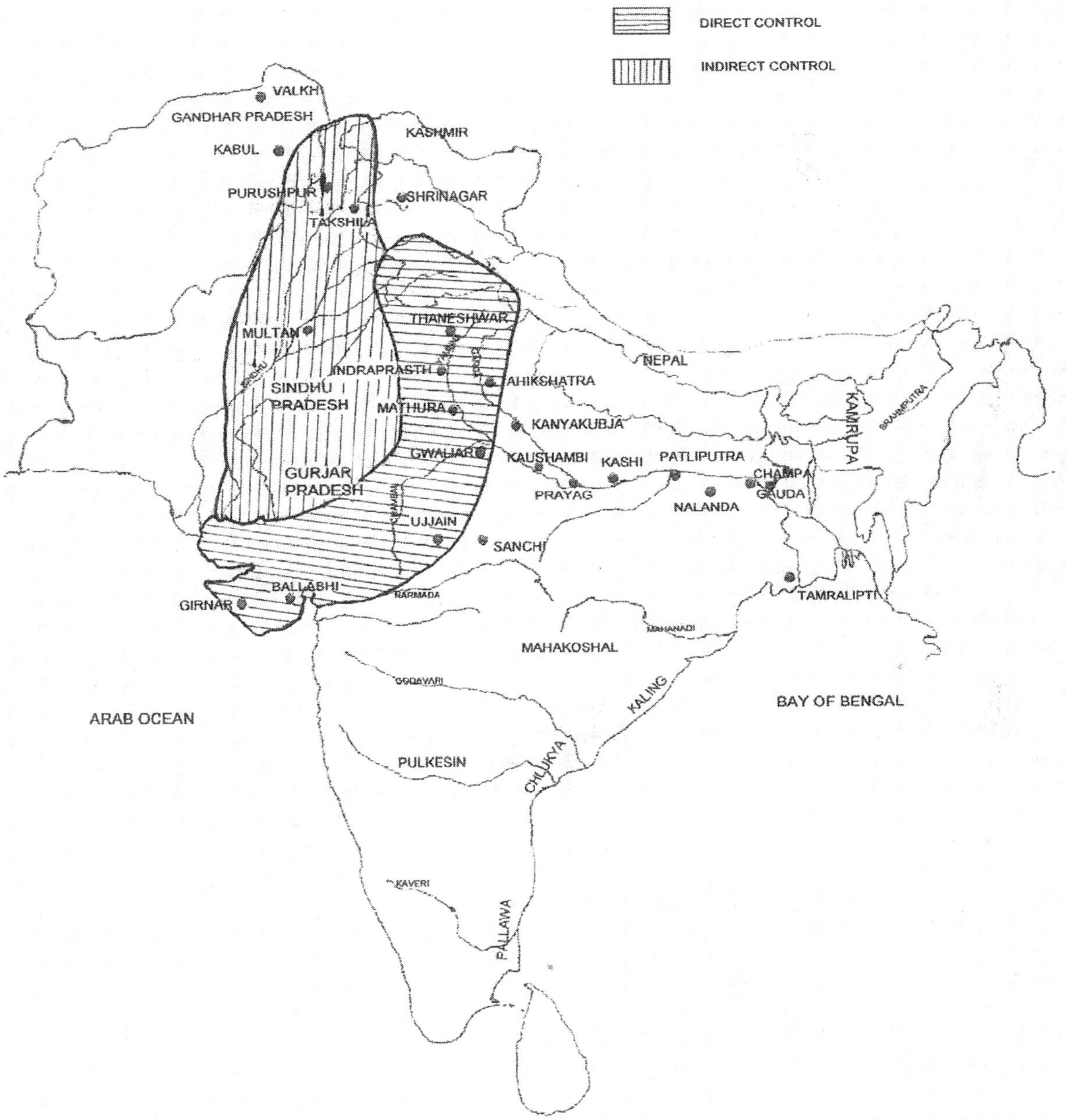

DIAGRAM OF SKANDHAVAR AND RAJKUL

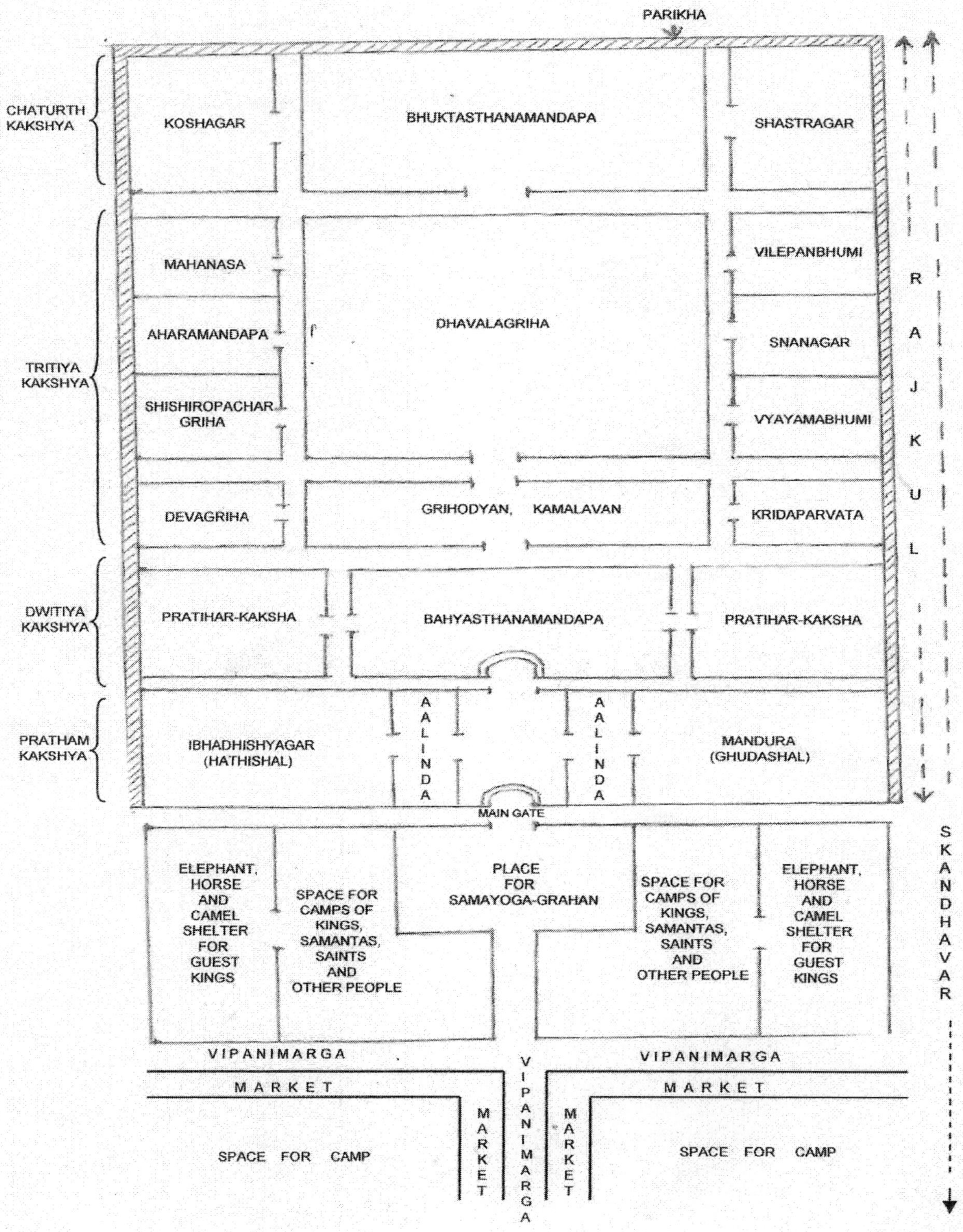

A calendar found in recent Indian markets which gives message like ***Yamapatta*** of Harsha-Period.

Tara, Kurkihar, Bihar. She has worn ***Balapasha*** on her head and put ***Tilaka*** on forehead.

Maitreya, Ahicchatra. He has worn ***Tarangita Uttariya*** which thin wrinkles are displayed.

Avalokitesvara,
Kurkihar, Bihar.
He has worn ***Kardhani*** in his waist and ***Keyura*** or ***Angada*** in upper-arm.

Lokesvara,
Nalanda.
He has worn ***Locket*** in neck made of nail of tigers.

Structure of Seventh Century Economy

Income of State

- Land revenue
- Tax on business & Foreign trade
- Tax on industrial products
- Tax on Forest Products

Expenditure of State

- Expenses on Royal family members & employees of state.
- Expenses on people's welfare work.
- Construction of palaces, buildings, ponds & expenses on plantation
- Internal and external security and weapons

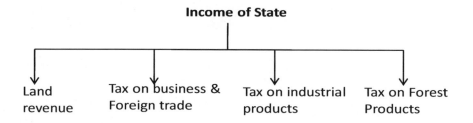

Coins of King Harsha

A Statue of King Kaniska, Mathura.
He has worn coat like ***Chinacholaka.***

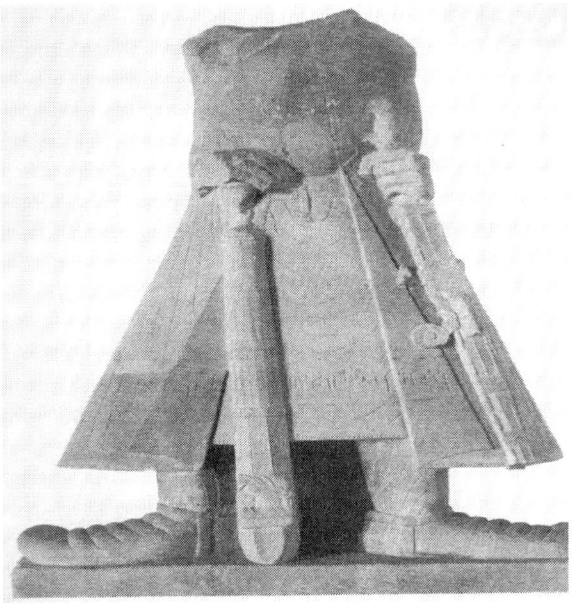

1***. Satula*** of blue strip, 2.***Satula*** of blue strip on white colour, 3. Chamaragrahini worn ***Kanchuka*** of lapis lazuli colour,4. ***White Kanchuka***,5. Saffron coloured ***Uttriya*** of head cloth and 6. ***Ekavali*** of pearl beads in neck.

Disciple of ***Bhairavacharya***(follower of Shaiva sect) & his dress.

Trikantaka jewellery of ear made of three emeralds and two pearls side by.

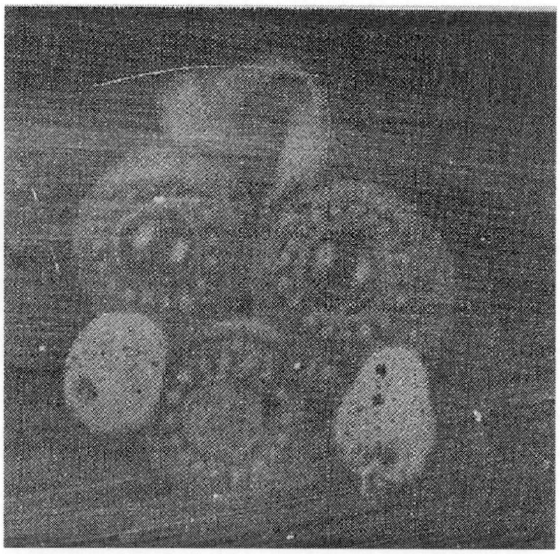

Apsaras , wall-painting ,Cave -17,Ajanta.
She has worn ***Ekavali*** of beads ,***Necklace*** in her neck, ***bracelet*** in wrist, ***Balapasha*** in locks of hair and ***Mangatika*** on parting of the hair.

The Stupa Site 3, Nalanda

Ruins of Ancient Nalanda University – A education centre supported by state

Printed in Great Britain
by Amazon

32783196R00197